1986

ROLAND BARTHES: A CONSERVATIVE ESTIMATE

ROLAND BARTHES

A Conservative Estimate

PHILIP THODY
Professor of French Literature
University of Leeds

First published 1977 by
THE MACMILLAN PRESS LTD
London and Basingstoke
Associated companies in Delhi
Dublin Hong Kong Johannesburg
Lagos Melbourne New York Singapore Tokyo

ISBN 0 333 21926 0

Typeset, printed and bound
in Great Britain by
REDWOOD BURN LIMITED
Trowbridge & Esher

To Brian and Vilma Hook

Contents

Acknowledgements

The author and publishers wish to thank the following who have kindly given permission for the use of copyright material from the works of Roland Barthes:

Jonathan Cape Ltd. and Farrar, Straus & Giroux Inc. (Hill and Wang) for the extracts from *Elements of Semiology*, translated by Annette Lavers and Colin Smith from *Eléments de Sémiologie*, © 1964 by Editions du Seuil, Paris, English translation © 1967 by Jonathan Cape Ltd. *Writing Degree Zero*, translated by Annette Lavers and Colin Smith from *Le Degré Zéro de L'Ecriture*, © 1953 by Editions du Seuil, Paris, English translation © 1967 Jonathan Cape Ltd. *Mythologies*, selected and translated by Annette Lavers from *Mythologies*, © 1957 by Editions du Seuil, Paris, English translation © 1972 by Jonathan Cape Ltd. *S/Z*, translated by Richard Miller, © 1970 by Editions du Seuil, Paris, English translation © 1974 by Farrar, Straus & Giroux Inc. and © 1975 by Jonathan Cape Ltd. *The Pleasure of the Text*, translated by Richard Miller from *Le Plaisir du Texte*, © 1973 by Editions du Seuil, Paris, English translation © 1975 by Farrar, Straus & Giroux Inc. and © 1976 by Jonathan Cape Ltd.

Preface

This introductory study of Roland Barthes is intended for English and American readers who have no previous knowledge of structuralism or semiology, but who would like to find out more about these disciplines by seeing them at work in one particular author. It has no pretence to being a complete analysis of the philosophical background to Barthes's work. Such an analysis would involve a detailed consideration of Marxism, Freudianism and Sartrean existentialism, as well as of the more unfamiliar and sometimes elusive ideas of Ferdinand de Saussure, Claude Lévi-Strauss, Michel Foucault, Jacques Derrida, Philippe Sollers and Julia Kristeva, and would go far beyond the aims I have assigned myself. These are, essentially, to try to see how the ideas which Barthes himself expresses in his own books can be applied outside the tradition within which he is immediately writing.

In thus trying to translate the implications of a body of theoretical and critical work from one intellectual context to another—to see, in other words, what becomes of Barthes's ideas when they are brought over to this side of the Channel—I have tried to avoid using the rather specialised vocabulary in which Barthes himself puts forward his views. English-speaking readers who wish to acquaint themselves with this vocabulary have an excellent guide in Jonathan Culler's *Structuralist Poetics*, and a good introduction to some of the figures in Barthes's world in Michael Lane's *Structuralism: A Reader*. Barthes's own *Eléments de Sémiologie* is also available in an English translation, and provides both a theoretical basis for the analysis of fiction in *S/Z* and a guide to the precise technical terms which Barthes himself uses in his writings. My aim has been to approach Barthes from the other side, trying to see how his ideas work in specific contexts without always necessarily bringing in the exact terms which he himself uses.

Fundamental to the account of language put forward by one of the most important thinkers to have influenced Barthes, the Swiss philologist and linguist, Ferdinand de Saussure, is the distinction between *la langue* and *la parole*, between English as a complete structure for the expression and communication of thoughts and the specific brand of English that any one individual speaker may use. No one, in Saussure's way of looking at language, can ever possess the whole *langue*. This is a corporate and virtually anonymous treasure which enables communication to take place, but which can never have more than a potential existence in any actual speaker. The *parole* which a specific individual may employ and exploit to make his meaning clear to his listeners can nevertheless exist only by virtue of the underlying *langue* that provides both a community of shared linguistic experience and the very thought-patterns by means of which the members of that community make themselves understood. This is a distinction which can serve, by analogy, to express and justify what I have tried to do in this book. The essays which Barthes has published are, as it were, his *parole*. They are the way in which his particular vision of the world takes shape, but they exist only by virtue of reference to an overriding general philosophy whose constituents I enumerated in the first paragraph of this preface: Freudianism, Marxism, Sartrean existentialism, the structuralism of Lévi-Strauss, the rejection of the idea of man as a communicating individual in the work of Michel Foucault. And just as no one could ever hope to give a complete description of the *langue* known as English or the *langue* known as French, so it is difficult if not impossible to evoke every detail of the *langue* made up by the world views of these thinkers. All that one can hope to do is describe a particular *parole*. This is what I have tried to do for Roland Barthes.

I should like to thank Elisabeth Bousfield for the exemplary care and patience which she showed in preparing the typescript of this book.

I should also like to thank Gwilym Rees for suggestions about Barthes's debt to Ferdinand de Saussure, and for his most valuable comments on the final version of this book.

Much of the incidental research was made easy for me by the extremely co-operative attitude of the *Service de Presse* of the Editions du Seuil and of the publicity department of Jonathan Cape.

As always, my thanks go to the staff of the Brotherton Library of the University of Leeds for their constant helpfulness; as well as to my hard-pressed fellow tax-payers in the United Kingdom. Without their readiness to maintain large provincial universities, I should never have enjoyed the comparative leisure which has enabled me to write this and other studies.

PHILIP THODY

Leeds, May 1977

1 Biography, writing and method

I

Roland Barthes was born in Cherbourg on 12 November 1915. On 26 October 1916 his father, Louis Barthes, was killed in a naval battle in the North Sea, and Barthes spent his early childhood in Bayonne, brought up by his mother and maternal grandmother in what he depicts as an atmosphere of genteel poverty. His mother's family, however, was one where cultural values, and especially music, were taken very seriously. His aunt was a piano teacher, and an anonymous contributor to *L'Echo du Sud-Ouest*, writing in 1973, recalled how the family house in the Allées Paulmy represented in the 1920s the centre of the musical life of the town, the place where all the famous performers could be heard on their visits to Bayonne.[1] Barthes himself learned to play the piano in his very early childhood, composed little pieces of music before he could even read, and commented later that he never found it boring even to practise scales.

Unlike Sartre and Camus, who also lost their fathers when they were young, Barthes has neither commented in detail on the effect which his fatherless childhood had on his personality nor written books that show an obvious obsession with the father-figure. When, during his later schooldays at the Lycée Louis-le-Grand, in Paris, his form-master solemnly inscribed on the blackboard the names of the boys whose relatives had died for their country, Barthes felt no pride at being the only one able to claim a father. All he felt was an emptiness, a lack of social anchorage, the absence of a father whom he might, like Oedipus, oppose and kill—a frustration, in fact, as he later observed, at not being able to live out a Freudian childhood to the full. In an interview in 1973, however, he also made a remark which confirmed what critical readers of his work had long since suspected: that an Oedipus with no Laius to kill will invent one; and that in Barthes's case his Laius was what he calls the *Doxa*, the stifling set of received and ready-made opinions, of stereotypes and fixed ideas, that he sees as characterising the bourgeoisie.[2] Indeed, his attack on what is not, after all, so very unusual a target is so violent and unreasoning that it cannot have wholly conscious origins. Significantly enough, he makes a point of saying that his mother cut herself free of her original bourgeois milieu by learning a manual trade, and also bears no personal grudge against Bayonne itself. Like all good middle-class Parisians, he spends his holidays with his provincial relatives.

In his later work, however, the target for his aggression begins to change. It becomes the ideological discourse of the Left, what he actually calls 'a kind of father whose vigilant function would be to prevent people enjoying themselves'.[3] For an English reader, this is a particularly interesting remark since it highlights one of the many similarities which his work has with that of George Orwell. Not only is Barthes the first major French writer to offer a serious analysis of popular culture, presenting in *Mythologies* (1957) the French equivalent of 'Boys' Weeklies' or 'Raffles and Miss Blandish'. He now seems to be becoming, if not what Orwell himself called 'one of those people who are driven into a perverse Toryism by the follies of the progressive party of the moment',[4] at least a man who sees that the threat to freedom can come as much from the supposed enemies of capitalism as from capitalism itself.

There is nevertheless something very paradoxical about beginning a book on Roland Barthes with facts and speculations of this essentially biographical type. His favourite author is Marcel Proust, and one of the ideas in Proust that he most enthusiastically endorses is expressed in a phrase from *Contre Sainte-Beuve*: 'a book is the product of a different self from the one we exhibit in our habits, in society, in our vices.'[5] Indeed, Barthes goes a good deal further than Proust ever did in denying the connection between an author's life and the books he writes. He even prefers to the traditional term of *auteur*, with everything he says it implies by way of recognition of the individual as sole source of truths and values, the new term of *scripteur*: simply the being in whom the written text originates. What such a being produces, he claimed in 1968, in an article entitled *La mort de l'auteur*, 'has no origin but language itself, that is to say the very thing which constantly calls all origins into question'. The *scripteur* has in him 'neither passions, humours, feelings nor impressions. Only this immense dictionary from which he takes an *écriture* [writing, verbal activity] which can never cease. Life does nothing but imitate books [*le livre*], and books themselves are merely objects woven out of signs.'[6] Literature, for Barthes, is a self-contained and self-sufficient linguistic activity. As will be seen later, he maintains that what are generally known in English as 'works of the imagination' contain neither moral truths, nor information about society, nor living characters, nor revelations about the author. The aesthetic which he and his disciples are developing is one where books do not contain a solid centre of guaranteeing truth but work by setting into motion an infinite interplay of ideas in the mind of the reader.

There are nevertheless some good reasons for writing about Barthes in a traditional, almost Lansonian manner, and for seeking an ascertainable content in his work. Like Valéry, he maintains that once a text is published an author has no intellectual property rights over it. The critic and reader are free to make of it what they can, and to apply what methods they please to bring out what the official English translation of *S/Z* calls 'the plurality of its systems, its infinite (circular) "transcribability" '.[7] And if Barthes can write about Racine, as he did in the early 1960s, in terms of the recurring and unconscious structures in his work, there is no reason why I should not write about Barthes as if he were a man and not what he calls a mere 'emitter of codes'. Moreover, Barthes himself has not stuck rigidly to the principle set out in his *Manteia* article: that 'the modern *scripteur* is born at exactly the same moment as his text', and is thus 'in no way endowed with a being that precedes his act of writing [*écriture*] or continues after this has finished'. In 1975, he published, in *Roland Barthes par Roland Barthes*, one of the best volumes in the Editions du Seuil *Ecrivains de toujours* series, and indeed the only one so far in which a living author has presented himself and his work. Admittedly, he genuflected towards his principles by insisting that 'biography can deal only with the unproductive part of life'. As soon as his career as a writer begins, in 1947, photographs of his private family life disappear, and *Roland Barthes par Roland Barthes* is certainly intended to be an 'anti-biography'. But few other books go so effectively against these formal Barthesian principles and fulfil the classical ideal formulated by Pascal when he noted how we sometimes expect an author but are delighted to find a man.

A biographical approach does, of course, always carry with it the danger of reductionism. Barthes even laid himself open to this in the signed review which he himself published in *La Quinzaine littéraire* of *Roland Barthes par Roland Barthes*. He remarked there on how the book is thrice dominated by the figure of the mother, recalled that the text is enthusiastic about 'the Goddess Homosexuality', and thus reminded his readers that both *Sur Racine* and *S/Z* lay considerable emphasis on the theme of the castrating mother figure.[8] But for the English-speaking reader for whom this study is intended, the introduction of biographical elements is essential to one of my main themes: that Barthes is a fascinating example of a modern French left-wing literary intellectual. His career, attitudes, intellectual interests and political assumptions are at one and the same time so characteristically French and yet so extraordinary when looked at from this side of the Channel that one often wonders, when reading him, whether phrases about 'a common European culture' have any meaning at all. It is against this background that I am writing, and I feel I am obeying Barthes's own injunctions in *Critique et Vérité* (1966) in thus laying my own cultural and critical cards on the table before I begin.

It is not that Barthes's education or career have anything particularly exotic about them, or that some of his arguments about the nature of literature do not occasionally have an unconsciously English or American ring. When he was eleven, his mother moved to Paris in order to exercise the trade of book-binding which she had learned to support herself in her widowhood. She and her two sons—Barthes has an elder brother, who makes one appearance in *Roland Barthes par Roland Barthes*—then settled in the *sixième arrondissement*, at the corner of the rue Mazarine and the rue Jacques-Callot. It is a part of Paris that Barthes has never really left, and he now lives within a mile of the street where he spent his childhood. In 1926, he moved from the *lycée* in Bayonne to the Lycée Montaigne, where he stayed until making the quite conventional change to the Lycée Louis-Le-Grand in order to benefit from its more specialised teaching of literature and philosophy. The *lycéens* of those days, he notes in a comment to one of the best photographs in *Roland Barthes par Roland Barthes*, were young gentlemen, and there is no mistaking the intellectual superiority with which the thin, adolescent Barthes looks out at the world as he walks down the boulevard Saint Michel with a friend. A longer passage in *Roland Barthes par Roland Barthes*, however, both heightens the similarity with Orwell and consciously suggests a personal reason for the hostility that Barthes was to adopt towards the commercial theatre in the mid 1950s. His childhood was marked, he notes, not by downright poverty but by the more subtle lower-middle-class experience of not quite being able to afford holidays, new shoes and even, occasionally, food. Orwell's remark that there is often 'more sense of poverty, more crust-wiping and looking twice at sixpence in the shabby genteel families than there ever is in the working class' offers a further parallel between the two writers, and Barthes follows up his comment with what is again a very human, perceptive and rather Orwellian observation. It is only in later life, he observes, after he has fully rejected the three moral systems which condemn money most rigorously—Marxism, Christianity and Freudianism—that he can glory in the unreflective, uncritical, spontaneous expenditure of money which characterises the rich.[9]

The academic career on which Barthes was launched by his undoubted intelligence and literary sensitivity—one of the schoolboy essays reproduced in *Roland Barthes par Roland Barthes* was given the almost unheard-of mark in French scholastic circles of 9 out of 10—would have led in normal circumstances to his entering the Ecole Normale Supérieure. There, he would have taken the competitive examination known as the *agrégation* and become one of the élite of highly paid schoolteachers who put in twelve hours a week as against their colleagues' eighteen and receive twice their salary. But on 10 May 1934 he fell ill with his first attack of tuberculosis and could not compete for entry into the Ecole Normale Supérieure. Instead, he had to be content with what is still very much a second-best in France, and study at the ordinary university, where there has never been selection or competition for places and where the first degrees awarded carry little prestige. He spent the four years from 1935 to 1939 reading French, Latin and Greek at the Sorbonne, and devoted much of his spare time to putting on classical plays with the student company entitled *Le Groupe de théâtre antique* that he had helped to found.

In 1937, Barthes had been declared unfit for military service, and this additional exclusion from the life and experience of Frenchmen of his own generation also serves as background to his later, semi-ironic question: 'Who does not feel how *natural* it is in France to be Catholic, married, and well qualified academically?'[10] For Barthes had been brought up a Protestant in a predominantly Catholic country, and he also comments wryly, when presenting in *Roland Barthes par Roland Barthes* a number of photographs clearly taken from the family album, that his own sexually unproductive body marks the finishing point beyond which his line will be continued no further. On a less fundamental level, Barthes also suffers from the slight feeling of exclusion and persecution common to many left-handed people obliged to adjust themselves day after day to living in a right-handed world, while another autobiographical fragment in *Roland Barthes par Roland Barthes* speaks of how stupid he often feels at possessing a mind that understands only aesthetic or ethical concepts, not scientific, political, practical, philosophical or mathematical ones. It is not that Barthes makes any appeal for sympathy by presenting himself as something of an oddity or suggesting why he is or feels excluded from conventional established French society. His freedom from romanticism is one of the most attractive features of his work and personality, and he seems at times to be at the opposite extreme from the romantic writer who claims universal validity for his ideas precisely because he is excluded from the society of his fellows. He even hints on occasions that one of the central themes in his work, his hostility to what is 'obviously the case', to 'the accepted view', to 'what goes without saying', to *la Doxa*, to orthodoxy in all its forms, may well have its origin in his private experience and perhaps be suspect for that very reason. What he finds most objectionable is what is known in French as *l'évidence*: that which is self-evident and which—like a father's word in happier times—lies therefore beyond the possibility of being called in question.

But until the publication of *Roland Barthes par Roland Barthes* in 1975, none of Barthes's essays showed any lack of confidence in his own ideas. It is, on the contrary, the dogmatic tone of his book *Le degré zéro de l'écriture* (1953) that is most surprising to anyone brought up in the more hesitant tradition of Anglo-Saxon empiricism. His interpretation of the literary history of France is presented as the central truth about the situation of the writer in the mid-twentieth century, and there is no hint that any other tradition either exists or is worth considering. The rather strident political tone of the essays may be a result of personal experience. Barthes had been compelled to spend most of the war years shut away in a sanatorium, and had thus been unable to follow out his political preferences and take part in the resistance to the German occupation and right-wing Vichy government. The intensity with which he applied a number of Marxist and Sartrean ideas to the study of literature can thus be interpreted as an attempt to compensate for the political inactivity to which he had been condemned. The enthusiasm he showed in the 1950s for the theatre of Bertolt Brecht might also have something of the same origin, and the fact that the articles which make up *Le degré zéro de l'écriture* first appeared in *Combat*, the newspaper then still closely associated with the name and reputation of Albert Camus, is again an indication of the political sympathies and ambitions of the early Barthes.

The basic idea of what the official English translation calls 'writing degree zero', of a literary style devoid of all ornament, had first occurred to him in 1942, when he wrote an article on Camus's *L'Etranger* in the review *Existences*, published by the patients at the *Sanatorium des étudiants de France*.[11] Originally, *Le degré zéro de l'écriture* had been offered to Gaston Gallimard, who published Sartre, Camus and Malraux, and represented the tendency dominant in immediate post-war literature. Gallimard rejected the book on the grounds that it was too abstruse and technical, but it was accepted by the Editions du Seuil on the recommendation of Albert Béguin and Jean Cayrol. *Le degré zéro de l'écriture* was clearly seen to fit into the new, more formalistic tendency that was already making itself felt in French literature, and the Editions du Seuil have since provided a home for two reviews closely associated with the approach which Barthes has adopted towards literature: the weekly *La Quinzaine littéraire* and the quarterly *Tel Quel*. *Le degré zéro de l'écriture* enjoyed considerable success with the critics, and Barthes no longer had to hawk his wares around. Since 1953, he has written only when commissioned to do so.[12]

II

Le degré zéro de l'écriture has strong similarities to Jean-Paul Sartre's *Qu'est-ce que la littérature?*, published in review form in 1946 and made available as a book entitled *Situations II* in 1947. Like Sartre, Barthes presents as universally valid his own view of how French literature has evolved over the last three hundred years, and uses this as a basis for an argument as to how literature ought to develop now. For the Barthes of *Le degré zéro de l'écriture*, there are two decisive dates in

French literary history: 1650 and 1848. Before 1650, or thereabouts, French had not settled down as a language, and writers had not therefore discovered the nature of what Barthes calls *l'écriture*: a specifically literary mode of expression. But once French had acquired a universally accepted syntax and vocabulary, works of the imagination came to be written in language which was immediately recognised as 'literary'. Such language reflected, according to Barthes, the attitude towards life of the new dominant middle class, and remained basically the same whether it was used by a man of genius like Racine or a hack like Pradon, by a quietist Bishop such as Fénelon or a specialist in romantic realism like Mérimée. All these writers, in Barthes's opinion, shared the view that the aim of literature was communication. Literature consisted of forming perfectly clear ideas and then finding words that expressed or translated what the writer wanted to say. Barthes does not actually quote the famous lines from Boileau's *L'Art poétique* (1674) that embody this view of the relationship between ideas and language:

> Ce que l'on conçoit bien s'énonce clairement,
> Et les mots pour le dire arrivent aisément

but he constantly assumes a thorough acquaintance on his readers' part with the classical authors dinned into them at school. Barthes's own view, of course, completely contradicts that of Boileau. For him, as for Tristan Tzara, 'la pensée se fait dans la bouche', and there is no way of separating the thought from the language that expresses it. The two come into existence simultaneously just as the author, as Barthes explained in *La mort de l'auteur*, is born at the same moment as his text. But earlier French writers, argues Barthes in *Le degré zéro de l'écriture*, did not recognise the obvious truth that thought cannot be separated from the words expressing it. Even the Romantics, who claimed to be carrying out a complete revolution against the classical aesthetic, kept 'l'essentiel du langage classique, l'instrumentalité'[13] (still saw language as an instrument). The real break in literary history came some fifty years after the Romantic revolution, and was the product of what happened in 1848.

It was then, maintains Barthes, that French society split into three antagonistic classes: the industrial working class; the land-owning aristocracy; and the dominant middle class which effectively controlled the production and distribution of wealth. Until the events of June 1848, the middle class had lived in a state of social and intellectual euphoria. Any defects in the private enterprise system could, they assumed, either be ignored or put right by arranging for the state to provide useful temporary employment for those who happened to be thrown out of work. The fundamental brotherhood of man and the ability of human beings to communicate one with another would then be proved by the ability of state intervention and private enterprise to live side by side. But in June 1848, the newly established *ateliers nationaux* went bankrupt and the workers employed in them were thrown out into the street. They refused to disperse; and far from demonstrating the continued existence of social harmony by continuing to pay them for doing nothing, the middle class hired General Cavaignac to shoot them down.

When the class war thus came so obviously into the open, the middle class could no longer persist in the view that 'language is always fundamentally persuasion, presupposing dialogue, instituting a universe in which men are not alone, in which words never have the terrible weight of things, in which speech always offers a meeting place with other people.[14] The inevitability of social conflict had destroyed the intellectual euphoria symbolised by Descartes's statement that 'le bon sens est la chose du monde la mieux partagée' ('common sense is the most widely shared commodity that exists'). Instead, the class war revealed a universe in which neither literature nor human communication could be taken for granted. If one looks solely at the content of their work, claims Barthes, Balzac and Flaubert differ from each other without ceasing to belong to the same school. But if one looks at their *écriture*, at the way they write and at their attitude towards writing, they are separated by the watershed of 1848. The first still belongs to the classical tradition, and takes language for granted as the natural instrument for communicating facts and ideas about human experience. The second already has a suspicious and self-conscious attitude towards language. He can write only by openly proclaiming the artificial nature of the literary activity he has happened to adopt. Literature has ceased to be something taken for granted as natural. It is no longer the inevitable result of people's ability to talk or write. It is seen as a cultural product of particular societies, varying with them as laws or religions vary, and in no way guaranteed as an automatic and integral part of the human condition.

The argument in *Le degré zéro de l'écriture* is clearly Marxist in the importance it gives to the influence of socio-economic factors on the development of literature and literary styles. It is because the first industrial revolution created an urban proletariat whose existence challenges middle-class supremacy and makes the class war inevitable that the *écriture* that had dominated French literature since 1650 ceases, in Barthes's view, to be a viable mode of expression. Barthes also follows Sartre in seeing a fundamental change between the historical role of the middle class in the seventeenth century and the place it occupied after 1789. Before the first French revolution, the demand of the middle class for equality before the law and for the abolition of feudal privileges had been a progressive factor. But once its seizure of power had coincided with the industrial revolution and the rise of the urban proletariat, the middle class became an objectively reactionary force whose world vision could no longer animate a unified culture. But while Sartre saw the writer's duty as that of allying himself with the movement for socialist democracy, of writing committed works of art that would constitute 'the subjective self-consciousness of a society in permanent revolution',[15] the Barthes of *Le degré zéro de l'écriture* put forward a different view of how the writer might react to this new situation. It is in the expression of this view that *Le degré zéro de l'écriture* resembles *Qu'est-ce que la littérature?* It is a literary manifesto for the present day as well as an attempt to rewrite the literary history of France from a basically Marxist standpoint.

Barthes outlines several possible ways of responding to the challenge of the new situation created by the fact that literature has, as he puts it, 'become dissociated from the society consuming it'. The first of these, admittedly, he presents as fairly valueless. It is what he calls 'l'écriture réaliste', which he sees as characteristic of writers such as Maupassant, Zola and Daudet. It consists, Barthes alleges, of 'an amalgam of formal signs of literature (past definite, free indirect speech) and of equally formal signs of realism (examples of popular speech, swear words, dialect words, etc.)', and he asserts that 'no mode of writing [*écriture*] is more artificial than this one, which claims to give the closest account of Nature'.[16] Lord Henry Wotton remarks in the first chapter of Oscar Wilde's *The Picture of Dorian Gray* that being natural is only a pose, and the most irritating one he knows; and from the frequency with which Barthes attacks people who present cultural and therefore artificial phenomena as though they were spontaneous, natural and inevitable, it is clear that he shares this opinion. He repeats his attack, as will be seen, in *Mythologies*, the *Essais critiques*, *Système de la Mode* and *S/Z*, and it is this insistence on the artificial nature of all communication systems which links together all the thirteen books he has so far published. It is also the opening essay of *Mythologies*, an analysis of all-in wrestling entitled *Le monde où l'on catche*, which presents what he regards as the best way of overcoming the fact that no mode of expression, except perhaps the grunt or the fart, is 'natural' in the strictest and narrowest sense of the word.

Thus what all-in wrestlers do, in Barthes's view, is openly proclaim that nothing they do is to be taken entirely seriously. The violent gestures they make are so obviously artificial that nobody can possibly mistake them for anything but an elaborate convention, and Barthes argues that the spectators at an all-in wrestling match are as fully aware of the complete artificiality of it all as a man who goes to the theatre to see a Molière play. The Latin tag which Barthes uses to express this idea is *Larvatus Prodeo*: 'I come forward pointing at my mask'. It was thus that the actors in the Roman theatre emphasised to the audience that they were playing traditional roles and not representing real people, and it is an attitude which Barthes recommends as a means whereby the author can be honest with his readers. He must, Barthes contends, constantly remind them that he is telling a made-up story, and that the language he is using is the one which the conventions of his society reserve for prose fiction. He does not pretend that it is natural and inevitable to use the past definite or the imperfect of the subjunctive, to present events in a chronological order or to explain the actions of his characters by reference to universal psychological laws.

Barthes calls this intensely self-conscious attitude towards literature 'la flaubertisation de l'écriture' [the Flaubertisation of writing], and describes it as the means whereby writers can obtain their 'redemption'. There is again a well-known phrase in English literature which makes Barthes's meaning more familiar and suspiciously easier to grasp: Coleridge's remark about the 'willing suspension of disbelief which constitutes poetic faith'. Such a suspension is certainly necessary if the theatregoer is to avoid the twin dangers of not enjoying the play and of thinking that what he sees on the stage is really happening, and is in fact applicable to all forms of literature. Barthes's vision of the author openly accepting the artificiality of his calling is indeed a fairly familiar one, and it is true that he does not, for all his enthusiasm for Flaubert, present 'la flaubertisation de l'écriture' as a very revolutionary concept. The same could also be said of the third reaction which he presents in *Le degré zéro de l'écriture* to the situation in which the writer finds himself now that literature has lost the innocent self-assurance whereby it could present itself as a wholly natural activity which everybody took for granted.

In classical times, he argues, there was no fundamental difference between prose and poetry. The latter was merely a rhymed and decorated version of the former. But since Rimbaud, poetry has changed its nature. It has become an activity which places men in contact 'not with other men, but with the most inhuman images of Nature: heaven, hell, the realm of the sacred, madness, pure matter, etc.'[17] There consequently exists, for Barthes, a profound difference of nature between prose and poetry. The former communicates ideas, and uses words as a vehicle for something that transcends them. The latter uses words as things in their own right, with all their many-sided richness and ambiguity. Each word, he claims, is like a Pandora's box, containing all the potentialities of language, holding at one and the same time 'all the different meanings among which a relational language would have required a choice to be made'. Yet although this view of how language works in a poetic context offers an interesting anticipation of Barthes's more complex theory, elaborated in *S/Z* in 1970, of how literature works, it is not a particularly new idea in the study of French poetry. The notion that prose communicates facts or ideas—and perishes in the process—whereas poetry offers the reader language in a non-utilitarian form is a critical common-place in the work of Paul Valéry, and was taken over lock, stock and barrel by Sartre in *Qu'est-ce que la littérature?* Where Barthes is being more original is in the view of literary style which gives the book its title, the idea of 'writing degree zero', of what he calls the *écriture blanche* which occurs in its most perfect form in Camus's *L'Etranger*.

There is once again a phrase in English literature which suggests something of the idea that Barthes is putting forward: George Orwell's statement that 'good prose is like a window pane'. For this is very much the notion that is brought to mind by the remark in *Le degré zéro de l'écriture* that this neutral or 'zero-term' is like the indicative as opposed to the subjunctive or the imperative mood. In the jargon of the late 1960s, it 'tells it like it is', and Barthes comments that the *degré zéro* could be described as a journalist's mode of writing 'if journalism did not usually employ optative or imperative (that is to say pathos-ridden) forms'.[18] For Camus, as he himself willingly acknowledged, learned the style for *L'Etranger* from Hemingway, and Hemingway himself had developed it in an attempt to render exactly what he saw, felt and heard. Barthes's great objection to the language of traditional French realism is precisely that it does not do this. Instead, it filters events through a preconceived network of cultural, moral and intellectual references, and makes no such attempt to cut through established clichés. In Camus's *L'Etranger*, on the other hand, argues Barthes, there is a 'transparent language'—shades of Orwell's window pane—which enables the ideas to stand by themselves. 'La pensée garde alors toute sa responsabilité' ['Thought then keeps its full responsibility'], is how *Le degré zéro de l'écriture* puts it, and Barthes claims that this enables the writer to become an honest man presenting honest wares. Of course, Barthes recognises, such a state of innocence cannot last for long. Writers easily fall back into the habit of using language in the form which literature offers to them, and the text of *L'Etranger* itself is by no means free of very literary devices such as imagery or metaphor. Indeed, Barthes himself later published a very different study which saw *L'Etranger* as carefully constructed to bring out an obsession with the sun.[19] The 'zero degree' in his first book of essays is in fact finally presented as a distant ideal rather than a current achievement, and the closing pages suggest that it is only when society has resolved its conflicts that literature will be able to go beyond the alienation which has characterised it ever since the class war in nineteenth-century France revealed the true nature of bourgeois society.

III

Le degré zéro de l'écriture received a wide and fairly enthusiastic welcome in the French literary press. Admittedly, there were some dissenting voices. The anonymous contributor to the *Bulletin critique du livre français* argued that 'the real problem posed by this little book is that of finding who is going to be helped by such deliberately obscure pages, in which the ideas constantly hide themselves away behind an exaggerated, grandiloquent, metaphorical and wholly illogical mode of expression',[20] but in *Critique, Le Monde, Les Lettres Nouvelles* and *Cahiers du Sud* Barthes was welcomed as a stimulating and perceptive thinker. Indeed, Dominique Arban commented that the difficulty of translating genuinely original writers such as Dostoyevsky or William Faulkner into French showed how the language had been fixed for too long in its confident perfection, while Jean Piel admired Barthes for his concern with the proper object of literary criticism, the relationship between literature and language.[21] *Le degré zéro de l'écriture* has also been translated into more languages than any of Barthes's other books: Spanish, Dutch, Japanese, Italian, Swedish, Czech, Portuguese, Catalan, German and English. Quite what it can mean to readers in these cultures is, however, something of a problem, since it concentrates on a situation and set of issues which are almost exclusively Parisian. Indeed, it is partly because of his overwhelming concern for the dilemmas confronting the French writer that Barthes is so fascinating an example of the modern French literary intellectual. John Fletcher commented in his recent book on Claude Simon on how monolingual and insular contemporary French literary intellectuals[22] are, and *Le degré zéro de l'écriture* illustrates this remark very aptly by generalising about poetry without mentioning a single non-French poet and about the novel without referring to Tolstoy, Dickens or Dostoyevsky.

It is indeed very tempting to criticise Barthes in terms of the English empirical tradition pointing out that the whole of the argument about *l'écriture blanche* or *l'écriture degré zéro* rests upon the first fifty pages of Camus's *L'Etranger*, and faulting almost all his arguments on the ground that he just does not offer enough evidence to support his thesis. Such criticism, however, misses the originality of what he is saying. For when he writes that there is only 'the slenderest difference between the *écriture* of a Fénelon and that of a Mérimée', he is not suggesting that they have the same style. He fully recognises that they do not. What he is doing is to draw our attention to the fact that two French writers who are so different when judged by the traditional criteria of stylistic analysis nevertheless belong to the same general tradition by the use which they both make of prose as an instrument of rational communication between human beings whose minds are all assumed to work in basically the same way. There is a perfectly valid observation, and there are other remarks in *Le degré zéro de l'écriture* which have the virtue of compelling us, precisely by their superficially outrageous content and the unfamiliarity of the terms in which they are couched, to look both at the history of French literature and at the way we communicate in a new and potentially very fruitful way.

Thus when Barthes observes that the revolutionaries of the eighteenth century 'had no reason to want to change *l'écriture classique*, they in no way envisaged calling into question the nature of man',[23] one's first reaction is to say that he is as sweeping as he is inaccurate. There is, if one looks at the content of their work, all the difference in the world between the concept of man in Pascal or Bossuet and the wholly new approach exemplified by Rousseau or Diderot, and Barthes initially seems merely perverse in suggesting that this is not the case. His originality as a literary thinker nevertheless lies in his readiness to carry an exclusive concern for form to its logical conclusion, and thus to make us realise that the agnostics or Nature-worshippers of the eighteenth century in no way rejected what had perhaps been the most important intellectual as well as literary conquest of their pious if tormented seventeenth-century predecessors: a mode of writing based upon Descartes's claim that since common sense is the most equally distributed commodity in the world, all human beings are the same in their ability to follow and be persuaded by a coherently presented set of arguments. In 1938, Jean-Paul Sartre declared when discussing the work of William Faulkner that 'the technique of a novelist always implies a metaphysic', and *Le degré zéro de l'écriture* is in many ways an attempt to carry this claim over into the wider realm of prose literature in general. Admittedly it puts forward a view which is inevitably over-familiar to the English and American reader when couched in a more popular form. The popular 'it ain't what you say, it's the way that you say it', like the more elaborate formulation of the same idea in Marshall McCluhan's *The medium is the massage*, represents a very similar way of looking at the experience of communication. What Barthes does, however, is to show us how the truisms which we are quite prepared to take for granted in the realm of popular culture or the electronic media can also be used to cast new light on an area which is often considered to be more important for its content than its form: that of descriptive, narrative or ideological writing. Perhaps, he suggests, we have always fooled ourselves by thinking that we use language. Perhaps it is language that uses us. This is something much more far-reaching than Sartre's claim about the metaphysic implied in a technique, since it effectively denies that any useful distinction can be made between form and content.

The Barthes of *Le degré de l'écriture* also differs both from Sartre and from most previous literary critics in another essential respect: he changes the emphasis from the writer as an individual to the writer as the almost anonymous mouthpiece of a social group. Essential to Saussure's concept of *la langue* is the idea that no individual can ever hope to alter its basic structure. This is something which is completely out of the control either of the individuals or of the social groups using it, and Barthes's vision of *l'écriture* as a mode of expression transcending and dominating virtually every writer over a fairly long historical period is a fascinating example of how the insights of structuralist linguistics and Marxism can occasionally coincide. For it is only, in the account which Barthes presents of the history of French literature, when the 'bourgeois consensus' established in the mid-seventeenth century begins to disintegrate under the effect of the contradictions which revealed themselves in the 1848 revolution that the *écriture* which had served as an instrument for class communication and domination starts to lose its self-evident validity. It is not, as it would have been from the standpoint of a bourgeois or romantic view of history, because some outstanding individual revolutionises the awareness which human beings have of themselves that literary language begins to change. It is the shift in economic and political power brought about by the industrial revolution which suddenly makes the way authors as different as Balzac or Mérimée write seem suddenly out of date, and *Le degré zéro de l'écriture* is a profoundly Marxist work in the expression which it gives to the view that it is changes in the mode of economic production which determine forms of literary and artistic activity.

There is however a difference between the Saussurian and the Marxist elements in *Le degré zéro de l'écriture*. Structuralism, as Sartre was to argue with considerable force in the nineteen-sixties, is a fundamentally a-historical way of looking at experience. Saussure himself contrasted the synchronic approach to language, that is to say the one which studied the way it worked here and now, with the diachronic approach which earlier scholars had adopted in order to discover how it had evolved over a period of time, and structuralism itself has generally preferred to adopt the former method. Barthes himself, on the other hand, has tended to vary in the emphasis which he gives to historical factors, and *Le degré zéro de l'écriture* is, from this point of view, his most historically-minded and diachronic book. Yet because it is also concerned with one particular communications system, that of the language used in French literature, it is relatively immune to the criticism of excessive gallocentricity suggested above. If Barthes talks about the novel without mentioning Cervantes and Thomas Mann, it is because the linguistic medium which these authors use, the *écriture* of seventeenth-century Spain or of twentieth-century Germany, is so completely different from the language which he is studying in *Le degré zéro de l'écriture* that mention of it would be a total irrelevance. What he is talking about is the continuity of written French between the establishment of classical prose in the mid-seventeenth century and the wholly new attitude to language implicit in the work of Flaubert, and this is, by definition, a purely French phenomenon. It is difficult, in a Marxist or post-Marxist age, not to notice that this period is sandwiched between the taming of the hereditary nobility by Richelieu and the rise of the industrial working class, and there is again a peculiarly French aspect to this experience which would make any extrapolation of it into the literature of other countries highly misleading.

One of the essays in *Mythologies* also effectively cuts the ground away from under the feet of anyone who tries to extend English empiricism to the point where it becomes an apparently devastatingly 'plain man' approach to Barthes's work. *Critique muette et aveugle* argues how someone who declares in all apparent honesty that he has not been able to understand Robbe-Grillet's *Les Gommes* or Samuel Beckett's *En attendant Godot* is in fact elevating his own mental laziness into an intellectual criterion. 'An intelligent man like me', such a critic tells his audience, 'whose job it is to understand works of art can see nothing in this one. You needn't therefore bother to look for anything either. Since you understand nothing either, you are as intelligent as I am.' This is very fair comment, especially since Barthes himself has always made a point of going to the opposite extreme. In the early 1950s, he was one of the first French critics to write enthusiastically about Bertolt Brecht, and rescued the nineteenth-century historian Michelet from near-oblivion. A number of critics have suggested that it was Barthes who first secured for the novels of Alain Robbe-Grillet and Michel Butor the wide reputation they now enjoy, and he has always been a leading innovator in French literary fashion.[24] To judge him in the terms of the plain man approach of English empiricism, expecting him to produce a multitude of examples to substantiate each generalisation, would be as inappropriate as to expect Schoenberg to compose a good tune to whistle in the bath.

There is also a way in which a sympathetic reading of Barthes does change one's ideas: by creating an acute awareness of how one's own mode of thinking can be imprisoned in a language which is so constantly taken for granted that it appears absolutely natural. To quote Wittgenstein's remark, 'The limits of my language are the limits of my world', is perhaps to fall into the very trap of which Barthes should make one most aware, for it shows how automatically one lapses into the assumption that Barthes can be understood and absorbed in a mode of thought already well established on this side of the Channel. It is regarded as axiomatic in England that a book setting out to express ideas should be written in the clearest possible language, with a multitude of specific examples to make the argument easy to understand or to refute. But English empiricism itself can also sometimes be a Procrustes bed which chops and stretches heretical thinkers until their originality disappears, and it is significant that the best book to be written so far on Barthes should have come from an Englishman who deliberately decided not to write in his own language. For as Stephen Heath explained when talking about his *Vertige du déplacement: lecture de Barthes*, it is only by giving up the language in which he thinks naturally that a writer can see things in a genuinely new and free manner. Indeed, Heath himself goes so far as to write about Barthes not only in French but in the rather particular kind of French that Barthes himself uses.[25]

There are still, however, a number of reasons to justify writing about Barthes without forsaking the English tradition. When an author is so exclusively French by his literary interests, it is useful to consider, in a supposedly international age, what relevance his ideas might have for another culture. When he is so intensely intellectual, it may be salutary to test his assumptions on more middlebrow examples. When he is so typically a French left-wing intellectual in his enthusiasm for Marx and the violence of his hostility to the bourgeoisie, it is interesting to speculate on how differently the middle class has sometimes behaved—or been made to behave—outside France. And when the richness, complexity and originality of his prose style sometimes make his meaning so difficult to grasp, it is challenging to see whether his ideas can be expressed in a more direct form. The style he favours has the unintended but real advantage of shielding him from certain kinds of criticism. He and his admirers can always say that he has been misunderstood. The style in which I shall try to relate Barthes to the English tradition will not, I hope, offer this particular protection.

The presentation of Barthes's ideas in an immediately comprehensible form can nevertheless be a mixed blessing, both for him and for his presenter. It shows, to begin with, that Barthes's literary theories often reflect ideas commonplace in Anglo-Saxon literary discourse since the 1920s. There is, for example, little in *S/Z* that is not more clearly expressed in L. C. Knight's *How many children had Lady Macbeth?*, while his views on the Death of the Author are a repetition in more grandiose terms of an attitude axiomatic in the American 'New Critics' of the 1930s and most elegantly expressed in the early essays of T. S. Eliot. Once the content of Barthes's work has been brought into the clear light of day, his books all seem to express a relatively small number of rather simple ideas, each of which can be illustrated by the same fairly straightforward examples. This has an obvious disadvantage for the person writing about Barthes: he constantly runs the danger of seeming to repeat himself when he is merely trying to bring out the basic ideas around which Barthes's work is constructed.

But this, in turn, is itself a vindication of Barthes's most firmly held belief: that the way of saying is all-important, the thing said banal to the point of non-existence.

2 Criticism, obsessions and the theatre

If one believes Barthes himself, he is not a great reader. He explained this, in an interview published in 1974, by saying that one of two things always happened: either the book interested him so much that he stopped reading in order to think, or he found it so boring that he put it down. Understandable though this may be, it is nevertheless a curious revelation to come from a man who is generally classed as a literary critic, especially when he remarks elsewhere that he rarely has much time for reading.[1] But whatever his reputation, Barthes does not actually look upon himself as a literary critic. He stated in *Critique et Vérité*, in 1966, that 'so long as criticism kept its traditional role of judging, it could only be conformist, that is to say acting in conformity with the interests of the judges', and it is clear that he sees all previous forms of literary criticism as merely so many tools in the hands of the ruling class.[2] He is in fact best seen rather as a new type of literary intellectual: a man who applies sociological, philosophical, psychological or linguistic categories to works of art, and does so with the intention of finding out what makes them tick rather than of judging them. Judgements do of course come through, and they often merge political and literary preferences inextricably together. But Barthes presents himself not as a traditional critic—someone who can offer an informed and balanced judgement because he has read a lot of other books—but as a man who, as he says of himself in *Roland Barthes par Roland Barthes*, suffers from his own particular illness: he *sees* language.[3] This image which he has of himself as someone obsessed with language, with the medium rather than the message, applies even to those works which, like the book on the nineteenth-century historian, Michelet, which he published in the *Ecrivains de toujours* series in 1954, might appear at first sight to be concerned with content rather than with form.

In fact, Barthes makes a point of summarising and dismissing Michelet's ideas in less than half a page. Michelet, he observes, believed that social classes would join together amicably but without disappearing; entertained the pious hope that labour and capital would work together in harmony; disliked machinery; combined

Voltaire's anti-clericalism with Rousseau's deism; held the people to be infallible; considered Béranger to be the greatest poet of the nineteenth century; regarded Germany (without Prussia) as a pleasant, genial country; looked upon England as a perfidious Albion; and held that France had two enemies: priests and English gold. Barthes clearly regards all this as a typically middle-class vision, quoting to illustrate his view the criticism which Marx made of the petty bourgeois mentality in the pamphlet which he published in 1853 entitled *Le 18 Brumaire de Louis Napoléon*.[4] He comments that Michelet has only 'the standard ideas of the *petite bourgeoisie* round about 1840', and quotes with apparent approval the French Marxist historian Mathiez's view that 'at the time Marx was writing *The Communist Manifesto*, Michelet was bleating about class unity'.[5] He both summarises his method and makes explicit his own prejudices in the declaration: 'Otez à Michelet sa thématique existentielle, il ne restera plus qu'un petit bourgeois' [Take away the existential thematics from his work, and Michelet is just a petty bourgeois];[6] and *Michelet par lui-même* is a book that contains, from a political point of view, virtually all the themes which make Barthes himself so typical a French left-wing intellectual of the mid-twentieth century: the belief that the term 'petty bourgeois' is the ultimate insult, the view that the touchstone of political thinking lies in the ability to detect the class war as the ultimate explanation of all historical events, the assumption that the events of nineteenth-century French history offer a paradigm capable of explaining all other modern societies, the readiness to see both Napoleons as very wicked and Maximilien de Robespierre as a great man, and a vigorous contempt towards anyone who does not agree with Balzac's diagnosis of money as the decisive element in modern society. But in the same way that certain of the passages which Barthes quotes from Michelet show him to have been, as it were, 'pas si petit bourgeois que cela'—especially in his anticipation of the attitudes inspiring a dictatorship of the proletariat[7]—so Barthes himself goes beyond both his own self-projected stereotype of a modern French literary theoretician who doesn't actually read many books. He may, indeed, be happy at times to see applied to himself Stendhal's remark that 'for anyone who has tasted the delights of writing, reading is but a pale pleasure'.[8] But one of the great merits of *Michelet par lui-même* lies in the fact that Barthes had clearly read each one of the forty volumes which make up Michelet's complete works.

Barthes's lack of interest in Michelet's ideology is, of course, fully in keeping with his frequently stated view that the contents of a work of art are less important than its form and structure. His remark in *Roland Barthes par Roland Barthes* that 'j'ai ma maladie, moi: je *vois* le langage', is also highly applicable to *Michelet par lui-même*, though possibly in a more conventional and accessible sense than it assumes

in his later work. For what interests him in Michelet is the richness
of the historian's language. It is this which contains the 'organised
network of obsessions' that Barthes is principally concerned to analyse,
and it is significant that his interest in Michelet should have originally
been aroused by reading the famous passage on the egg.[9] It was the
way Michelet entered into an almost symbiotic relationship with the
physical objects he described which fascinated Barthes and led him
to devote one of his long periods of convalescence from an attack of
tuberculosis to reading his work. It is this relationship with physical
objects and physical qualities that most interests Barthes, and which
he calls Michelet's 'existential thematics'. He dwells at length on the
way Michelet devours documents, virtually eating his way through
history; emphasises his liking for closed, warm, smooth objects like
the interior of a Dutch ship; relates his dislike of the Bourbon dynasty
to his horror of everything gross or swollen and his rejection of the
Napoleonic empires to the revulsion he feels in the presence of *la cirosité*
[waxiness]; quotes the famous passage in which, at the moment of
death, the dryness and sterility of Robespierre are exposed to the
triumphant warmth of the mob; and introduces the theme that was to
give *Michelet par lui-même* something of the same *succès de scandale* later
enjoyed by *Sur Racine* when he writes that 'for Michelet, Blood is the
cardinal substance of History'.[10]

   This approach to an author through the dominant features of his
physical sensitivity made a number of the critics who wrote about
Michelet par lui-même compare Barthes's method to the one inaugurated
and practised earlier by Gaston Bachelard. Thus in *L'Eau et les Rêves*
(1942), Bachelard had argued that if certain primitive philosophical
systems keep the ability to convince us of their truth, it is because
their formal, abstract principles are linked to one of the four fundamental elements that lie at the root of all human experience: earth,
water, fire, air. The poet, argues Bachelard, imposes his dreams and
visions upon us by associating them with the experience of the four
basic elements which we all keep in our unconscious mind, so that
any intellectual objections which we might have are swept aside by
the depth of the response which comes from our earliest and most
primitive memories. Barthes himself later observed, however, that
Michelet par lui-même actually owed very little to Bachelard's work.[11]
In 1954, he had not read Bachelard, and it is more probable that the
actual term *thématique existentielle* came from Sartre. *L'Etre et le Néant*
(1943) argues that our attitude towards certain physical qualities
such as *viscosité* [stickiness] reveals a great deal about how we ourselves
come to terms with existence, and Sartre's own analysis of Baudelaire
in 1946 had dwelt at some length on the 'existential significance' of
Baudelaire's dandyism, his cult of rich perfumes and his refusal to
lose himself in the sexual act.

Michelet par lui-même, however, also seems to contain a strong personal and subjective element in the importance which Barthes attributes to certain recurrent physical themes. Barthes himself is clearly fascinated by unctuous, all-enveloping surfaces, and the pages in which he dwells on Michelet's vision of the world as 'un objet délicieusement lisse' [a deliciously smooth object] and speaks of his presentation of the People as living in 'la nappe d'incubation où tout naît' [the enclosed incubation chamber in which everything comes to life] seem to show his own physical and linguistic obsessions rather more than those of Michelet. For his description of Michelet's sexual ideal as 'la conjonction des sexes adverses dans un ultra-sexe, troisième et complet ... la réfection magique d'un monde lisse, qui n'est plus déchiré entre des postulations contradictoires' [the conjunction of opposing sexes in an ultra-sex, third and complete ... the magical reconstruction of a smooth world, no longer destroyed by contradictory tendencies] is not the only passage in his work in which he seems almost pathologically obsessed by smoothness. In *Roland Barthes par Roland Barthes* he describes his most detested object, the *Doxa*, or established opinion, as 'un nappé général, épandu avec la bénédiction du Pouvoir' [a smooth coating spread out with the blessing of the Powers that Be], while in *Mythologies* his account of how, in the kind of recipes recommended by the magazine *Elle*, 'la catégorie substantielle qui domine, c'est le nappé' rises to a veritable crescendo of descriptive, obsessive lyricism. 'On s'ingénie visiblement', he writes,

> à glacer les surfaces, à les arrondir, à enfouir l'aliment sous le sédiment lisse des sauces, des crèmes, des fondants et des gelées. Cela tient évidemment à la finalité même du nappé, qui est d'ordre visuel, et la cuisine d'*Elle* est une pure cuisine de la vue, qui est un sens distingué.
>
> [The 'substantial category' which prevails in this type of cooking is that of the smooth coating: there is an obvious endeavour to glaze surfaces, to round them off, to bury the food under the even sediment of sauces, creams, icing and jellies. This of course comes from the very finality of the coating, which belongs to a visual category, and cooking according to *Elle* is meant for the eye alone, since sight is a genteel sense.][12]

One of the reviewers of *Michelet par lui-même* was clearly annoyed by the frequency with which Barthes came back to this and other themes. 'These words: smooth, equation, death/sleep, sun/death, are maniac's words', wrote an anonymous reviewer in *Le Monde*. 'Say: "man does not wholly understand himself". But, for Heaven's sake, say it in French! You would then see that your discoveries are commonplaces, to which comic labels give a false appearance of being scientific.'[13] Barthes had already been attacked for writing jargon when *Le degré zéro de l'écriture* was published, and the accusation is one that has followed him throughout his literary career. But at least nobody has even been able to accuse him of reductionism, of claiming—for example—that all Michelet's ideas about Joan of Arc as the personification of French history, about the wickedness of the priesthood or about the long-term benefits of the Barbarian invasions, are merely the product of a particular set of physical obsessions, and are therefore nothing more than an attempt to rationalise a purely personal and subjective vision. Indeed, the Barthes of *Michelet par lui-même* goes to the opposite extreme. In his view, it is only because Michelet's ideological preferences have so firm a basis in his direct physical apprehension of the world that they are worth discussing. This is what he means where he says, 'Take away his existential thematics, and all that is left of Michelet is a petty bourgeois', and *Michelet par lui-même* could be seen as yet another sign of how completely the existentialist attitude carries romanticism to its logical conclusion. For the romantic, the more intense the experience, the more valid the ideas based upon it. For the atheistic existentialist such as Sartre, no set of ideas can be ultimately true, since there is no God to guarantee it. What takes the place of God is the intensity and authenticity which the individual attains through his relationship with his own body and his own physical experiences. Michelet's ideas, in other words, may be utter nonsense, but they attain a certain validity through the network of physical obsessions which gives them life. Viewed in this context, as a symptom of a general tendency rather than as something which exists in its own right, the central argument in *Michelet par lui-même* can be seen as characteristic of certain attitudes current in mid-twentieth-century French literature.

Michelet par lui-même is indeed very much the product of French intellectual life in the 1950s, with its Sartrean or Bachelardian existentialist overtones and its automatic presupposition that Marx is always right and the lower middle classes [*la petite bourgeoisie*] always wrong. Neither can an outside observer avoid seeing a parallel between *Michelet par lui-même* and the intellectual movement with which Barthes later came to be most frequently associated, that of structuralism. Thus for structuralist linguistics, the historical process—or set of historical accidents—which led to a language being what it is today holds only an anecdotal interest. What matters is the way the language functions here and now. Similarly, for Claude Lévi-Strauss, there is no point in speculating on how the myths which he presents as incarnating certain permanent features of the human mind came to assume the particular form in which he found them. They are simply there, as the means whereby human beings make sense of their own experience, and must be studied without reference to their genesis. And, for the Barthes of *Michelet par lui-même*, the question of what accidents in Michelet's life led him to think and feel as he did never arises. What matters is the existence in Michelet's work of the 'organised network of obsessions' that enabled him to give organic unity to a set of social and intellectual ideas which have no general validity whatsoever. Had the language which Michelet used not embodied the intensity with which he saw the world in terms of smoothness, appetite, fatness, 'cirosity' and blood, his ideas would have merely an historical interest. They would have done little more than reflect what Barthes calls 'l'ensommeillement radical-socialiste',[14] the shallow confidence of the non-Marxist progressive parties which flourished in nineteenth-century France that progress could be achieved without the class struggle.

This refusal to speculate as to why Michelet happened to feel in terms of 'delicious unctuosity', why he disliked tobacco because he thought it would put people off sex, or why he constantly reverted to 'the few essential movements of matter: liquefaction, stickiness, emptiness, dryness, electricity' fits in with Barthes's insistence elsewhere that the author comes into existence only from the moment that he puts pen to paper. He dwells a good deal on Michelet's susceptibility to migraine—an 'essentially civilised' ailment which he shares with Barthes himself[15]—and conjures up a magnificent vision of Michelet eating his way through history, producing forty volumes while living as a perpetual invalid. But he does not indulge in the type of speculation practised by more biographical critics, and suggest that Michelet was like this because he once saw something nasty in the woodshed. It is not that Barthes completely refrains from talking about Michelet the man. Indeed, his speculations on the nature of Michelet's sexual life were to cause something of a minor scandal when the book appeared. But the starting-point for his analysis of Michelet's sexuality lay in the printed word as it was publicly available. He worked backwards from the text, inferring the existence of personal tastes from the work as it existed, not arguing that the work stemmed from the personal tastes and could therefore be discounted as mere rationalisation.

The inferences which Barthes drew from his study of Michelet's work were nevertheless rather surprising. Michelet, he argued, was obsessed by the menstrual cycle. 'For Michelet', he wrote—adding that there were a 'multitude of indiscreet professions of faith' on this point—

femininity is complete only at the moment when the woman is having her periods. Which means that the aim of love is less to possess woman than to uncover her secrets: the keenest spur to love is not so much beauty as the storm. Michelet's erotic system clearly takes no account of the pleasures of the orgasm, while he does attribute considerable importance to Woman at her times of crisis, that is to say to Woman humiliated. It is an erotic system based on seeing, not on possession, and Michelet in love, Michelet satisfied, is nothing other than Michelet the peeping Tom.

What Michelet called pity, Barthes argued, was never anything but the 'erotic spectacle of Woman in a state of humiliation', and he quoted long passages from Michelet's books on *L'Amour* and *La Femme* to show that the genuine privilege of the husband lay not in making love to his wife but in usurping the chambermaid's function of looking after the woman at the time when she was having her periods. The orgasm, wrote Barthes, was excluded from Michelet's erotic paradise 'precisely in so far as it is foreign to the ceremony of devotion with which men should surround women.'[16]

This is all good clean stuff for the psychiatrist's couch or a Soho bookshop, and helps to explain why *Michelet par lui-même* should have made something of a stir at the time. One leading scholar of Michelet's work, Claude Digeon, accused Barthes of presenting Michelet as an 'obsédé sexuel',[17] and the situation might have become quite embarrassing for Barthes's reputation had it not been for one important factor: the existence of Michelet's then unpublished *Journal*. Like everyone else, Barthes knew of its existence, but unlike other critics he had sufficient confidence in his own method to pronounce on its contents. It was virtually certain, he wrote in *Michelet par lui-même*, that this diary has no other theme than what Michelet called 'the love crisis which makes woman what she is, this divine rhythm which, month by month, marks out time for her.'[18]

Shortly after the appearance of *Michelet par lui-même* in the spring of 1954, an article was published in *Combat* by the two historians, Lucien Febre and Daniel Halévy, who were then preparing an edition of Michelet's diary. It stated that from what they had seen of the *Journal* so far, Barthes's analysis of Michelet's sexual peculiarities was not wholly fanciful, and recalled some of the circumstances of his married life. Michelet had met his second wife, Athénaïs Mialevet, in 1948, when he was fifty years old and she twenty. She—not surprisingly—survived him, and presented so imposing a figure that André Hébraud is said to have observed that she enabled you to understand why the guillotine was popularly known as *La Veuve* [the Widow].[19] In addition to rewriting his unpublished works to make sure they fitted in with what she thought Michelet ought to have said, Athénaïs also did everything in her power to ensure that his wishes as far as the appearance of the *Journal* was concerned were respected. She was posthumously helped in this by Gabriel Monod, who was equally anxious that nothing should appear which damaged Michelet's memory. It was thus not until 1950 that work could begin on publishing it in its entirety, and the two volumes which it eventually constituted did not finally appear until 1959 and 1962. The fact that Michelet did note down when his wife was having her periods appeared to lend support to Barthes's thesis, and led one of his former critics, V. H. Debidour, to confess that he would now be inclined to treat Barthes's 'irritating and, in the last resort, unintentionally cruel'[20] essay on Michelet less severely than he had done in the past. When even the ranks of Tuscany are thus prepared almost to cheer, the Barthes of *Michelet par lui-même* might seem at first sight to have achieved a victory comparable to those of his fellow pioneers in structuralism, Ferdinand de Saussure, Charles Mauron and Lucien Goldmann.

Saussure, whose methods Barthes was to emulate more systematically later on in his career in *Mythologies* (1957) or *Système de la Mode* (1967), had begun his career with an essay which is now regarded as one of the first attempts at structural linguistics. In his *Mémoire sur le système primitif des voyelles dans les langues indo-europeénnes* (1879), published when he was only twenty-one, Saussure had set out to solve the problem of why the Proto-Indo-European vowel system, which was thought to be the same as that of Sanskrit, nevertheless contained the four vowels of a, e, o and ā as opposed to Sanskrit's three: a, a2, ā. He did this by postulating, as Maurice Leroy puts it, 'the existence in Indo-European of a phoneme (later called *shwa* and represented by ə) which had been an integral part of the very flexible system of sonants but which had disappeared in the historically attested languages'. It was only in 1927, forty-eight years after the publication of Saussure's original *Mémoire*, that the hypothesis which he had formulated on structuralist grounds was confirmed by independently acquired empirical evidence. Jerzy Kuryłowicz observed that the Hittite consonants transcribed with a ẖ corresponded to the ones which Saussure had argued must have existed in order to create the situation in which the short Indo-European a became ā and subsequently e and o.[21]

A similar case history illustrating the virtues of structuralism had also been provided in a literary context by the critic Charles Mauron, whose book *L'inconscient dans l'œuvre et la vie de Racine* (1957) was later to supply the source for a number of the ideas which Barthes expressed in *Sur Racine* in 1963. In 1940, Mauron had argued in *Mallarmé l'Obscur* that both the 'irresistible nostalgia' of Mallarmé's early poems and certain features of his private life and later work stemmed from a childhood fixation on a young girl, whom he had known and loved and who had died. 'All these features', he wrote, analysing Mallarmé's early work, 'fit together to indicate *en filigrane* [as a watermark] precisely this deep childhood affection, deeper even than the love felt by a man, and which must have linked Mallarmé to his wife by the most secret bonds.'[22] In the very next year, 1941, Henri Mondor published his monumental *Vie de Mallarmé*, and included in it the following phrase from a letter which Mallarmé had written at the age of twenty-seven to his friend Cazalis: '. . . ce pauvre jeune fantôme qui était ma sœur et qui fut la seule personne que j'adorasse avant de vous connaître tous' ['. . . this poor young ghost who for thirteen years was my sister and who was the only person I adored before meeting all of you'].[23] The reference was clearly to Mallarmé's sister Maria, who had died in 1857 at the age of thirteen, and whom no previous critic or biographer of Mallarmé had so much as mentioned. Although there were, as Mauron was the first to acknowledge, a great number of other features in Mallarmé's poetry that this memory of his dead sister did not explain, his approach had both identified a number of previously unnoticed patterns and explained why they were there. In 1963, when Mauron presented his book entitled *Des métaphores obsédantes au mythe personnel* for the Doctorat-ès-Lettres at the Sorbonne, Marie-Jeanne Durry praised him for having inaugurated a method which produced results that were, like those of a real scientist, directly verifiable ('directement contrôlables').[24]

It was a method which, like the one first practised by Saussure in 1879, depended not on a deductive but on an inductive process of reasoning. It was also one that was to be practised in another literary context by Lucien Goldmann in a book which appeared shortly after the publication of *Michelet par lui-même*. For it was in 1956 that Goldmann published both *Le Dieu caché*, his study of the tragic vision in the work of Pascal and Racine, and the correspondence of the Abbé Martin de Barcos. Early on in his researches, Goldmann had inferred from his study of Pascal and Racine that the Jansenist movement in seventeenth-century France must have contained an ecclesiastical hard-liner, a neo-Augustinian hawk. If such a person had not existed, there would have been no ideological inspiration for the extremist wing of the movement whose influence on Pascal was so very strong. Goldmann too had validated his method by following the indications it offered him until he came across the person of Martin de Barcos, and was able to edit the correspondence in which this intransigent cleric had insisted upon the uncompromising nature of the true Christian's rejection of all worldly concerns.

For the admirer of structuralism, albeit in this early and suspiciously understandable form, the similarities between the *Mémoire sur le système primitif des voyelles dans les langues indo-européennes*, *Mallarmé l'Obscur*, *Le Dieu caché* and *Michelet par lui-même* are indeed striking. Even though Saussure, Mauron, Goldmann and Barthes might not have recognised it themselves—a very structuralist situation—they were all following modes of enquiry which had pronounced similarities. In each case, they began by examining not the circumstances surrounding or preceding the existence of the phenomenon that interested them, but the phenomenon itself. Each then adopted what is known in linguistics as a synchronic rather than a diachronic approach. That is to say, each studied the phenomenon as a system which works here and now, and postulated the existence of unseen or previously unknown factors by arguing that it would not work without them. Even Goldmann, a convinced Marxist if ever there was one, studied Jansenism as a system before turning to its possible historical origins, and it is not difficult to see why Jean-Paul Sartre later denounced structuralism as essentially a-historical and consequently opposed to the interests of the revolution. In the case of *Michelet par lui-même*, however, there is no need to invoke so historically-minded an ideology as Marxism to point out the weakness of Barthes's approach. In one of his earliest works, *Aesthetics and Psychology* (translated into English by Roger Fry and Katherine John), Charles Mauron had himself told the charming story of how an Eastern prince, attending a number of European balls, asserted that they were invariably followed by scandalous orgies as soon as the lights went out. 'Did you witness the orgies?' someone asked. 'No', he replied, 'but it was obvious'.[25] It is an anecdote which has some applicability to Barthes's *Michelet par lui-même*, since the actual reading of Michelet's *Journal* is less flattering to Barthes's critical perspicacity than either these structural parallels or Professor Debidour's palinode might suggest.

Thus so long as Michelet's first wife is alive, the menstrual cycle is absent from his diary. It is only after he has married Athénaïs, and has discovered that her enthusiasm for his ideas is not matched by an ability to enjoy the sexual act, that he begins to note down a number of details about the frequency and quality of her menstrual flow. But he also comments with even greater frequency on the fact that she has toothache, that he himself has frequent attacks of flu and gastro-enteritis, and that Athénaïs is often distressingly constipated.[26] Indeed, as Jacqueline Piatier observed in her review of Michelet's *Journal* in *Le Monde*, the entries concerning Athénaïs are rather more clinical in tone than *Michelet par lui-même* might have led one to expect, and really betoken little more than the natural concern in a passionate man over his wife's inability to enjoy sex.[27] Had the whole of the *Journal* been available when Barthes wrote *Michelet par lui-même*, he might have been less confident in claiming that Michelet's obsession with the menstrual cycle constituted its main and even exclusive theme. But his own intellectual preoccupation with what he calls 'the death of the author' would still have prevented him from giving a more balanced account of Michelet's attitude to sex. For he would still have attributed to Michelet's 'organised network of obsessions' something which a more orthodox critic would have more convincingly explained by reference to an unwise and fundamentally rather unhappy marriage.

Where *Michelet par lui-même* offers a rather more genuine insight into women's condition is in the passages which Barthes quotes to show how fully Michelet adopted the typically nineteenth-century vision of woman as a being entirely different from men. 'She does not eat as we do', writes Michelet, 'neither as much nor the same dishes. Why not? Above all because she does not digest as we do. Her digestion is constantly disturbed by one thing: she loves 'from the very depths of her being' ['du fond de ses entrailles'].[28] This complete 'otherness' of woman reveals itself particularly, according to Michelet, when she goes sea-bathing, and when the male spectators on the beach see her emerging 'pâle, hâve, effrayante, avec un frisson mortel' ['pale, haggard, terrifying, with a deadly shiver'][29] from the waves. It is then, Michelet adds, that a devoted and indispensable person should be there, 'ready to help, watching over her, rubbing her at the harsh moment of the return to land with a very warm towel, giving her a light cordial or a warm drink, in which he has put a few drops of a powerful elixir'. One of the major themes in Barthes's *Mythologies*, his most accessible and probably his most influential book, is the way petty bourgeois civilisation consistently presents cultural and therefore transient phenomena as if they were natural, permanent and inevitable. In no other aspect of his work does Michelet more completely deserve the strictures which Barthes reserves for the petty bourgeois mentality, for nowhere else does he show how completely he regards the cultural patterns of his society as establishing an unalterably natural model.

Michelet par lui-même confirmed the reputation which Barthes was acquiring as one of the leaders in the new school of criticism growing up in France. Gaëtan Picon[30] compared him to Georges Poulet and Jean-Pierre Richard, both of whom were making a similar attempt to analyse the way in which literary creation reflects the fundamental emotive and psycho-physiological categories of the human mind. Jean-Pierre Richard's *Littérature et Sensation* was in fact published in the same year as *Michelet par lui-même*, and resembled it in analysing Stendhal, Flaubert, Fromentin and the Goncourt brothers in terms of this physical sensation dominant in their work. In Stendhal, for example, Richard found a constant tendency to divide and circumscribe matter, in Flaubert what he called a 'passive voracity', in Fromentin an obsession with landscapes and in the Goncourts an intense concern for the most minute details in surfaces. In a broader context, both *Littérature et Sensation* and *Michelet par lui-même* can be seen as part of the greater awareness which human beings now have of themselves as complex psycho-physiological phenomena, an awareness all the more interesting in the France of the 1950s because it constituted not only a continuing escape from the nineteenth-century taboos on discussions about sex but also a reaction against the predominantly Cartesian model of the human mind. For Descartes, body and mind are distinct and separate entities, the second nobler than the first because it is the only possible source of true ideas. Even Sartre, with his insistence that the mind has the duty and ability to dominate the body—you are sea-sick only if you accept that you will be, he told Simone de Beauvoir[31]—belongs in a way to the Cartesian tradition, and it could be argued that it is only with the works of Merleau-Ponty and books like *L'Eau et les Rêves, Littérature et Sensation* or *Michelet par lui-même* that the hold of Cartesian image on the French mind has really begun to be broken. Except for some interestingly dissentient voices, *Michelet par lui-même* was well received, and there is nowadays no shortage of reviewers prepared to agree that Michelet's own recently revived popularity is partly the result of Barthes's essay.[32]

II

Yet while Barthes may have been partly responsible for a revival of fortune as far as Michelet is concerned, a more likely explanation lies in the extraordinary ability of late capitalist civilisation both to support those who set out to destroy it and to revive thinkers whose work might appear at first sight to have only a tangential relevance to the last third of the twentieth century. The other writer who most preoccupied Barthes in the early 1950s belonged, albeit in what nowadays seems a rather mild way, to the destroyers. From the foundation of the review *Théâtre Populaire* in May 1953, Barthes led a veritable campaign in favour of Bertolt Brecht, and rounded off his campaign by writing a long commentary on a superb collection of photographs of the performance given in Paris at the *Théâtre des Nations* in 1957 of *Mother Courage and her Children*. He remarked in an interview published in 1971 that Brecht was 'a Marxist who had reflected on the value of signs; something of a rarity' ['un Marxiste qui avait réfléchi sur la valeur du signe: chose rare'],[33] and his writings about Brecht bring together two of his fundamental interests: his Marxism and his concern for the way in which signs can, do and should work in modern society. These writings also form part of a general theory of what the theatre itself can and should do, and an account of the contribution which Barthes made to *Théâtre Populaire* is not only interesting on general aesthetic and political grounds. It is also a good introduction to the more systematic analysis of how communication systems work in modern society which he undertakes in *Mythologies* and *Système de la Mode*.

Barthes is naturally hostile to the commercial theatre and he would scarcely be a representative intellectual of any modern Western society if he were not. The editorial that he wrote for the fifth number of *Théâtre Populaire*, in January 1954, proclaimed that he and his colleagues 'spewed out' the theatre based on money ['le théâtre que nous vomissons, c'est le théâtre de l'Argent'], and he expressed himself in similarly vigorous terms when he declared in a lecture entitled *Les maladies du costume du théâtre* that plays in which you couldn't see the action for the costumes were those where 'the terrible cancer of wealth'

had completely devoured the theatre itself.[34] Albert Camus said much
the same in his lecture on Jacques Copeau in 1953, and Barthes also
shared Camus's distaste for dramas based on adulterous intrigues
among the upper middle classes. This distaste was also linked, in
Barthes as in Camus and Sartre, to a preference for a theatre in which
the issues at stake were not those of man's private conscience but of his
moral and political destiny. For Barthes, any theatre which concentrated on the individual psychology of the characters on stage or on
the expression of the author's own personal dilemmas merely reinforced the bourgeois illusion that literature must inevitably concern
itself with the exquisite complexities of the human heart. He much
preferred the classical Greek drama in which, he claimed, the 'feelings'
of the characters (pride, jealousy, rancour, indignation) are 'in no
way psychological, in the modern sense of the word'. He continued:

> They are not individualist passions, born in the solitude of a ro-
> mantic heart. Pride here is not a sin, a marvellous and complicated
> form of evil; it is an offence against the city, an example of political
> excess; rancour is never anything but the expression of a former
> right, that of the vendetta, while indignation is never anything but
> the rhetorical demand for a new right, the sign that the people
> have reached the stage of judging and condemning the ancient
> laws.[35]

The theatre, for Barthes, is not an evening's entertainment that takes
our minds off the mortgage. It is a means whereby we participate, at a
higher level of awareness than can be found elsewhere, in the collective
passions and political dilemmas of our time.

There is again a resemblance between Barthes's ideas and the theory
and practice of Jean-Paul Sartre as a playwright. Sartre explained in
1946 that the recourse which he and his contemporaries had had to
Greek myths stemmed from their desire to replace psychological
analysis by the treatment of moral and political issues such as conflicts
of rights. He too, like Barthes, preferred what he called a 'theatre of
situations' to a 'theatre of characters',[36] and in a theatrical context
this attack on psychologising also leads to a wholly different view of
the actor's role. This is no longer to establish a kind of magical communication between himself and the audience, enabling them to
share each mood and emotion that he incarnates. It is to enable the
audience to understand intellectually what the situation is. When the
theatre is based on money, there is a contract whereby the playwright
and producer guarantee the spectator a sumptuous spectacle and a
good laugh—or cry—in return for the five pounds he has paid for his
seat in the orchestra stalls. The theatre which Barthes envisages is
more intellectual and austere.

If Brecht had not existed, Barthes would surely have had to invent him. What seems to have happened, however, is that Barthes was already thinking in these terms when the Berliner Ensemble came to Paris in May 1954. The experience of seeing Brecht acted as Brecht intended served as a kind of catalyst which enabled Barthes to develop his vision of what the theatre should be like. Indeed, Barthes himself uses the words 'illumination', 'incendie' and 'éblouissement' [he 'saw visions', was 'set on fire', 'dazzled'] to evoke the overwhelming effect that the Berliner Ensemble had on him, and the visit seems to have been a major intellectual event in his life.[37] In particular, the Brechtian notion of *Verfremdung* [*distanciation, distancement,* estrangement, alienation] provided the basis for a whole new conception of the theatre as a place where the audience is made to see things happening rather than encouraged to enjoy vicarious emotions. This conception of the theatre also has two other striking parallels with the rest of Barthes's work: by its initially unexpected resemblance with his analysis of all-in wrestling; and by the imagery that it leads him to use in order to express the unpleasant experience from which the Brechtian notion of *Verfremdung* provides an escape. This again highlights the extent to which Barthes's analysis of some of Michelet's apparently obsessive imagery may well reflect some of his own physical preoccupations, as well as reinforcing the impression that his apparently very complicated way of thinking is centred around a number of relatively simple ideas.

The essence of all-in wrestling, for the Barthes of *Mythologies,* lies in the openness with which the wrestlers present their performance as obviously faked. There is, he argues, no pretence at the realism that exists in boxing matches. What the wrestlers offer their public in place of this realism is a world that is made intelligible with a completeness that can never exist in real life, intelligible because of the openly histrionic nature of their gestures and attitudes. Like the Roman actor whose mask and motto of *Larvatus Prodeo* provide the illustration for the central argument in *Le degré zéro de l'écriture* about the need for the writer to proclaim the artificial nature of literature, the all-in wrestler proclaims from the very outset that nothing he is doing is genuine or real. Like the ideal Brechtian actor, he does not invite or expect the spectator to sympathise with him. The romantic concept of sincerity, of the actor moving the audience because he is moved himself, is at the furthest possible remove from the aesthetic which Barthes derives from Brecht's theory and practice in the theatre. 'What the whole Brechtian concept of the theatre implies', he wrote in 1956, 'is that today at least, dramatic art tends less to express reality than to signify it' ['tend moins à exprimer le réel qu'à le signifier'].[38]

One of the shortest and most interesting articles in which Barthes put forward this view about Brecht is entitled *Mère Courage Aveugle.* It analyses the way in which Helene Weigel played the name part, and uses this as a basis for Brecht's ideal of how the actor should perform. What Barthes especially singles out is Mother Courage's apparent inability, when played by Helene Weigel, to understand what is happening around her. Not only does she not see the horrors of the Thirty Years War. She is not emotionally involved in them either, and it is precisely as a result of the almost somnabulistic way in which, according to Barthes, she moves through history without understanding it that the audience is compelled to see and understand on her behalf. Were she involved in what is happening and were we, in the audience, emotionally caught up with her sufferings, invited to the tears, sympathy, connivance and participation still sought by actors performing in the bourgeois tradition, we should not be detached enough to be able to see and understand everything that is happening. We should—the word recurs three times in the three pages occupied by the article—be 'empoissés' [stuck down][39], unable to stand aside and judge. The sticky sentimentality of petty bourgeois culture would, in Barthes's view, so bog us down in our own and the actors' emotions that the free and vital understanding of our historical alienation brought about by the Brechtian *Verfrèmdung* could not take place.

There is thus in Barthes, as there is in Sartre, a passion for liberty which takes the form of trying to protect freedom at its very source: in the human mind. This is why Barthes develops an aesthetic of the theatre which reduces its hypnotic effects to a minimum, and also perhaps why he differs on at least one point from his fellow left-wing French intellectuals—including Sartre himself—by having little enthusiasm for the cinema. Films, in his view, envelop the spectator in what he calls, in *Roland Barthes par Roland Barthes*, a 'smooth, unremitting continuum of images',[40] and it would clearly be difficult, in practice and in theory, to have a film star practising a Brechtian *Verfremdung*. Perhaps Marilyn Monroe did it in *The Seven Year Itch*, where she effectively defused her own sexuality by playing it as a joke, but a more common experience in the cinema is the one that Barthes analyses in his article on Elia Kazan's *On the Waterfront* in *Mythologies*. There, he observes, we are made to identify ourselves entirely with Marlon Brando, 'empoissés dans une communion de destin avec ce docker qui ne retrouve le sens de la justice sociale que pour en faire hommage et don au capital américain'[41] ['stuck down in a shared destiny with this docker who rediscovers the meaning of social justice only to hand it over in respectful homage to American capitalism'], and the kind of non-participatory, detached understanding which is Barthes's dramatic ideal is possible only in a theatre which goes against all prevailing fashions in popular entertainment. For Barthes, it is only when we are not filled with admiration for the beautiful costumes and elaborate scenery, or hypnotised by the electric personality of the leading lady, that we can make full use of our intellectual freedom.

In 1943, Sartre had given a new twist to the Orestes legend by using it as the basis for a play, *Les Mouches*, in which the French were fairly explicitly urged to reject the reactionary cult of guilt and remorse encouraged by the Vichy government and told, instead, to take their fate into their own hands. In the article which he published in *Théâtre Populaire* in 1955, *Comment représenter l'antique*, Barthes again seemed to be following Sartre's example in arguing that the Aeschylean original itself, the *Oresteia*, was—when replaced in its historical context—'an unquestionably progressive work'. It bore witness, he maintained, to 'the passage from a matriarchal society, represented by the Erinyes, to the patriarchal society represented by Apollo and Athena'.[42] What it showed, in Barthes's view, was men's ability to escape from the weight of the past and create new values with which to confront and transcend new political situations, and the determinedly progressive cast of Barthes's own thought was to recur in *Sur Racine*, in 1963, when he put forward a similar interpretation of the character of Pyrrhus in *Andromaque*. Pyrrhus's famous question to Andromaque, 'Peut-on haïr sans cesse? et punit-on toujours?', was not, for Barthes, a piece of self-interested emotional pleading by a man ready to use any and every argument to persuade his enemy's widow to go to bed with him. It was part of an attempt to begin a *vita nuova* in which all the values of the past are consciously rejected.[43] Perhaps naturally, Barthes also finds this concept of an open future in Brecht, arguing on a number of occasions that Brecht's dramatic technique underlines the extent to which men can take control of their own history, and both he and Sartre are here writing well within the Marxist tradition. The essential fear from which man suffers, argued the Sartre of *Matérialisme et Révolution* in 1947, is neither death nor the existence of a stern God. It is 'simply the idea that the state of things from which he suffers should have been created and maintained for transcendent and unknowable ends'.[44] Barthes, in comparably progressive temper, maintains throughout his whole work, and especially in his approach to Brecht, that the intellectual understanding of what is happening to them through the action of other men in history is the first and essential step which people must take if they are to realise that society does not exist for 'transcendent and unknowable ends' and that it can therefore be changed.

What Brecht teaches by his theory and practice in the theatre is thus, in Barthes's view, that the sufferings which men undergo are historical and not natural in origin, that they stem from the action of other men and not from some inescapable fate or from the unalterable nature of things. These are concepts which Barthes will exploit and explain in more detail in *Mythologies*, developing more fully an idea which he only begins to adumbrate in his writings on the theatre. For when he remarks, in one of his articles on Brecht, that the signs used in the theatre must be 'partly arbitrary, for otherwise one relapses into an expressionistic art, an art of essentialist illusions',[45] he is suggesting just why it is important that Brecht is 'a Marxist who has reflected on the nature of signs'. If all signs meant exactly one thing, only one thing and inevitably one thing, then an essential part of human liberty would disappear. Man would no longer have the ability given to him by the ambiguity of language to interpret events in different ways and constantly to see things differently. A world in which the word 'table', for example, had only one possible meaning, defined for all eternity in exactly the same way in all the dictionaries, would be a world in which human speech would be so predetermined that the very idea of freedom simply could not arise. And if, in a less rigorous manner, the audience in the theatre were held captive by the signs displayed before them, by the décor and the costume, then the theatre could never become what Barthes would like to make it: the place where men encounter and become conscious of the freedom which, as individuals, they have to understand and alter history.

Barthes wrote relatively little on the theatre once he had made out the case for Brecht against what he frequently presents as an anti-intellectualist conspiracy to deny his importance.[46] In 1955, however, he did come to the defence of Jean-Paul Sartre's *Nekrassov* when it was receiving a mauling from the critics, and his article was later reprinted in the collection entitled *Sartre et les critiques de notre temps*.[47] For Barthes, the hostility shown towards *Nekrassov*, a play which satirised the excesses of professional anti-communists in the French right-wing press, was basically political. While pretending to criticise Sartre on aesthetic grounds, comparing his failure to write a well-constructed play to the common middle-class experience of realising that 'l'ouvrier français a perdu le goût du travail' ['French workmen just don't *want* to work nowadays'], the bourgeois writers who were trying to kill off *Nekrassov* were obeying a far more fundamental intellectual tendency. 'The bourgeoisie', wrote Barthes, 'has always had a very tyrannical but very selective idea of reality: reality is what it sees, not what exists',[48] and its hostility to the Sartre of 1955 stemmed from a refusal to see French society as it really was: dominated by a conspiracy which the press, the police and the government had invented in order to slander the Communist Party. For Barthes, Sartre was absolutely right to denounce this conspiracy, and he himself found consolation for the poor critical reception of *Nekrassov* in the thought that it would, each evening, liberate 'des Français qui, comme moi, souffrent d'étouffer sous le mal bourgeois'[49] ['French people who, like myself, suffer from being stifled by the sickness of bourgeois society'].

III

Both in his articles on Brecht and in his later discussion of prose fiction in *S/Z*, Barthes exhibits a puritanical zeal which invites a reply based upon Sir Toby Belch's question to Malvolio: does he think, because he appreciates Brecht, that we shall have no more Terence Rattigans? For Barthes to detest a theatre based on money is fine. It is his right in a free society. For Barthes to extend our range of dramatic appreciation by showing us how interesting Brecht's plays can be is even better. It is part of the essential role which the intellectual plays in society. But when he sneers at 'les salles de cinéma s'amollissant aux aventures du couple de *Brève Rencontre*' ['cinema audiences going all gooey over the adventures of the couple in *Brief Encounter*'] or of 'les questions byzantines du théâtre bourgeois relatives aux droits internes du cocuage' ['the Byzantine questions of the bourgeois theatre about the private rights of cuckoldry'], one wonders what entertainment will be allowed when he is the philosopher-king. Racine and Corneille will clearly do no better than Noël Coward or André Roussin, for he is equally dismissive about 'la fausse tragédie du XVIIe siècle', in which 'L'essentialisme classique a substitué un théâtre de types à la dramaturgie des grandes idées morales, qui seules peuvent s'imposer avec passion à l'intelligence d'une communauté' ['Classical essentialism has substituted a theatre of types to the dramaturgy of great ethical notions, which alone can impose themselves with passionate force on the mind of a community'].[50] Later on in his career, when he becomes associated with the *Tel Quel* group, Barthes's views on what constitutes acceptable literature become even more dismissive of earlier aesthetic achievements, and it is interesting to speculate on why he is so aggressive towards books and writers that he does not like. Is it, as I suggested earlier, part of the quest which all orphan Oedipuses must undertake for an identifiable Laius whom they can slay? Is it yet another symptom of the lust for power which inspires left-wing intellectuals, and which finds its satisfaction in imposing literary norms when the successes of capitalist society block the way to political action? Is it merely a piece of rhetorical exaggeration, something said to attract attention but not to be taken seriously? Or is it, to revert to one of the main themes of this study, because Barthes is so French a left-wing intellectual?

Thus it may well be that French society is more oppressive towards its intellectuals than the outside admirer might think. In an article in the special number which the *Times Literary Supplement* devoted in 1971 to the problems and nature of literary criticism, Barthes argued that the bourgeoisie such as Marx defined it, the class of landowners, employers, high-grade executives, senior civil servants, had been evicted from power not by the proletariat or by the lower middle class but by the State. It was the State which had become the new source of economic power and of intellectual influence and cultural prestige. The State was prepared to slacken its hold on the universities, because it knew that it was not there that 'the new conquering culture is made'. But never, argued Barthes, would it give up its hold on radio and television. 'If it owns these cultural channels', he wrote, 'then the culture to which it can dictate is the real one, and by dictating to it, it makes it its culture, a culture within which the class which has handed in its intellectural resignation (the bourgeoisie), the class which is being promoted (the lower middle class) and the silent class (the proletariat) are all obliged to meet together.'[51] In the 1950s and early 1960s the hold of the French State on the mass media was even more powerful than it is today, and it may be that the sense of ideological claustrophobia which makes Barthes and his followers feel so persecuted by their society is due to nothing more complicated than the absence of a French equivalent to the BBC.

Barthes's own reply to anyone who drew his attention to the intolerant nature of some of his literary pronouncements would undoubtedly run parallel to Sartre's apology for revolutionary violence. Sartre maintains that all violence stemming from the oppressed is merely a 'counter-violence' triggered off by the violence constantly exercised against them by the very structure of bourgeois imperialist society, and Barthes would argue that his intolerance of the commercial theatre is merely a legitimate response to the intolerance which the commercial theatre is said to show towards the avant-garde. There is, however, a more literary aspect to the intense Frenchness of Roland Barthes as left-wing intellectual, and that is his conformity to the long-established tradition whereby French writers form themselves into categories and mutually denunciatory schools. The most famous *évidence* or self-evident truth in English literary theory, Kipling's observation in 'In the Neolithic Age' that

> There are nine and sixty ways of constructing tribal lays,
> And–every–single–one–of–them–is–right!

has never been regarded as axiomatic on the other side of the Channel. There, the struggles between classical and romantic concepts of literature, between realists, symbolists, Parnassians, existentialists, rationalists and surrealists take place in a welter of proclamations of faith, excommunications and *pronunciamientos* which always assume that everybody is wrong except the last speaker and that only one kind of literature is acceptable. The two schools with which Barthes has been most closely associated, the *nouveaux romanciers* of the 1950s and the *Tel Quel* group in the sixties and seventies, have almost carried this substitution of manifestos for creative writing to an art form in its own right, and it is therefore not surprising that he should so delight in nailing his theses and opponents to the church door of Saint-Germain-des-Prés.

3 Signs, myths and politics

The first of the fifty short essays which make up the volume entitled *Mythologies* was published in the monthly review *Esprit* in October 1952, at a time when Barthes was still relatively unknown. It was entitled *Le Monde où l'on catche*, and is still one of the most entertaining of the *mythologies*. In 1958, it was reprinted in its entirety, accompanied by some superb photography, in the semi-official monthly review *Education Physique et Sport*, and is one of the few serious attempts to analyse a phenomenon which lies on an interesting borderline between sport and popular entertainment.[1] It attracted sufficient attention for Maurice Nadeau, who had already played some part in Barthes's career by taking the essays in *Le degré zéro de l'écriture* for *Combat*, to ask him to contribute a whole series of shorter *Mythologies* to *Les Lettres Nouvelles*. These appeared fairly regularly in review form in 1954 and 1955 before being published in one volume in March 1957. This was reprinted in 1965 and reissued as a paperback in 1970, but without including any of the essays which constituted the second series, published when *Les Lettres Nouvelles* briefly became a weekly review in the spring of 1959.

Mythologies, taken as a whole, is a profoundly political work. It accepts the Marxist view that all cultures are political ideologies reflecting the interests of the class in power, sees French society as still dominated by the industrialists and landowners who had seized power in the early 1800s, and maintains that the bourgeoisie still uses the legal system essentially to defend and perpetuate its own values and interests. It is equally hostile to Franco's Spain and to French colonialism in Indochina and North Africa, is instinctively anti-American, and strongly opposed both to formal religion and to the conformist, conventional values said to be put out by the mass media. It denounces the way bourgeois society hides the reality of economic exploitation behind an official belief in universal human brotherhood, and anticipates an important later development in left-wing thought by the implicit but real support which it gives to the then nascent movement for women's liberation.

Inevitably, the political content of some of the essays now gives them a rather dated air. Only professional historians remember

Pierre Poujade, the small shopkeeper who led a neo-fascist movement in the mid 1950s. His frequent recurrence in *Mythologies* is perhaps due rather to the unwitting evidence which he provided for Barthes's thesis about the anti-intellectualism of the *petite bourgeoisie* than to his actual importance as a politician, but he was so exclusively a figure of the mid 1950s that the way he keeps popping up in the essays is a perfect illustration of Sartre's view that the writer who does concern himself with the immediate issues of his time must accept that some of his books will be quite incomprehensible to the next generation. If *Mythologies* as a whole avoids this danger, it is because it also deals with a more permanent problem: the relationship between signs and the things they signify. Its presiding genius is not only the furious, boil-ridden, aggressive, heavily-bearded bourgeois-hating Marx. It is also the mild, aristocratic, scholarly Swiss linguist Ferdinand de Saussure.

Saussure was the first to postulate the existence of what he called semiology, 'a science which studies the way signs behave in social life' ['une science qui étudie la vie des signes au sein de la vie sociale'].[2] Although his own professional interest was primarily with words, he nevertheless regarded language as only one of the systems, albeit the most important one, which enable human beings to communicate with one another. The deaf-and-dumb alphabet, symbolic rituals, social conventions, military salutes are other ones which he mentions himself, and it is not difficult to adduce others. Traffic signals are perhaps a misleading example because they are such a simple creation which remains so obviously under people's conscious control. They nevertheless are a very convenient illustration of one of the points on which Saussure most insists: that all sign systems are essentially arbitrary. There is nothing inevitable about using red for stop and green for go, or zig-zag white lines rather than interrupted yellow ones to indicate that it is illegal to overtake. However natural we may feel it is to associate red with danger and green with security (bulls charge at red, green is said to make us feel secure), the system would work just as well if everything was the other way round. This idea of the arbitrary nature of signs is fundamental to Barthes's argument in *Mythologies*, since it fits in so very well with his attack on what he regards as the bourgeois view that everything holds together through natural, inevitable and unchanging links. Whether he really took this particular notion from Saussure is perhaps another matter. Although he said in his preface to the 1970 paperback edition that he read Saussure just before writing *Mythologies*, he contradicted himself in an interview which he gave to *Tel Quel* in the following year.[3] There, he declared that he had really begun to study Saussure only after having written the essays in *Mythologies*, and his professional rival Georges Mounin would certainly endorse the validity of this confession.

Indeed, Mounin went so far as to say that Barthes had begun to study semiology so late in life that he would never, however hard he ran, catch up with what it really meant. What Barthes did, in his view, was social psychoanalysis, an activity which did not merit the intellectual prestige associated with a scientific discipline such as linguistics.[4]

If there is, however, one fly that Barthesian analysis has let out of the bottle of literary argument, it is the idea that an author's achievement is in some way diminished if it can be shown that he has been unfaithful to his sources. All that matters is what an author has managed to create, and the same thing is true of a thinker's intellectual achievement. If Barthes did in fact distort Saussure's method in *Le Monde où l'on catche* or *Iconographie de l'abbé Pierre*, then so much the better for Barthes. These are essays which tell us something about the way in which certain kinds of communication take place in modern society, and they certainly fit in with the spirit of Saussure's ideal if not with the practice recommended by his more zealous disciples. What they also do, which is perhaps even more important, is carry the style of thinking inaugurated in *Le degré zéro de l'écriture*, or in the essays on Brecht, into the realm of the mass media. In the France of the 1950s, this was a relatively new activity. The England of the 1930s and 1940s had had its George Orwell and Q. D. Leavis, while in North America, Marshall McLuhan's *The Mechanical Bride, Folklore of industrial man* had appeared in 1951. *Mythologies* applied the attitudes and insights already developed in *Le degré zéro de l'écriture* to a France emerging into a period of affluence. While this showed Marx the prophet wrong in forecasting the collapse of capitalism, it nevertheless gave Marxist critics some fascinating new examples of alienation to analyse.

In *Le degré zéro de l'écriture*, Barthes had argued that the slogan of the Roman actor, *Larvatus Prodeo* ('I come forward pointing at my mask'), expresses the only really honest attitude for the writer to adopt. Rather than trying to claim that he is telling the story in the only way possible, that his narrative technique is justified and inevitable because it is natural to human beings to tell stories, the writer whom Barthes admires never ceases to remind his readers that everything he does is artificial and conventional. This, for Barthes, is also exactly how all-in wrestlers behave. They do not expect the audience to believe in what is really happening. If they did, they would not signal their triumphs, manoeuvres and defeats with such obviously histrionic gestures. They are not fighting each other in the way that boxers do. It would be absurd to wager on the result of an all-in wrestling match. What they are doing is acting out situations and emotions which can never exist so perfectly in real life. What dominates there is what Barthes calls 'l'ambiguïté constitutive de la réalité quotidienne' ['the ambiguity which makes up the stuff of everyday reality'].[5] Like the type of writer whom Barthes admires, the all-in wrestlers are not imitating life. They are making it intelligible, and one could apply to the really good all-in wrestlers the remark which Barthes was to make later on, in 1971, in his essay on the Marquis de Sade: that theirs is not a mimetic art but a semiotic one. 'Etant écrivain et non auteur réaliste', he writes, 'Sade choisit toujours de discours contre le référent; il se place toujours du côté de la sémiosis, non de la mimésis: ce qu'il "représente" est sans cesse déformé par le sens, et c'est au niveau du sens, non du référent, que nous devons le lire.' ['Since he is a writer and not a realist author, Sade always chooses speech rather than the subject matter. He always writes from a semiotic rather than a mimetic standpoint. What he "represents" is constantly distorted by what the meaning is, and it is at the level of what he means, not what he is talking about, that we should read him.']⁶

The all-in wrestlers are not like the Balzac of *Le Père Goriot* who claimed in a quotation which he attributed to Shakespeare that 'All is true'. They openly declare in fact that it is all a put-up job. But it is a put-up job which presents a world that is immediately meaningful, in which signs instantly make sense, in which human beings see not what their life is actually like but what it might, in certain privileged, unusual and artificial situations, really mean. To the amateur of literary influences, Barthes is once again obviously carrying on the debate in Sartre's *La Nausée* about the incompatibility between life and art. Roquentin comes to realise that nobody can actually experience 'an adventure' because nobody, at the time, can say with absolute certainty: 'This is the decisive moment in my life'. Literature cannot be like life because it is an essential characteristic of life to be formless and of literature to have form. Only by consciously abstracting himself from 'l'ambiguïté constitutive de la réalité quotidienne' can either the writer or the all-in wrestler tell it like it really is: by lying.

The almost instinctive anti-Americanism of the French Left comes out in Barthes's claim that this self-conscious over-simplification of life's normally highly complex issues takes a specifically political form on the other side of the Atlantic. There, he says, it presents 'a kind of mythological contest between Good and Evil (of a para-political nature, the baddie always being assumed to be a Red)'.⁷ In France, on the other hand, the contest emphasises more moral issues. The aim is to present the audience with the finished portrait of what Barthes calls 'le salaud parfait', the 'absolute bastard', a specific social and psychological type characterised by his total instability. Such a man breaks the rules when it suits him, but claims their protection when it is in his interest to do so. He protests if he is attacked when an inch outside the ropes but then proceeds to use this official protection in order to hit his opponent himself. When such a living example of the defiance of society's rules is finally defeated—as he generally is— the audience goes into a paroxysm of delight. 'La salópe'—the feminine gender is essential, observes Barthes, whatever Littré may say[8]—is punished and degraded with an ultimate finality rarely encountered in real life. And even if, as occasionally happens, the 'salope', whose mounds of white, flabby flesh and long, uncombed greasy hair proclaim his contemptible a-sociality, actually wins, then the public is given a different kind of opportunity for enjoyment. It can give vent to a desire to protest against an obviously unfair order of things which again can rarely be assuaged with such gratifying certainty and impunity in the complex and ambiguous society that we actually inhabit.

Barthes thus presents all-in wrestling as a spectacle whose main function is to enable people to take time out from the real world. His analysis cannot, of course, be carried over lock, stock and barrel into the world of Rugby League or Association Football. Although these games do not always conform completely to Barthes's description of boxing as 'un sport janséniste, fondé sur la démonstration d'une excellence'[9] ['an austere sport, based on the mathematical proof that one of the contestants is superior'], it is nevertheless true that the better side generally wins and that there is a real contest. But one only has to witness the delight with which the Kop applauds an incident in which certain players act out the drama of injured innocence or the frenzy with which it welcomes the brutal insistence on the right to revenge to see what a useful approach Barthes has adopted towards the psychology of modern spectator sports. Such sports create myths which enable their worshippers to see the world as intelligible, and it is perhaps this aspect of mass culture and mass entertainment which most fully justifies the title of *Mythologies* which Barthes gave to the essays. Either honestly, as in the case of all-in wrestling or of non-mimetic art, or dishonestly, as in most of the other examples which he discusses, the sign system used in modern society creates a state of affairs which oversimplifies life's complex issues. When it does this consciously, as Brecht also does, this is a good thing. It is precisely what the original Greek myths did when they told improbable stories which were quite blatantly untrue in any realistic sense of the word. The stories of King Midas, of Orpheus and Eurydice, of Persephone and the six pomegranate seeds, could obviously never have happened in the way that the plots of realistic novels like Balzac's *Le Père Goriot* might have happened and are claimed to have done. But they nevertheless possessed the quality which Barthes finds attractive in all-in wrestling and which an agnostic admirer of the Old Testament can also find in the Book of Genesis. They satisfied a basic human need by explaining to people why and how things are as they are. And they did so by fulfilling one of the classic paradoxes of art: that of telling the truth by appearing to tell, if not exactly lies, at least exceedingly tall stories.

We all want to make sense of our own experience. The spectator sports which are, as Barthes would put it, 'diacritique' [diacritic, sketching out patterns] enable us to do this. Nothing is really happening in an all-in wrestling match. All that exists is what the spectator sees: the aeroplane twizzles, the double and single Nelsons, the forearm smashes and the obvious cheating. Similarly, there never was—for Barthes—a real Père Goriot or Emma Bovary. There are only the verbal signs, the plots, conversations, descriptions and codes whereby Balzac or Flaubert point our minds in the direction of old age, greed, miserable married women and the stultifying dullness of French provincial life. Semiosis (signs) and not mimesis (imitation of reality) is what Barthes calls it, and Mick McManus, who must have earned a fortune by appearing alternately to slaughter other people or to be knocked senseless himself three times a night for twenty years, would doubtless see what he meant.

The other forms of communication analysed in the rest of *Mythologies* do not come up to the curiously paradoxical standards of honesty set by all-in wrestling. None is so perfect an illustration of Saussure's theory about the arbitrary nature of signs, for in no other is there so clear a dividing line between reality and the means used to represent it. The contemporary cinema, represented by the 1953 Mankiewicz version of *Julius Caesar* and by Elia Kazan's *On the Waterfront*, is as unsatisfactory in its use of signs as it is in its political implications. Why, asks Barthes, do Brutus and Cassius have such visible fringes on their foreheads, Portia and Calpurnia such ostentatiously disarranged curls? Because fringes are seen as a natural sign of *la romanité* [Roman-ness] and an elegantly disordered hair style the inevitable concomitant of an aristocratic lady being woken up in the middle of the night. Such signs are presented as the absolute and natural accompaniment of being Roman, just as sweating betokens either anguished thought—as in the case of Brutus—or—as for the crowd—its intense bafflement as it is swayed this way and that by Brutus's and Mark Antony's speeches. In no case is the audience given the credit for being intelligent enough to interpret events for itself, to stand back and understand. Because the sign is presented as the natural emanation of a real state of affairs, the audience is held entirely captive by an art which makes no distinction between fiction and reality. At any moment, it might bombard the baddies with tomatoes. And when Marlon Brando, at the end of *On the Waterfront*, staggers towards the capitalist employer who stands straddling the entrance to the warehouse, the audience is caught up in a system of signs which deprives it of its political as well as its imaginative freedom. Because it is wholly identified with Brando, it hands over its liberty at the very moment he does. Only Charlie Chaplin plays the working class as Barthes thinks it should be played: blind to the reality of its condition, yet with a blindness that—as he also argues in *Mère Courage Aveugle*—stirs us even more profoundly to

revolt because we are made to see and understand the full horror of
this oppression when the person suffering from it cannot.[10]

Neither does the Barthes of *Mythologies* find still photographs any
more honest than moving ones. When an actor has his photograph
taken by the famous Harcourt studios, the ostensible aim is to present
him as he actually is in real life, off-stage. But this pretence at being
natural only emphasises how intensely artificial the photographs really
are. Nobody ever really looks like a Harcourt photograph, and this pretence at naturalness is infected with the same kind of dishonesty which
Barthes finds in photographs of authors on holiday or stories about the
crowned heads of Europe actually cleaning their own shoes. By
presenting as deserving of particular comment the fact that an author
takes a holiday or a princess wears a printed cotton dress, the media
are in fact elevating these already unusual beings on to an even higher
plane. By insisting on their everyday qualities, the photographs which
show them pursuing the activities of ordinary mortals give them the
status which the heroes of the past enjoyed when they put on human
attire. Such heroes, however, never pretended that their disguise was
ever anything but a disguise, and the main burden of Barthes's attack
against modern mythology is that it constantly blurs the edges between
what is real and what is artificial. It would be all quite acceptable—to
translate his analysis of France in the fifties to the England of the
seventies—if Prince Charles were honestly presented for what he is:
a prince playing one day at being a subaltern, on another a helicopter
pilot and on another a mountaineer. It is when we are expected to see
him at one and the same time as a real prince and a real helicopter
pilot that the problems arise, since we all know—as he must know
himself— that he would never be allowed to take the same risks as the
serving officer who has to fly in all weathers.

There is clearly not much harm in this in contemporary England,
where the distinction between the real power of the trade unions and
the apparent authority of the Crown is clearly recognised by everyone.
But the France of the 1950s had, in Barthes's view, a less endearing
ability to use the mass media in order to create an obviously false
vision of itself. Indeed, when the French organisers give the grandiose
title of *La Grande Famille des Hommes* to a collection of photographs
known in English simply as *The Family of Man*, the results are totally
opposed to a free and unalienated vision of what modern society is
really like. For what characterises human experience, argues Barthes,
is the fact that poor men work for rich men. Wherever you look,
human cultures contain conflict, the rich live and the poor die. In the
photographs brought together under the title of *La Grande Famille des
Hommes*, on the other hand, all human activities are depicted as wholly
natural, all types of work as basically the same, all sorts and conditions
of men as harmoniously united in a common brotherhood. But Barthes

tells the inventors of this title to 'Go and ask the parents of Emmet Till, the young negro murdered by white men, or the North African workers who live in the slum of *La Goutte d'or* what *they* think of *The Great Human Family*'[11] and the answer which he would give for them is clear: It's all a great con. By presenting cultural events realistically, as natural, spontaneous and inevitable ones, the authors of the collection are imprisoning their readers in a vision of human society eternally fixed in its present mode by the very nature of things. By not accepting that signs are arbitrary and cultures subject to historical change, they are limiting the freedom which human beings can obtain only by being able to stand aside from their own experience and see it as relative and subjective.

In this particular instance, of course, Barthes's attack is as much against the use of language as against the misuse of the camera. It is the French organisers of the photographic exhibition who have, by translating *The Family of Man* as *La Grande Famille des Hommes*, 'moralised and sentimentalised'[12] what was originally a neutral zoological expression. Similarity, it is the French popular illustrated press which makes such a song and dance about the crowned heads of Europe showing their ordinariness by cleaning their own shoes. It is also, according to *Mythologies*, the French mass media which reveal such a determination to keep the lower classes in their place by persuading them that true happiness can be found only in the acceptance of things as they are. This eminently conservative ethos used to be expressed in the verse from 'All things bright and beautiful' which went:

> The rich man in his castle
> The poor man at his gate
> God made them high or lowly
> And ordered their estate,

and such a formulation has, in Barthesian terms, the immense advantage of being intellectually honest. What he finds so dishonest, and what he denounces in *Astrologies*, *Celle qui voit clair*, and *Conjugales*, is the way that horoscopes, the 'Advice to Readers' page in women's magazines, and the place given to marriages in the French popular press all disguise their plea for social conformity beneath an apparently objective and even progressive style of presentation. In each case, argues Barthes, the aim is to convince the working and lower middle classes that private, domestic happiness is the only valid ideal, and that unhappiness is never the result of the way society is organised. It is still the world analysed by George Orwell in 1940 in his famous essay on 'Boys' Weeklies'. There, Orwell wrote of the stories in the *Oracle* or *Peg's Paper* that:

The major facts are simply not faced. It is admitted, for instance, that people sometimes lose their jobs; but then the dark clouds roll away and they get better jobs instead. No mention of unemployment as something permanent and inevitable, no mention of the dole, no mention of trade unionism. No suggestion anywhere that there can be anything wrong with the system *as a system*.[13]

In 1974, when *Le Magazine littéraire* devoted a special number to Barthes, Robert Louit observed not quite correctly that Orwell's essays were unknown in France. Unfamiliar, yes; unconsciously imitated, yes; untranslated, no.[14]

It would nevertheless be rash to insist that the analysis in *Mythologies* applies only to the France of the 1950s. When thirty of the *mythologies* appeared in translation in 1972, John Berger devoted almost the whole of his review in *New Society* to a demonstration of just how applicable Barthes's approach could be to the situation in this country. Thus the *Observer* for 2 February 1972 had carried a photograph on its front page of policemen arresting a Protestant demonstrator during a civil rights march in Glasgow. The officers involved looked calm, responsible and normal, the outward and visible sign—in John Berger's view— of what Barthes, following Saussure, would have called *le signifié*: the Impartiality of the British Forces of Order. 'In the myth of the *Observer* front page', continued the *New Society* review, 'the policemen in Glasgow represent eternal Order; and the dead in Derry—despite four centuries of the most violent history of colonialism—remain eternally the exception', and rarely could an author have felt happier than Barthes at such a perfect extrapolation of his views.[15] In less politically oriented journals, however, Barthes was less enthusiastically received. Graham Hough, in the *Times Higher Educational Supplement*, commented that 'in some of the pieces, the depth of actual social observation is not much beyond that of the sophisticated women's page: sharper than Jilly Cooper, but not smarter than Katharine Whitehorn', while Christopher Ricks observed in the *Sunday Times* how 'the sense that it all seems randy [sic] and commonplace is a recognition that it belongs to the heyday of Marshall McLuhan'.[16] French critics show a similar tendency to be more enthusiastic for Barthes's work if they are on the left and more detached if they are on the right or in the centre, and here again he himself would doubtless be disappointed if it were otherwise. Indeed, if Barthes had read the reviewer in the *New Yorker* who commented that 'the author's repeated and humorless attacks on the bourgeoisie take on the quality of a vendetta', he would have been delighted. Nothing pleases a left-wing French intellectual more than the refusal of the middle class to recognise itself for what it is or to acknowledge its own wickedness.[17]

What is equally fascinating about *Mythologies* is the portrait which it gives of French society in the 1950s, and in this respect it is almost as though Barthes were compensating for the deliberate refusal of the 'nouveaux romanciers' to offer any account of what their own or indeed any other society was like. For central to the theory which Alain Robbe-Grillet put forward in his essays and fiction was the view that the novel ought to concern itself solely with physical objects and not at all with sociology or psychology. These, it was argued, were best left to the professionally qualified specialists, and the support which Barthes himself gave to Robbe-Grillet, like his attacks on supposedly realistic literature, tended to support this view. But in *Mythologies*, albeit unintentionally, he goes against his theory of what the *scripteur* should offer, and does for the France of the Fourth Republic almost what the despised Maupassant did for the first twenty years of the Third.

It is, of course, a different kind of portrait from the one which a Balzac, a Zola or a Flaubert might have given. Barthes's point of departure is the vision which French society tries to project of itself rather than of society itself, and his method could be a very fruitful one for the study of television. For while *The Waltons, Coronation Street, Porridge, Dad's Army* or *The Likely Lads* may not tell us much about what American or English society is really like now or actually has been in the past, they are immensely informative of how their millions of admirers would like to see themselves. In *Mythologies*, it is especially the essays directly or indirectly concerned with France's colonial ambitions and misadventures which show how the French were encouraged to see their situation and themselves at this particularly frustrating period of their history. Their enemies, as Barthes observes in *Vocabulaire africain*, were invariably described as 'bands of outlaws', representing a 'certain minority element of the population'. Such people, to put it in the style which Barthes analyses, cannot, by the very nature of things, lead their 'groups of malcontents' to the 'true independence which would represent the authentic aspirations of communities that have been indissolubly linked together in a century-old relationship'.[18] France is a country with a mission, and only what Pierre Poujade calls the 'rootless intellectuals' call into question the visceral certainty with which true Frenchmen, with their feet firmly planted on the ground, know that they have to fulfil it. One of the many virtues of *Mythologies* is to show how supposedly natural and eternal French characteristics such as Voltairean scepticism can disappear when a culture goes through a profound political and economic crisis, and the analysis which Barthes provides of the new self-images which then arise is one of the most intriguing features of his book. For when the general responsible for a major military disaster seeks to be 'reintegrated into the national community' by asking for a plate of steak and chips, and is applauded by the mass media for so doing, then the myth of what Barthes calls *la francité* (Frenchness) does indeed reveal a society which is comic as well as dangerous in its self-indulgent illusions.[19]

The analysis which Barthes makes of the obfuscating language in which French colonialist policies are defended again has a strongly Orwellian air. Thus when he observes that nouns are much more useful than verbs in hiding reality behind a smokescreen of verbiage, he comes very close to repeating what George Orwell said in his essay 'Politics and the English Language': that when you are trying to defend the indefensible, 'political language has to consist largely of euphemism, question-begging and sheer cloudy vagueness'.[20] There is also a marked similarity with *Nineteen Eighty-four* when Barthes singles out for a comment General de Monsabert's statement at the time of the Algerian conflict to the effect that: 'War does not preclude measures of pacification',[21] and his thesis that a dishonest policy inevitably reveals itself by the language which it uses is again a view which Orwell had argued some fifteen years earlier.

The way in which Barthes tried to change society through an analysis of its myths and language rather than by more direct forms of political action did not, however, always endear him to other opponents of French colonialist policies. François Mauriac, for example, uncomfortably aware of having exposed himself to some of Barthes's strictures on *L'écrivain en vacances* by allowing himself to be photographed for *Le Figaro littéraire* wearing blue pyjamas, but strong in the knowledge that he had tried to influence government policy on specific issues such as the torture of political prisoners, pointed out in *L'Express* that Barthes would have more right to criticise his literary colleagues if he too had actually done something.[22] It is an interesting observation, since Barthes is in fact one of the few French literary intellectuals who did not take a formal stand either for or against the war of 1946–54 in Indo-China, the Algerian struggle for independence between 1954 and 1962 or the imposition of the Fifth Republic on the French nation by military blackmail in 1958. He did not, for example, sign the *Manifeste des 121* supporting French soldiers who refused to serve in Algeria (*Déclaration sur le droit d'insoumission dans la guerre d'Algérie*), and it is very difficult to find out what he actually thought on such issues as the return to power of General de Gaulle in 1958 or the tactics de Gaulle successfully used to end the Algerian war in 1962.[23] Such abstention from public statements is, of course, fully consistent with his view that the writer should try to destroy society by attacking language. He should, for Barthes, make people think differently by changing the dominant instrument—language—in which they do their thinking.

This is, of course, a very un-Marxist approach. For classical Marxism, it is the economic infrastructure which creates such supra-structures as legal systems, philosophical concepts or literary forms, and it would be fully consistent with its deterministic temper for it to regard language as being just as much the product of socio-economic conditions. Barthes, however, seems to adopt the completely opposite view, both in his practice in *Mythologies* and in his later theories. His dissipation of the myths created by the new Citroën, by advertisements for detergents, by the 'common sense' objections to strikes put forward in *Le Figaro*, is ultimately aimed at changing society only by making people realise intellectually how fully they are being duped. Such an attempt to change people's minds by constantly swimming against both the linguistic tide and the more insidious pressure of visual advertising is naturally a very long-drawn-out process. Poujadism did not disappear from French political life because Barthes showed up Poujade for the fool he was by analysing the clichés he used. It faded away because the Fifth Republic offered, from 1958 onwards, a very much more satisfactory and successful type of right-wing politics, and reappeared in the person of Gérard Nicoud only when the attractions of Gaullism had begun to fade. The lot of a left-wing intellectual in France is very hard. Jean-Paul Sartre himself spent eight years of his life supporting a left-wing solution to the Algerian problem, only to see the Communist Party's recommendations for total Algerian independence imposed by an ageing, Catholic, conservative general. *Mythologies* may have been, as Jacques Bersani observes,[24] the bedside book of many French students in the 1950s. It is improbable, however, that it did more than strengthen the opinions they would have had anyway. Preaching to the converted is not an activity which creates either in the performer or the spectator any great sense of permanent achievement or intellectual adventure.

Sometimes, Barthes's verbal exuberance also runs away with him. This was especially the case when he wrote of the then revolutionary Citroën DS: 'I think that cars today are almost the exact equivalent of the great Gothic cathedrals: I mean the supreme creation of an era, conceived with passion by unknown artists, and consumed in image if not in usage by a whole population which appropriates them as a purely magical object.' Indeed, this particular passage led Christopher Ricks to greet Barthes with the only half-ironic remark of 'what a copywriter', and his comment was taken up by at least two other English critics of the 1972 translation of *Mythologies*. John Casey wrote in the *Spectator* that 'Barthes seems very much at home in the consumer society, the grotesqueness of which he delineates with such loving attention', and added that the net result of such a book was that the 'vulgarities of such a society are endowed with a sort of glamour'. An equally common reaction was to observe that we had been here before and even to prefer the description of all-in wrestling in Kingsley Amis's *Girl 20*. Some prophets clearly lose originality as well as honour the moment they move from their own country; and when the *New York Review of Books* stated that Barthes 'investigates "petit bourgeois culture" (what we call "Pop")', it also became apparent that the semiologist Barthes was not very well understood either.[25]

There are fifty *mythologies* in the original French edition, and it would be tedious to analyse how Barthes's technique works in each case. When they were collected and published in book form in 1957, a number of critics made the somewhat wry comment that nobody would have suspected French society of harbouring quite the number of myths which Barthes had found in it, and there were other discordant voices. In *La France Catholique*, for example, Jean-Pierre Morillon attacked Barthes for making fun of marriage in the *mythologie* entitled 'Conjugales', and made a comment repeated in a number of other periodicals when he wrote that Barthes attributed 'a great deal of cunning to the bourgeoisie and an amazing simple-mindedness to the proletariat'.[26] It was also predictable that other critics should reprove Barthes for not attacking the greatest myth of all in the France of the 1950s, the claim of the Communist party to represent the working class and to be 'le parti des 75,000 fusillés' ['the party of the 75,000 people shot by the Germans'], and there was an element of fair comment in the frequent remark that Barthes himself was guilty of inventing the greatest myth of the lot. He had, after all, ascribed the most alienating features of modern mass communications to a nefarious but ill-defined conspiracy entitled the bourgeoisie and had never paid his readers the compliment of saying who the bourgeoisie actually were, where they got their money from, and where the supposed plethora of *idées reçues* was actually to be found.[27]

Barthes's own later formulation of his fundamental ambition as being the desire to 'battre en brèche la naturalité du signe' ['attack and destroy the idea that signs are natural'] is a misleadingly abstract way of describing his achievement in *Mythologies*, and the further he moves away from the specific examples given in the individual *mythologies*, the less satisfying does his method become. The long theoretical essay which closes the volume, *Le mythe, aujourd'hui*, contains, admittedly, some interesting remarks. It describes Sartre's *Saint Genet, comédien et martyr* as offering, in its 'simultaneously formal and historical, semiological and ideological description of sainthood', one of the best examples of 'total criticism', and thus sharpens one's appetite for the more relative and less ambitious kind.[28] It makes the interesting claim that 'genuinely revolutionary language cannot be mythical language' since it is linked to an effort to 'change the world rather than to preserve it in images',[29] but is unfortunately unable to substantiate this by any specific examples. And it provides, in a long discussion of how a photograph of a negro soldier saluting the French tricolour dishonestly exemplifies the supposedly non-ethnic nature of *la francité*, yet another instance of Barthes's indefatigable hostility to right-wing modes of thought. But *Le mythe, aujourd'hui* never comes anywhere near a short *mythologie* entitled 'Iconographie de l'abbé Pierre' either as suggesting a starting-point for other analyses or in explaining just why the 'naturalness' of signs should be such a bad thing.

L'Abbé Pierre was a well-known figure in the Paris of the 1950s. When, in February 1952, the bitter cold threatened to kill some of the weaker down-and-outs who still slept under the bridges, it was he who organised a rescue service for them. He—and the Church—derived almost as much prestige from this operation as they did from the Abbé's appearance, and it is with this latter aspect that Barthes is concerned. L'Abbé Pierre had a superbly austere short haircut and a flowingly apostolic beard. Between them, they proclaimed the intensity of his devotion to the Christian ideal and his sublime indifference to the mere social usages of the secular world. And what is more, they appeared to do so with complete naturalness. It was inconceivable, one thought on looking at him, that he had deliberately chosen both haircut and beard as outward and visible signs of an inward and spiritual grace. And yet this, argued Barthes, was precisely what they were: signs which had been consciously chosen but which were now passing themselves off as spontaneous and inevitable. Had l'Abbé Pierre contented himself with the official uniform of his calling, Barthes would have had no objection. Uniforms are open, honest signs of what one is, and the clergyman who wears a dog-collar is exemplifying the Barthesian ideal of *Larvatus Prodeo*. But to go around pretending that one is too busy to shave, so much one of the boys that one's natural garb is a leather wind-cheater and not a sober clerical black, and so oblivious of appearances that one's intensely spiritual haircut is a sheer accident, shows a complete lack of intellectual honesty. 'Bourgeois charity', Sartre once wrote, 'keeps alive the myth of fraternity'. Barthes goes one further in completing his neo-Saussurian analysis of society when he concludes by asking whether the splendid and affecting iconography of L'Abbé Pierre is not the alibi which a large section of the nation uses, once again, in order to feel quite innocent in replacing justice with the signs of charity'.[30]

When, in 1971, Barthes was asked to preface a special number which *Esprit* was devoting to myths he commented that 'demythifying' had become its own *Doxa*, and this remark provided an interesting anticipation of one of the main themes in *Roland Barthes par Roland Barthes* in 1975. There, he comes back on a number of occasions to the theme that uniformity, ideology, orthodoxy, the cult of *ce-qui-va-de-soi* [the obvious, what goes without saying], the refusal and inability to understand what other people are really like, are now far more characteristic of the Left than of the Right, and it is clear in this respect that any new series of *mythologies* would be very different from those published between 1952 and 1954. Then, as he explains, the myths that he found in French society differed from those which existed in other cultures in that they formed no coherent system. Myth, in twentieth-century capitalist society, was 'anonymous, evasive, fragmented, loquacious, vulnerable at one and the same time to ideological criticism and to semiological analysis'.[31] Were the Left really to succeed in imposing its mythology, Barthes would doubtless find both of them—if he survived—somewhat more monolithic.

It would nevertheless be a mistake to see this shift of political intention too much in Orwellian terms. If Barthes is to be believed when he told Raymond Bellour, of the Communist *Les Lettres Françaises*, that he rejected contemporary society 'jusqu'à la nausée',[32] he is unlikely to write the French equivalent of *England, your England*, and like most of those who share his current literary ideals he remains thoroughly alienated from the society which has accorded him such fame for criticising it. If his two most recent books, *Le Plaisir du Texte* and *Roland Barthes par Roland Barthes*, constitute any precedent, his attack on the ideology and *Doxa* of the Left will be aphoristic and fragmented, based more upon the hedonistic appreciation of reading and writing than on the systematic defence of the open society which Orwell provided when he moved from the denunciation of capitalism to the analysis of the greater lie of left-wing totalitarianism. Indeed, a number of the essays in *Mythologies* already show this almost physical delight in the handling of language which is one of Barthes's most attractive characteristics and which, together with his driving ambition to make people realise how arbitrary signs are, gives the book a genuine aesthetic unity. Yet although it is Barthes's rich and complex language which gives his ability to define precisely what is wrong about certain forms of intellectual cheating its ultimate appeal, his style is not one that keeps all its charm in translation. One has only to compare the original French of the *mythologie* entitled *Publicité de la Profondeur* with the translation to see how inadequate an instrument English is to render the rhetorical wealth and precision of Barthes's *écriture*.

> Toute la publicité des produits de beauté prépare donc une conjonction miraculeuse des liquides ennemis, déclarés désormais complémentaires; respectant avec diplomatie toutes les valeurs positives de la mythologie des substances, elle parvient à imposer la conviction heureuse que les graisses sont véhicules d'eau, et qu'il existe des crèmes aqueuses, des douceurs sans luisance.
>
> La plupart des nouvelles crèmes sont donc nommément *liquides, fluides, ultra-pénétrantes*, etc.; l'idée de graisse, pendant si longtemps consubstantielle à l'idée même de produit de beauté, se voile ou se complique, se corrige de liquidité, et parfois même disparaît, fait place à la fluide *lotion*, au spirituel *tonique*, glorieusement *astringent* s'il

s'agit de combattre la cirosité de la peau, pudiquement *spécial* s'il s'agit au contraire de nourrir grassement ces voraces profondeurs dont on nous étale impitoyablement les phénomènes digestifs.

[The whole publicity put out for beauty products thus opens the way for a miraculous reconciliation between hostile liquids, declared henceforth brothers in arms. While diplomatically respecting all the positive values of the mythology of substances, it nevertheless manages to impose the happy conviction that grease contains water, that certain creams are aqueous, and that there are smooth materials which do not shine.

Most of the new creams are thus pointedly referred to as *liquid*, *fluid*, having *extra-penetrative powers*, etc.; the idea of cream, so long consubstantial with the idea of beauty product, is veiled, complicated, corrected by the notion of liquidity. Sometimes it even disappears, giving way to a fluid—a *lotion*—or is endowed with a spiritual *tonic* quality. When it has to combat the greasiness of the skin, it becomes gloriously *astringent*. If, on the other hand, it is called upon to give rich nourishment to those voracious depths whose digestive capacities are so pitilessly exposed to our eyes, it acquires the modest adjective of *special*.][33]

But even in translation, this is much better than saying that advertising is all lies. Barthes, Bachelard and Saussure here have the great merit of helping people to free themselves, through a rhetorical exuberance of language, from the myths in which language constantly threatens to imprison them.

4 Racine, quarrels and criticism

I

If Barthes had been a British academic, he would have been securely settled in a university teaching career very soon after the publication of *Le degré zéro de l'écriture*. However hard the pundits protested, his *Michelet* would have confirmed this position, while the publication of *Mythologies* in book form in 1957 would certainly have got him his Readership. In the France of the 1950s however, stricter habits of more formal academic respectability still held sway. To teach in a university, one had first to have passed the *agrégation*. Barthes had never even competed. To become a university lecturer and move on to the first rungs of the ladder eventually leading to a chair, one had to have written two hundred pages of one's thesis, and had them formally approved by one's *directeur de thèse*. In 1954, Barthes had had the scholarship earlier awarded to him to do research in lexicology withdrawn because he had not made sufficient progress. Published work, especially in books, newspapers or periodicals which people buy with their own money, still counts for little in the official French academic world, and the system did not allow Barthes to do what any literary intellectual with a fraction of his gifts could have done in England: apply for an openly advertised post in a university and be appointed on the strength of his controversial but highly stimulating books and articles. These were what are still slightingly known in official circles as 'des livres sans bibliographie', and in 1955 Barthes entered what he euphemistically terms a period of 'professional instability' which did not really come to an end until he was appointed, in 1960, as 'chef de travaux à la VIe section de l'Ecole pratique des Hautes Etudes'. In 1962, he was promoted Director of Studies, and has taught there—with tenure—ever since.

The slightly ironic tone in Barthes's later remark about how natural it was in France to be 'catholique, marié et bien diplômé' is thus perhaps explicable by the fact that he was almost fifty before he secured a permanent teaching appointment. The preceding paragraph should also further clarify, should this be necessary, Barthes's frequent distinction between nature and culture. For it is written in a tone which implies that the way in which English universities recruit their staff is the natural prototype from which other, culturally defined, systems vary at their peril and to their disadvantage. The Frenchmen of Montesquieu's day apparently had comparable difficulty in understanding how anyone could really be a Persian, and it is curious how often Barthes's strictures on the petty bourgeois mind for its 'incapacité à comprendre autrui'[1] ['inability to understand other people'] apply in real life to the failure of French, British and American academics to understand how one another's appointments and promotion system works.

It is nevertheless useful to begin a study of what is up to now the most notable episode in Barthes's life, his quarrel in 1965 with Raymond Picard, by a further brief glance at his career and at the institution where he eventually ended his period of 'professional instability'. For the Ecole pratique des Hautes Etudes had been founded in 1886 by Victor Duruy precisely in order to get round the refusal of the Sorbonne to include such revolutionary disciplines as sociology in the curriculum. But in France the State alone has the right to grant formal certificates at any level (it enjoys what is called *le monopole des diplômes*), and it was not until 1974 that the degrees which the Ecole pratique des Hautes Etudes awarded were officially recognised within the official higher educational system (*l'Université*).[2] The decision of Lucien Febvre, in 1948, to set up the VIe section, one which would take account of the contribution which Marxism could make to the study of history, literature and philosophy, cannot have endeared the School itself to the academic powers that be, and it is difficult for an outsider to believe that it was a pure accident that Raymond Picard should have been a Professor at the traditionally-minded Sorbonne. His thesis, *La Carrière de Jean Racine*, represented all that was best in the established tradition of literary scholarship. But it did not indicate a frame of mind likely to be impressed either by Barthes's *Sur Racine* or by the more philosophical and sociological approach to literature adopted at the upstart institution in the rue de Varennes. In addition to being a *querelle de clercs* [squabble among the dons], and in the minds of Barthes's supporters a *querelle de classe* [episode in the class war], the dispute between Raymond Picard and Roland Barthes was also a *querelle d'institutions* [dispute between institutions].[3]

Like *Le degré zéro de l'écriture* and *Mythologies*, Barthes's book on Racine was not originally conceived as a unitary study. The first and by far the longest part, 'L'Homme racinien' (*Homo Radicinus*) dated from 1960, and had first appeared as a preface to an edition of Racine's plays published by the *Club français du livre*. Barthes was subsequently to reveal that he would have much preferred to write the preface to the volume on Michelet, and gave a further hostage to fortune by suggesting, in the second essay in the book, that he did not actually enjoy seeing Racine's plays performed. The second part of *Sur Racine* was in fact a reprint of an essay which had originally appeared in *Théâtre populaire* in 1958, and clearly owed a great deal to the ideas which Barthes had been developing about Brecht. The mistake which most actors made when they performed Racine, he argued, was to show the audience that they understood every line they were speaking, and to invite it to participate in their understanding. This led to a kind of diction analogous to what music critics call *rubato*, an expressive insistence on the emotion contained in each note. Barthes had already found this objectionable in the French baritone Gérard Souzay, denounced in the *mythologie* entitled 'L'art vocal bourgeois', and was to criticise it in another context in 1971 when he described Fischer-Dieskau as 'indiscret' ['brash, intrusive'].[4] Whether justified or not, it is a criticism which fits in with Barthes's liking for a style of communication which leaves the audience free to feel what emotion it finds appropriate to the spectacle presented to it. When Barthes first began to go to the theatre, in the early nineteen-thirties, the reigning genius was Louis Jouvet, the interpreter of Giraudoux. In 1965, Barthes recalled how he had admired the 'clarté passionnée'[5] of Jouvet's diction, his constant readiness to let the text speak for itself, and there is here a direct relationship between a performing artist's conscious intention and Barthes's enthusiasm for him. 'Dis ton texte, mon petit' ['Just say your lines, laddie'] was the advice which Jouvet gave to all his actors.

Neither was the 'préjugé indéracinable qui veut que les mots traduisent la pensée',[6] and which led actors to squeeze every ounce of meaning out of their lines, the only obstacle Barthes found to his enjoyment and appreciation of Racine. He thinks it wrong to see words as translating a meaning which is hidden so deep inside the text that every effort must be made to bring it into the clear light of day. And it is this mistake which, for him, is responsible for the exaggeratedly expressionistic manner in which actors—and, more particularly, actresses—perform Racine's plays. But the fault, according to Barthes, also lies in Racine himself, in the impurity which makes him oscillate between genuine tragedy and the beginnings of psychological, bourgeois drama, and he goes so far as to say in *Sur Racine* that his theatre is perhaps already three-quarters dead as far as any possible performance is concerned.[7] It is not even certain, in Barthes's eyes, that the role of Phèdre herself is a very good one, and the only actor for whom he has a good word to say in what is, in fact, an extended review of a recent performance of *Phèdre* at the Théâtre National Populaire, is Alain Cuny in the part of Thésée. Cuny, in Barthes's view, played Thésée as someone who had recently been in contact with the Gods, and who therefore felt cut off from his own earthly personality, wandering in an almost somnambulistic style through a world that had become wholly alien to him. It is in this way that

Barthes thinks that actors and actresses should perform Racine's plays, and there is an obvious similarity between this approach and the praise he bestowed on Helene Weigel for playing Brecht's Mother Courage as a person who did not understand what was happening to her. To suggest that Racine was virtually unplayable if not performed like this was nevertheless not quite the way for Barthes to endear himself to the more conservative members of the French literary establishment. The equivalent in England would be to say that Shakespeare could now be understood and acted only in accordance with the views of the Polish critic Jan Kott. The enemies whom Barthes had already made in the near-incestuous world of French literary criticism must, on reading this part of *Sur Racine*, have rubbed their hands and repeated the words of Job XXXI, 35: 'My desire is that mine adversary had written a book.'

The third essay in *Sur Racine*, 'Histoire ou Littérature', was also not calculated to please the pundits. It too had first appeared as an article, in 1960 in *Annales*, and consisted of a brisk critical gallop through a number of recent works on Racine and the seventeenth century generally. The fact, as Raymond Picard pointed out, that Barthes did not appear to know that certain crucial monographs even existed deprived some of his complaints about the inadequacy of recent scholarship of a good deal of their validity. Thus Barthes had implied that nobody really knew who went to the theatre in Racine's days, when a glimpse either at John Lough's book *Paris Theatre Audiences in the Seventeenth and Eighteenth Centuries* or at Picard's own review of it in the *Revue des Sciences Humaines* would have told him that two-thirds of the audience came from the aristocracy, that it was essential for a playwright to have his works performed at Court (which nevertheless preferred farce to Racinian tragedy) and that there were probably not more than a thousand people who were regular theatregoers in the sense of attending more than thirty performances a year.[8]

There is, of course, a good deal of academic one-upmanship of this type in the quarrel between Barthes and Picard which gave such excellent copy to the French literary press in the 1960s, and it is instructive, before giving a detailed analysis both of Barthes's 'L'Homme racinien' and of Picard's objections to it in *Nouvelle Critique ou Nouvelle Imposture*, to summarise the main incidents in the campaign. The publicity given to Picard's violent attack made Barthes, temporarily at least, almost a household name, and helped to make the general public more aware of the changes which had come over the literary scene now that the Second World War was well and truly over and the Algerian war itself beginning to recede into the past. In the immediate post-war period, the fame of Malraux, Sartre and Camus had given the impression that French literature was to remain dominated by political and moral problems. The Barthes/Picard quarrel showed that the emphasis had swung back to more intellectual, philosophical and essentially literary concerns. If the future of French society was in any way at stake, it was not in the obvious way that it had been when writers were involved in the Resistance movement or argued about the role of the Communist Party or the future of France as a colonial power. The Barthes/Picard quarrel was, as Henri Bonnier observed,[9] one of the happy results of a period of peace. It was none the less acrimonious and exciting.

The first official shot came from Raymond Picard, in an article which appeared in *Le Monde* on 14 March 1964. Although officially a review of Barthes's recently published *Essais critiques*, it concentrated in fact on two essays in particular: 'Les deux critiques', which had first appeared in *Modern Language Notes* in 1963; and 'Qu'est-ce que la critique?' originally published in a special number of the *Times Literary Supplement* entitled 'The Critical Moment' in 1963.[10] In the first of these, Barthes had distinguished, as the title implies, between two types of criticism: what he called 'la critique universitaire', perhaps best translated as academic criticism, and 'la critique d'interprétation', criticism which sought to interpret and analyse works of art from an openly proclaimed political or philosophical standpoint. Thus among the 'interpretative critics' whom he mentioned were Jean-Paul Sartre, whose *Saint Genet, comédien et martyr* (1952) Barthes regards as a master-piece, and who sets out from an existentialist position; Lucien Gold-mann, whose book *Le Dieu caché* [*The Hidden God*] was an attempt to apply a fundamentally Marxist methodology to Pascal and Racine; Gaston Bachelard, whose phenomenological approach had similarities with the method Barthes had adopted himself in *Michelet par lui-même*; and Jean-Pierre Richard, whom Barthes had greeted as a fellow spirit in an enthusiastic review of *Littérature et Sensation* in *Esprit* in 1955.[11] Whatever differences separated these various tendencies, argued Barthes, their practitioners had at least two virtues in common: they did not pretend to be neutral, objective and coldly scientific, but rightly acknowledged that all standpoints were committed and subjective; and they did not have the simple minded, 'ce qui va de soi' view of literature as first and foremost the expression of the author's feelings. It was in this way, Barthes maintained, that Sartre, Bachelard, Richard, and other interpretative critics differed fundamentally from those of their colleagues who stuck closely to the positivistic methods established some fifty years earlier in the Sorbonne by the great Gustave Lanson. These *critiques universitaires* were, in Barthes's view, fundamentally dishonest. To begin with, they did not acknowledge how fully their view that the prime duty of the critic lay in the estab-lishment of isolated facts represented just as arbitrary and committed an ideology as Marxism or phenomenology. They assumed that the only valid attitude towards cultural phenomena lay in the positivism which had flourished in the nineteenth century, and never called into question the presupposition that a literary work could always be explained by reference either to its literary sources or to the writer's own personal experience. Moreover, while pretending to be neutral and scientific, the Sorbonne was in fact hanging on to its power. The old-fashioned methods were invaluable in examinations.

In retrospect, *Les deux critiques* can be seen to have contained almost all the themes which Barthes and his admirers were to develop in the polemic which followed the appearance of *Sur Racine* and *Nouvelle Critique ou Nouvelle Imposture:* the accusation of bad faith levelled against unnamed establishment figures at the Sorbonne, the insistence that genuine criticism must concern itself not with biographical details but with the immanent structure of works of art, the need for ideology and the refusal to look for the meaning of an author's work anywhere but in the books he actually published. The article by Barthes in the *Times Literary Supplement* in 1963 put forward very much the same point of view, and expressed in these terms it has really very little to shock the ear of the English reader who knows his Empson or his Wimsatt and Beardsley. What Raymond Picard found objectionable, however, were two things: what seemed to him the unjustified division of the world of French literary criticism into the angels of structuralism and the old goats of the Sorbonne; and the gratuitous attacks, initially published abroad, on an institution which was doing its best in difficult circumstances. It was not, in view of what Picard was to say later, a particularly violent or even an especially perceptive attack, and it fell to a later correspondent to *Le Monde*, Edouard Guitton, to express the attitude which was later to be defended by virtually all Picard's supporters. 'Classical criticism', he wrote, refusing the derogatory appellation of *universitaire*, 'is based on an ideal of rigour and submission to nature. It concerns itself with the past for its own sake, and does not allow itself the liberty of revising it. It prefers to speak an everyday and universally comprehensible language... It looks for Racine in Racine and not in the metamorphoses Racine undergoes on coming into contact with ideologies or jargons'.[12]

With each side adopting such an eminently reasonable attitude, conflict was inevitable. *Sur Racine* was published in book form in May 1963. Picard could therefore have commented on it before attacking Barthes over his *Essais Critiques*, not published until early in 1964, and there is some force in his later statement that he decided to criticise the essay on Racine only after it had received what seemed to him to be an excessively uncritical reception. For it is indeed true that *Sur Racine* had a fair number of rave reviews, especially from the more radically-minded journals. René Matignon, in *Arts*, declared that Barthes had done brilliantly in the question paper on Racine which every French critic had to sit before finally establishing himself, and compared Barthes's presentation of Racine in eminently modern terms to the recent cleaning process which had restored their original beauty to the great architectural monuments of Paris. *Combat* quoted the definition which Barthes himself had given of the structuralist method in literary criticism in a recent number of *Les Lettres Nouvelles*, and applauded his success in putting it into practice. The aim of structuralism, Barthes had argued in an article entitled 'L'activité structuraliste', and republished in *Essais critiques*, was to provide a kind of working model which made the more complex patterns of the original artefact fully comprehensible. This, in *Combat's* view, was exactly what Barthes had done for Racine's theatre, and the *Tribune de Genève* added the significant compliment from abroad to the effect that the machine undoubtedly worked.[13]

The Barthes/Picard quarrel was later to be frequently interpreted in political terms as a clash between Right and Left, and Jean Thibaudeau, writing in *France Nouvelle*, even went so far as to describe it as a precursor of the events which were to shake the political structure of France as a result of the student rebellion of 1968.[14] The critical reception of *Sur Racine* was certainly more enthusiastic on the Left than on the Right, and a reviewer in Jean-Paul Sartre's *Les Temps Modernes* accused Picard of intellectual chauvinism for his supposed preference for Descartes over Kant.[15] Interestingly enough, however, *Nouvelle Critique ou Nouvelle Imposture* had not originally been intended either for a wider audience or for a readership which could be relied upon to side automatically with a progressive or with a conservative approach to literary criticism. The first eighty pages of its final rather slim format—it contains only 148 in all—had first appeared not in the highly traditional *Revue d'Histoire Littéraire de la France* but in the more eclectic and sociologically-minded *Revue des Sciences Humaines*. This was published in Lille and edited at the time by an independent-minded Protestant called Albert-Marie Schmidt, who until April 1966 also edited the Protestant newspaper *Réforme*. Picard's essay was originally called 'Nouvelle critique ou nouveau délire', and appeared in the January–February number for 1965. It emerged from this respectable haven of academic controversy only when Jean-François Revel spotted its existence and took it for the *Libertés* series that he directed at the publishing house of Jean-Jacques Pauvert.[16]

The fact that the pamphlet which then took on the name of *Nouvelle Critique ou Nouvelle Imposture* appeared in such a collection and under such an imprint ought perhaps to have made it very difficult for it to have been presented in *Tel Quel* and *La Quinzaine littéraire* as part of a Fascist plot. Jean-François Revel was—and happily still is—the most irreverent of men. In 1965, the very year of the *Querelle*, he published an essay entitled 'En France' which contained the phrase: 'Le général de Gaulle a parfaitement raison de penser qu'il incarne la

France, il a tort de croire que cela soit flatteur pour lui' ['General de Gaulle is not wrong in believing that he is the incarnation of France. Where he is mistaken is in the belief that this is flattering for him'][17] and the collection *Libertés* had also published recent translations of Bertrand Russell's *Why I am not a Christian* and Bakunin's essay on liberty. In addition to bringing out a completely new edition of Littré, Jean-Jacques Pauvert had also undertaken the publication of the work of the Marquis de Sade and in 1956 been prosecuted and fined for his pains. Barthes was thus very far from really being able to claim that he was being attacked by an organised right-wing conspiracy. The tone of Picard's essay, however, was rather sharp, and fully in keeping with Revel's determination to make *Libertés* as controversial a series as possible. He not only accused Barthes of systematically distorting Racine's works, of not understanding what the word 'respirer' actually meant in the seventeenth century, of inventing inaccurate jargon and of transforming Racine's characters into earlier and more sexually obsessed versions of D. H. Lawrence's. He also wrote, rather neatly in view of Barthes's insistence that an author's conscious intentions were quite irrelevant to a real understanding of his work, that he was 'like a man who was interested in women but who, by a curious perversion, could appreciate them only by an X-ray machine'.[18]

The Barthes/Picard quarrel gave rise to at least six other books, in addition to the publicity which it received in article form. In February 1966, Barthes published *Critique et Vérité*, an even slimmer volume than *Nouvelle Critique ou Nouvelle Imposture*, and the same year Serge Doubrovsky came to his defence in the longer and more complicated *Pourquoi la Nouvelle Critique. Critique et objectivité*. From Switzerland, in 1967, André Allemand was to act as another of the many self-appointed judges in the quarrel, with *Nouvelle Critique, Nouvelle Perspective*. He too finally came down on Barthes's side by putting forward the eminently reasonable view that there could not, as Raymond Picard had apparently argued, be any one ultimate criterion for judging the value of a critical method but only 'different types of possible coherence'.[19] A second critic taken to task by Raymond Picard,[20] Jean-Claude Weber, replied in *Néo-critique et Paléo-critique*, dealing with the charge that he had analysed *Monsieur Teste*, Paul Valéry's semi-ironic portrait of a man wholly devoted to the intellectual life, in terms of the child's longing for its mother's breast.

Even Charles Mauron, whose residence in Aix-en-Provence normally kept him aloof from Parisian polemics, added a long note to his latest book, *Le dernier Baudelaire*, to make his position quite clear. Psychocriticism, he argued, did not try to analyse the author. He agreed with Raymond Picard that this was an impossible task, especially for a writer who had been dead for hundreds of years and had left no private papers. Neither did it set out to take the place of classical criticism and establish its own aesthetic criteria for judging works of art. It saw itself as essentially a means of enriching traditional methods by showing how the underlying structure of certain works of art corresponded to patterns which existed in the author's unconscious mind, and which repeated themselves in a way that he himself had not intended.[21] Pierre Daix also supported Barthes from a Marxist standpoint in *Nouvelle Critique et art moderne*, while in 1971 Lucien Goldmann summed up what he felt from a slightly less orthodox Marxist standpoint in *Situation de la critique racinienne*. From the other ideological side, and as if to show that the battle line was geographically a little further-flung than the three-quarters of a mile separating the buildings of the Sorbonne in the rue des Ecoles from the offices of the Editions du Seuil in the rue Jacob, a charming and elderly French academic called Alfred Bonson emerged from his exile in São Paulo to publish *La Nouvelle Critique et Racine*, putting forward the view that Racine was best considered as the creator of the purest poetry and of the most perfectly finished tragedies in the French language.[22]

It had already been reported, by November 1965, that Georges Poulet and Jean Ricardou were organising a colloquium to be held at Cérisy-la-Salle the following summer on 'Les chemins actuels de la critique', and the issues raised by the Barthes/Picard quarrel naturally figured in a number of the papers. A further colloquium held in 1968 on 'L'enseignement de la littérature' was virtually dominated by the impulse which Barthes and a number of other 'New Critics' mentioned disparagingly by Raymond Picard—Charles Mauron, Lucien Goldmann, Jean-Pierre Richard—had given to the discussion of the closely associated problems of what literary criticism was and how it should be incorporated into the syllabus of schools and universities.[23] For a debate which called into question at a comparable level on this side of the Channel the image which society could or should have of its own culture and educational system one has to turn to the arguments sparked off by C. P. Snow's lecture on 'The Two Cultures and the Scientific Revolution' in 1959 and the reply made to it by F. R. Leavis in his Richmond Lecture for 1962, 'Two Cultures? The significance of C. P. Snow'.

II

In retrospect, the interpretation which Barthes put forward in 'L'Homme racinien' the first and longest of the three studies which made up *Sur Racine*, seems to have been almost deliberately calculated to arouse the ire of the French literary and academic establishment. Racine, as every French schoolboy knows and as Barthes therefore found it unnecessary to mention, wrote out his tragedies in prose before transcribing them into alexandrines, and took care to avoid any

appearance of forcing his rhymes by always composing the second
line of his rhyming couplets first. His tragedies were therefore generally
regarded, in Raymond Picard's own terms, as 'le triomphe de la
création volontaire et consciente' ['the triumph of deliberate and
conscious creation'],[24] and the fact that Racine always took great care
in his prefaces to justify what he was doing by reference to the Ancients
also lent weight to Picard's view that his tragedies 'belonged to a
literary genre governed by strict rules and conventions'. Barthes, in
contrast, wrote in a way which clearly implied that Racine did not
really know what he was doing. His principal theme in *Sur Racine* is
that the underlying patterns in Racine's plays are all reducible to the
same basic model. At the beginning of human society, he argues, men
lived in tribes. Only the chief, the original father, the leading dominant male, had the right to possess and enjoy the women, and his sons
(or other junior members of the tribe) did so very much at their own
risk. The more aggressive sons naturally rose up against this tyranny,
and tried to establish their independence through a revolt against the
father. The more submissive obeyed his rule, albeit reluctantly, and
waited until he was weak before trying to challenge the Law which he
incarnated. The more audacious rebelled before the time was ripe,
and were, as Barthes stylishly puts it, 'impitoyablement tués, châtrés ou
chassés' ['pitilessly killed, castrated or driven out'].[25] When the old
man was eventually killed, quarrels broke out among the sons for the
possession of his wives and authority.

The basic relationships within primitive early society were thus
those of power, possession, jealousy, rivalry, punishment and revolt;
and, argues Barthes, it is precisely this structure which provides the
emotional underpinning for the imaginative universe which Racine
created in his plays. If, he maintains, one looks at Racine's plays as
they really are, phenomenologically, one might say, and without
any preconceived ideas as to his debt to the Greeks, his relationship
to Port-Royal, his supposedly tumultuous private life, his acceptance
of the neo-classical doctrine of the three unities, one always sees the
same pattern emerging: there are those who are identified with power
and are truly virile—even, he maintains, if they are (like Agrippine in
Britannicus or Roxane in *Athalie*) biologically female; and, in contrast,
there are those who are weaker, but who nevertheless try to escape
from the Old Law, from the Authority of the Tribe, and establish
themselves as sons, fathers and human beings in their own right:
Pyrrhus in *Andromaque*, Pharnace and Xipharès (albeit in contrasting
ways) in *Mithridate*, Néron in *Britannicus*.

Naturally, Barthes maintains, the pattern does not recur in absolutely the same form in every play. It is nevertheless always accompanied by the 'typically Racinian' situation in which A has all power
over B—Pyrrhus over Andromaque, Mithridate over Monime,

Roxane over Bajazet—but is not loved in return. Indeed one can imagine cases in the primitive human horde when the younger women were not all that keen on being reserved exclusively for the Old Man of the Steppes. But the fact nevertheless remains—according to Barthes —that the fundamental structure of Racinian tragedy varies only superficially from play to play: it always contains relationships characterised essentially by force and authority; and it deals with a revolt that is frequently accompanied by feelings of guilt. For, argues Barthes—clearly if unconsciously following Freud—the son who rebelled against the father for the possession of the women generally felt guilty at what he was doing. Similarly, in *Phèdre*, the main character feels guilty over her love for Hippolyte—she, too, of course, is presented as an aggressive, masculine-type woman, of the type which Barthes calls *viriloïde*—and so interiorises her guilt that she commits suicide. If we follow out these recurring patterns in Racine's plays, suggests Barthes, we shall in fact discover a gradual renunciation of the idea of revolt, culminating in the punishment of Athalie (another virile, rebellious woman) and the triumph of the authority figure of Joad. So that if we, as readers of Barthes's essay, insist on reverting to the old-fashioned idea of the author as a real person and link this pattern to Racine's own career, we can see this rise, fall and punishment of the rebel as a reflection of his own initial attempt to escape from Port-Royal and his final repentant return to the fold.

Clearly, these patterns are not all that Barthes finds in Racine. He shares with the Lucien Goldmann of *Le Dieu caché* the view that any attempt to escape from a tragic situation by compromise—an attempt which he sees as represented by the *confidente*—is morally despicable and also claims that the asexual characters of Oenone, in *Phèdre*, and Acomat in *Bajazet*, represent 'l'esprit le plus contraire à la tragédie, l'esprit de viabilité' ['the attitude of mind most opposed to tragedy, that of viability'].[26] What interests Barthes are the metaphysical overtones and implications of Racine's plays, and he writes that 'the whole of Racine lies in that paradoxical moment when the child discovers that his father is evil and yet wishes to remain his child'.[27] Indeed, he moves on from this to see Racine's religious universe as virtually identical with that of Dostoyevsky or the Marquis de Sade, and by that point in his argument the author is not only dead but turning in his grave. For the Racine who thought of himself as the most devout of Christians is presented as depicting in all his plays a God who is a fundamentally evil, incomprehensible creature, towards whom the only attitude which a rational being could adopt would be one of revolt. Barthes also writes that it is 'always through the king that tragedy turns rotten',[28] and politically and metaphysically, *Sur Racine* is on the Left. There can be no question of Barthes ever seeing any possibility of redemption through suffering or of Racinian tragedy offering the kind of reconciliation which one finds in Sophocles, Shakespeare or Corneille.

In *L'enseignement de la littérature*, one of the several collections to emerge from the Barthes/Picard quarrel, one of Barthes's admirers and disciples, Michel Déguy, insists that it is fully legitimate to base one's interpretation of an author's work on one example as long as this is the best available, and rejects the notion that scholars ought to accumulate a large amount of information before putting forward their conclusions.[29] If, by a certain poetic justice, we apply this particular method to Barthes himself, and use *Sur Racine* as the basis from which to define the structuralist approach which Barthes was adopting in the early nineteen-sixties, we shall arrive at something like the following statement: what matters in a work of art is not the author's conscious intentions; these are irrelevant, as are most of the objectively ascertainable facts of his life and the aesthetic which he thought he was adopting. What matters are the patterns which recur in his work, its fundamental emotional structure, and this is something over which the author himself, in the last resort, has very little control. The patterns and structures in Racine's plays depend, for Barthes, upon the survival in the writer of the kind of collective unconscious which Jung identified as lying at the heart of the myths and legends which are common to all people. Any value which we may find in an author's work does not depend, in the aesthetic implied by *Sur Racine*, on its similarity to our own experience and certainly not on the skill of the author in creating character. It does not stem from the beauty of his language or the persuasive power of the images and metaphors he uses, from his ability to recreate a vanished epoch or depict the true workings of society, from his psychological perspicacity, or from the originality of his moral vision. It is not a result of his power to evoke emotions in the reader's mind, of the honesty and perception with which he analyses and comes to terms with his own past experience, and it certainly has nothing to do with his ability to use established literary forms. In the case of Racine, for example, Barthes dismisses his skill in handling the alexandrine as a mere epiphenomenon. What really matters is the reproduction, in apparently original terms, of the earliest psychic history of mankind. Almost by definition, this is something of which Racine's conscious mind could have known absolutely nothing. The theory of the 'primitive horde' is a late nineteenth-century, post-Darwinian concept, and there is every reason to believe that Racine shared Bishop Bossuet's view that the world was created in exactly 4004 B.C. It is nevertheless from this basic situation whereby individuals define themselves in terms of their loyalty towards the most ancient discipline of the tribe that Barthes presents Racine's theatre as deriving what he regards as its greatest aesthetic quality: its coherence. Structuralism, as far as the literary criticism derived from it in the France of the early

1960s is concerned, would thus seem to be the search for the repetition of coherent but unconscious patterns in an author's work, irrespective of his conscious intentions.

In the case of Barthes, this neglect of any possible link between Racine the man and the text of his tragedies anticipates his later views on the death of the author, and is in many ways a logical continuation of the views which Paul Valéry had expressed in 1933 when he declared that the author had no authority to pronounce for or against any interpretation of his work.[30] This rejection of the biographical approach also marks off *Sur Racine* quite clearly from the two other major attempts at reinterpreting Racine which had immediately preceded Barthes's and which will be analysed in more detail in the next chapter: Charles Mauron's *L'inconscient dans l'œuvre et la vie de Racine* (1957) and Lucien Goldmann's *Le Dieu caché* (1954). For both Mauron, writing from a fairly conventional Freudian standpoint and Goldmann, attempting to apply his own version of Marxism to seventeenth-century French literature, had set out from what seems in contrast the rather orthodox view that Racine's life did have something to do with his plays. For Mauron, it was of the utmost importance for understanding *Andromaque* or *Phèdre* to know that Racine's parents had died before he was four, and that he had been brought up in the Jansenist stronghold of Port-Royal. This had fashioned his whole sensibility, and led him to make sense of his experience by writing plays which brought all the unconscious traumas of his childhood to the surface. For Goldmann, it was also essential both for an understanding of Racine's work and for an appreciation of its aesthetic merit to know that the social group in which he had lived in his childhood was the legal nobility which had provided most of the recruits for the Jansenist movement. This was not because Goldmann was any great believer in the importance of the isolated individual as sole creator of works of art. Indeed, what he presented without false modesty as his own 'Copernican revolution' in the study of literature and philosophy lay precisely in the opposite view. He maintained that

> the social character of a work of art resides first and foremost in the fact that an individual could never work out, through his own efforts alone, a coherent mental structure known as 'a world vision'. Such a structure can only be elaborated by a group. All the individual can do is carry it to a very high level of coherence, transposing it into a work of imagination or on to the plane of conceptual thought.[31]

But he nevertheless regarded both Pascal and Racine as important as individuals in their own right precisely because they represented the culmination of a whole complex of social attitudes which would,

without them, have remained dispersed in the general body of society
and never attained the fully coherent expression which only a perfectly
finished work of art written by a particular person can give them.

Sur Racine, however, makes only one or two fleeting references to
Racine as an individual. Although Barthes assumes, by his comment
about the importance of ingratitude in Racine's life, that readers will
know about the disingenuous way in which *Alexandre le Grand* was
taken away from Molière's company when it suited Racine's book to
do so, his whole approach is dominated by the view that what matters '
is the overall structure of Racine's tragic universe and not its genesis
in his personal experience. Indeed, it is quite fascinating to compare
Barthes's approach in *Sur Racine* with that of Mauron in *L'inconscient
dans l'œuvre et la vie de Racine*. Mauron is still, in his insistence on the
importance of the individual, very much a man of the nineteenth
century. Barthes, in contrast, is moving towards what he and his
admirers would consider to be the more specifically twentieth-century
attitude represented by the claim of Michel Foucault, on the last page of
Les Mots et les Choses, in 1966, that 'l'homme est une invention dont
l'archéologie de notre pensée montre aisément la date récente. Et
peut-être la fin prochaine' ['Man is an invention which the archaeology of our knowledge can easily show to have been of recent origin.
And which may also shortly disappear'].[32] Foucault's argument that
individual thinkers matter less than the forms and language in which
they do their thinking has some interesting similarities with Claude
Lévi-Strauss's declared intention in *Le Cru et le Cuit*: that he was setting
out to show not how men think through the medium of myths but
how myths themselves 'se pensent dans les hommes et à leur insu'
['think themselves out in men, without men knowing what is
happening'].[33] These two thinkers were generally considered, along
with Barthes and Jacques Lacan, to form the tetrarchy of French
structuralism in the nineteen-sixties, and *Sur Racine* is in many ways
the most accessible example of how their particular mode of thinking
works in a literary context. Yet Barthes himself had not, in the early
1960s, moved wholly into the much more arcane and unfamiliar style
of discourse which was to inform *S/Z, Sade, Fourier, Loyola* or *L'Empire
des Signes*; and *Sur Racine* belongs sufficiently to the kind of thinking
about literature represented by *L'inconscient dans l'œuvre et la vie de
Racine* or *Le Dieu caché* for Barthes's approach to be meaningfully
compared with that of Mauron and Goldmann.

Indeed, in so far as the quarrel with Picard was so frequently represented by Barthes's allies and admirers as a struggle to carry French
literary criticism kicking and screaming into the twentieth century,
it is essential to an understanding of Barthes's position in the French
intellectual life of the sixties not to see *Sur Racine* as an isolated phenomenon. It was part of a general movement to link criticism with the

major ideologies of the late nineteenth and early twentieth century, and followed hard upon the attempt which Mauron had made to use Racine as an example to prove the validity of the Freudian approach and the effort of Goldmann to demonstrate the superiority of Marxism by showing how it led to a better understanding of Racine and Pascal. One of the many paradoxes of Barthes's work is that in spite of his own enthusiasm for literature and proclaimed hostility to ideology, he is much more interesting when discussed in a sociological or semi-philosophical context than in a purely literary one. It may even have been this pretence at writing literary criticism when really indulging in philosophical speculation which explains why Picard should have chosen *Sur Racine* rather than *Le Dieu caché* or *L'inconscient dans l'œuvre et la vie de Racine* as the object of his attack. For neither Goldmann nor Mauron made any secret of the fact that his interests were ideological and not literary, and each put his philosophical cards honestly on the table. They consequently represented less of what Picard clearly thought to be the essentially dishonest challenge to traditional literary criticism represented by the covert apology for the ideology of structuralism contained in Barthes's *Sur Racine*. Mauron and Goldmann also wrote a much more conventional French than Barthes, and it was as much the way in which *Sur Racine* was written as its actual content which attracted Picard's disapproval. This, of course, is fully consistent with what Barthes considers his principal originality. A man who sees language as intensely as he does, who believes that the only way to change society is to change the language in which people think, is inevitably led to write in a highly original manner and to annoy people by so doing.

5 Marxism, Freudianism and ideology

I

One of the most intriguing features of the Barthes/Picard quarrel was the eagerness which other critics showed to act as referees. This was just as true of the man principally responsible for it, Jean-François Revel, as it was of Lucien Goldmann, the person whose book constituted the first serious attempt to see Racine in the light of a new ideology. Thus Revel declared in April 1966 that he had sought only to open a debate and was disappointed at the failure of both sides to say whether the application of Marxism, psychoanalysis or structuralism to literary criticism actually worked, while Goldmann predictably declared in his summing-up that Picard was 'for order and orthodoxy, whether they were conservative or Marxist'.[1] Charles Mauron added a postscript to his latest book, *Le dernier Baudelaire*, to explain why he found both Picard and Serge Doubrovsky in error for systematically rejecting the importance of the role played by the unconscious in literary creation. At the same time, he showed his understanding of what matters in philosophical argument by writing that 'except for mathematics and theoretical physics, the only criterion for truth is experimental evidence'.[2] Goldmann also accused *Sur Racine* of too frequently substituting 'personal problems and perspectives for the objective and literal meaning of the text in question',[3] and if ever there was a case of the pot calling the kettle black it is this particular judgement. For in spite of the enthusiasm which *Le Dieu caché* has aroused on both sides of the Channel—Alistair MacIntyre, reviewing the English translation in 1966, described Goldmann as 'an original philosopher of great powers', while Raymond Williams spoke in 1971 of the 'exceptionally valuable emphasis which he gave, theoretically and practically, to the development of literary and social studies'[4]— his version of Racine is so partial as to make Barthes stand out in comparison as a representative of the most cautious and painstaking brand of English empiricism. It is nevertheless very relevant to a discussion of *Sur Racine* in that it shows how far French critics were prepared to go, in the mid-twentieth-century, in using works of literature to support a largely political and philosophical case. It illustrates how typical Barthes was of the left wing in the intellectual

French society of that time in setting out from the presupposition that an author could be meaningfully evaluated in terms wholly alien to the artistic tradition in which he had originally written.

Goldmann's interpretation of Racine is in fact only part of a much larger thesis about the general relationship between the fortunes of the legal nobility in seventeenth-century France and the religious movement known as Jansenism.[5] This was an extremely austere form of Roman Catholicism which was eventually condemned as a heresy in 1713, and which can be said to have begun its existence as a movement, as distinct from an ideology, in 1637. It was then that a very brilliant young lawyer called Antoine le Maître withdrew from public life and chose to live in penance and retreat in what was later to become a stronghold of Jansenism, the religious community of Port-Royal des Champs, some twenty miles from Paris in the Vallée de Chevreuse. He was joined there by a number of other men, all of whom placed themselves under the spiritual direction of the Abbé de Saint-Cyran, one of the leading Jansenist theologians, and who became known as 'les solitaires'. The authorities became worried at the effect which comparable withdrawals from the world might have on the public life of France and in 1637 Saint-Cyran was arrested at the order of Cardinal Richelieu. He died in prison in 1643.

The persecution of the Jansenist movement remained a more or less permanent feature of French life for the rest of the seventeenth century, but does not really seem to have affected the popularity which it enjoyed among the legal profession. Goldmann quotes, in *Le Dieu caché*, several instances where lawyers seem to have gone out of their way to give verdicts that were favourable to people with Jansenist leanings, and Louis XIV experienced the greatest difficulty in having his edicts against the movement registered in the Courts. This was not, in Goldmann's view, merely an accident, or simply an example of the critical attitude which lawyers always tend to have towards governments. An important event had taken place in the 1630s which had profoundly affected the previously harmonious relationship between the King and the legal profession: the creation, under Richelieu's guidance, of a number of career civil servants, the *Intendants de Justice, de Police et de Finances*. In the past, and especially in the sixteenth century, the King had tended to rely on the middle class, and especially the lawyers, in his struggle with the hereditary nobility. In return for their support, he had agreed to an extension of the system whereby the holders of certain legal posts were able to take out patents of nobility, and even—in return for an extra payment —to hand both their post and their new title on to their children. A new class had thus grown up, the legal nobility or *noblesse de robe*. Unlike the hereditary nobility, however, and unlike the new merchant class, it was not financially independent of the King. The value of the offices held by its members depended to a considerable extent on the work the King gave them to do. If he succeeded in having cases judged in his own courts, the fees went to his stipendiary judges, not to those who had purchased their offices. And if he chose to alter his earlier policy of seeking co-operation from the middle class, taking the administration of the country away from the *noblesse de robe* in order to entrust it to the new civil servants whom he had appointed and whom he could therefore dismiss, there was remarkably little that the legal nobility could do about it.

It was the situation thus created by the establishment of the *Intendants de Justice, de Police et de Finances* which, in Goldmann's view, explained why the Jansenist movement proved so attractive to the legal nobility. The Jansenists taught, among other things, that men could be saved only by Grace. No purely human action could attain merit in God's eyes, and God alone knew who the Elect were on whom he bestowed His grace. Even with the best intentions, man might find himself falling into sin. Indeed there were certain commandments that even good men could not obey, however hard they might try. It was, in other words, a theology of individual impotence; and, as such, it corresponded exactly to the situation of a class which, like the *noblesse de robe*, found itself deprived of the functions which it had earlier been its pride and privilege to exercise. The *gens de robe* were equally unable to break away from the King and to influence his decisions; and there was, in this respect, a strong structural similarity between their position and that of the Christian who was equally unable to attain salvation by his own efforts and to reject the God who could alone bestow Grace. There was, admittedly, between 1648 and 1653, an attempt by certain members of the legal nobility to rebel against the King by joining forces with the dissident nobles involved in the rebellion known as the *Fronde*. But the *Fronde* was defeated, and the possibility of France experiencing the equivalent of the constitutional changes which resulted from the Civil War in England disappeared.

The two writers most closely associated with the Jansenist movement were Pascal and Racine. Much of *Le Dieu caché* is indeed concerned with the former, and Goldmann goes to immense pains both to show how the *Pensées* give philosophical coherence to the world view which enabled the legal nobility to make sense of their condition and to demonstrate how close Pascal came to Marxism. He anticipated Marx, Goldmann argues, in adapting an essentially dialectical mode of thought, but was prevented from discovering the true way in which the dialectic works—through History—by the misfortune of representing the interests of a class whose social and economic position prevented it from envisaging the possibility of historical change. Goldmann does not try to do the same for Racine, but concentrates instead on showing how the impossible situation which the Racinian hero—or, more frequently, heroine—has to confront is structurally identical to the concept of the human condition elaborated in the tragic vision of the Jansenist movement. Thus, in Racine's first really successful play, *Andromaque* (1667), the heroine has to choose between two equally unacceptable alternatives. She is Hector's widow, and longs to remain faithful to the memory of her dead husband. But she is the captive of Pyrrhus, Achilles's son, who has fallen passionately in love with her. Indeed, his passion is so violent that he is threatening, if she persists in her refusal to marry him, to kill Astyanax, the son she bore Hector, and whom she longs to protect with the same fervour that she seeks to honour her husband's memory. Like the most intransigent of Jansenist theologians, she knows that this world is evil: Pyrrhus is the son of the man who killed her husband, he is threatening to murder her son, and all the other characters in the play behave, as he does, like ravening beasts. But she cannot simply reject the world, for to do so would lead to the death of her son. God's moral commandments are absolute, but He gives human beings no means of carrying them out. He is a Hidden God whose motives nobody can ever know, and whom an infinite and qualitative gulf separates from His creatures. Yet though hidden, He still exists; and by the side of what He commands, all earthly concepts of right and wrong are wholly inauthentic.

Andromaque herself, however, does not—in Goldmann's view—remain all the time on the tragic plane of moral absolutes. She is inspired, by a visit to her husband's grave, to adopt a subterfuge which will enable her to reconcile the contradictory demands laid upon her: she will marry Pyrrhus, and make him swear to protect her son; then she will kill herself before the marriage is consummated. From the moment that she accepts this compromise, Goldmann maintains, she ceases to be a tragic figure. Tragedy flies out of the window when compromise comes in at the door, and its is only in Racine's next play, *Britannicus* (1669), that he succeeds in creating what Goldmann regards as a wholly coherent tragedy. In this play, the tragic character is Junie, in love with the noble Britannicus but pursued by the wicked Néron. When Néron murders Britannicus, Junie's intuitive knowledge that one cannot live authentically in this world attains the level of a certainty; and she herself becomes a vestal virgin. Racine's next play, *Bérénice* (1670), is also a tragedy in the sense that neither of the two main characters is able or ready to envisage any compromise with the world. Titus, the new Emperor of Rome, is in love with Bérénice, Queen of Palestine. His love for her is absolute, but so is his recognition that the traditional Roman hostility to Kings and Queens must be respected. He eventually sends her away—'dimisit invitus invitam': against his will, against hers—knowing that they will never see each other again. 'The "long exile" of Titus', writes Goldmann, 'like the temple of the vestal virgins, is the refuge hidden behind the world, and the translation into tangible, pagan language of the real Christian and spiritual lives which Racine beheld as a schoolboy at Port-Royal and which profoundly influenced his way of thinking and feeling.'[6]

After *Bérénice*, a change is apparent in the patterns of Racine's tragedies. The rejection of the world is less absolute, and the final catastrophe is either avoided altogether or brought about by an unhappy accident. In *Bajazet* (1672) all might have ended happily if Roxane had not found Bajazet's love letter concealed in the bosom of the fainting Atalide. In *Mithridate* (1673) the central character dies triumphant, after having overcome his emotional problems by an access of positively Corneillian generosity, while in *Iphigénie* (1674) the heroine is saved by the intervention of the Gods and allowed to marry Achilles. Goldmann links this changed atmosphere to an improvement in the fortunes of the Jansenist group. A compromise patched up in February 1669 in what French historians call *La Paix de l'Eglise* and English ones the Peace of Clement IX led to a period in which the Jansenists were not persecuted quite so intensely, and could envisage a permanent *modus vivendi* with the French state. However, the presence in *Iphigénie* of the one character stated by Goldmann to be genuinely tragic—the young princess Eriphile, consumed by what she knows to be a hopeless and criminal passion for Achilles—indicates that these hopes were felt to be short-lived, and the appearance of *Phèdre* in 1677 reintroduces the theme of how impossible it is to live authentically in this world. Phèdre, passionately in love with her stepson, Hippolyte, allows herself to be seduced by the false rumour of her husband Thésée's death into believing that this passion can be satisfied without loss of honour. Thésée's return disillusions her, and there is a structural similarity between the failure of her hopes and the collapse of the compromise adumbrated in the Peace of Clement IX. After a long break with the theatre, between 1677 and 1688, Racine comes back to the stage with two dramas taken from the Old Testament: *Esther*, in 1689, and *Athalie*, in 1691. Both can be related to the hope that the Jansenists might, after all, succeed in imposing themselves in this world, but neither can be seen as a tragedy.

Goldmann's discussion of Racine's tragedies in these terms anticipates *Sur Racine* in a number of ways. It is, to begin with, totally unsupported by any evidence other than that provided by the recurring patterns in the plays themselves, and is based throughout on the presupposition that Racine did not really know what he was doing. *Le Dieu caché* also contains in a fully articulated form a definition of tragedy as the literary genre which presents compromise with the real world as impossible, and also defines the tragic hero as the person who recognises this to be the case. It was this somewhat narrow definition which was to form the unacknowledged basis for a number of Barthes's aesthetic judgements in *Sur Racine*, and which is undoubtedly the weakest point in both Barthes's and Goldmann's argument. For Goldmann not only refuses even to discuss any other definition, arguing that Racine wrote only three tragedies, *Britannicus, Bérénice* and *Phèdre*, when he in fact gave the title to eleven of his works and has, in the opinion of most other critics and theatregoers, been credited with at least five more than Goldmann will allow: *Andromaque, Mithridate, Iphigénie, Bajazet* and *Athalie*. He also insists, within the plays themselves, on regarding as 'tragic'—and therefore, by definition, centrally important—characters who play very little part in the action. In *Britannicus*, for example, Junie speaks only 156 lines out of a total of 1768, and is, when the play is performed, totally overshadowed by Agrippine and Néron. Similarly, in *Iphigénie*, the supposedly tragic Eriphile is offstage for a good two-thirds of the play, and has only 229 lines to Agamemnon's 350. It is certainly an interesting idea to define the 'tragic man' as someone who lives on the plane of absolute demands and refuses, to use Arthur Miller's terminology, to 'settle for half'[7]. It could even—though this is perhaps not a point in its favour— be used to make Anouilh's *Antigone* amenable to discussion as a tragedy. But as applied to the works of Racine, it is indistinguishable from Joe Gargery's account to Pip of the pleasures to be derived from reading. 'Give me', he says, 'a good book, or a good newspaper, and sit me down afore a good fire, and I ask no better . . . Lord, when you *do* come to a J and an O, and says you: "Here, at last, is a J–O Jo", how interesting reading is!' Goldmann leaps upon any character whose passion for moral absolutes fits his own definition of tragedy; and, like Joe Gargery passing over such interesting people in his own life as Pip, Estella, Biddy or Miss Haversham on the grounds that their names contain neither a J nor an O, relegates Pyrrhus, Oreste, Hermione, Agrippine, Néron, Roxane, Amurat or Thésée to the rank of 'wild beasts' or 'marionettes'.

While Barthes is not quite so exclusive in his judgements, he implicitly adopts the definition which Goldmann gives of the tragic hero: someone who recognises the impossibility of the situation in which he or she is placed and insists that there can be no way out through compromise. 'Tragedy', Barthes writes of the play *Iphigénie*, 'defeated on all sides by the rise of the middle class which is the dominant feature of the times ['battue en brèche de tous les côtés par le puissant courant bourgeois qui emporte l'époque'], is here entirely concentrated in the character of Eriphile'.[8] It is, to put it mildly, a narrow definition of the most famous 'hurrah word' in the whole vocabulary of literary criticism, and one only has to think of asking how this particular use of the word 'tragic' could be made to fit either Sophocles or Shakespeare to see how both Goldmann and Barthes have allowed themselves to be carried away by the worst form of *a priori* reasoning. What is even more extraordinary is the extreme insularity which both critics indulge in when they allow themselves to define a word such as tragedy by reference solely to one or two plays by Racine, and this again has strong if unintended political overtones. Thus I have already argued, in discussing Barthes's enthusiasm for Brecht, that the great danger of his approach lies in a puritanical zeal which allows no place for any works of art that he happens not to like, and this intellectual narrow-mindedness is even more clearly marked in the similarity between his view of tragedy and the one to be found in *Le Dieu caché*. When the Left was in permanent opposition, fighting against a genuinely oppressive capitalist society which tried to ban authors like Ibsen, Flaubert, Baudelaire or Zola, it both preached and practised intellectual tolerance. Now that it has come to represent what Barthes would call the prevailing *Doxa*, this has ceased to be the case. Both Goldmann and Barthes behave towards the word 'tragedy' exactly as the giant Procrustes behaved towards his guests. They expand or contract it to fit their own narrow definition of what it ought to be, just as he compelled unwary travellers to fit his bed by either stretching them or cutting off their legs. Similarly, in the countries where it has triumphed, the Left has imposed its own stultifying ideology on both political and literary life, and there is little either in *Le Dieu caché* or *Sur Racine* to indicate that it would ever act differently even in France.

The chief interest of *Le Dieu caché* is, of course, a philosophical rather than a literary one. Goldmann is putting forward a view about how works of art come to be written, and his thesis that the great writer is the person who gives complete intellectual coherence to the world-view of a particular social class at a specific moment in history is a very stimulating one. At a time when French fiction seemed to be deliberately abandoning any attempt to be interesting, the French literary critics took up the challenge of trying to give people a good exciting read; and both *Le Dieu caché* and *Sur Racine* have all the excitement and much of the improbability of the less subtle nineteenth-century novels. They are equally intriguing as examples of how literary criticism can be influenced by ideology as well as expressing it, since it is quite clear that neither Goldmann nor Barthes could take any enjoyment in a performance of Racine which did not fit their particular theories. These books also illustrate how a society with such a strong tradition of philosophical thinking as France makes a constant re-evaluation of its cultural heritage in fashionable political and ideological terms rather than in literary ones. There is, however, one really successful attempt to interpret Racine in the light of modern ideas: Charles Mauron's *L'inconscient dans l'œuvre et la vie de Racine*. This is a book which shows how a basically ideological approach can, on occasion, fulfil what G. K. Chesterton once defined as the aim of

criticism: to tell the author something which would make him jump
out of his boots. For Racine would have jumped out of his boots on
reading Mauron's book because he realised that it was all true.

II

Barthes acknowledges his debt to Mauron on the very first page of
Sur Racine, and there are a number of obvious similarities between the
two works. Both insist on the role of possessive women in Racine's
work, both regard Pyrrhus, in *Andromaque*, as the character invested
with Racine's own aspirations and problems, and both point out how
inadequate the fathers or father-figures generally are in Racine.
Barthes's description of the role of Junie in *Britannicus* derives equally
directly from Mauron's more soberly written analysis. 'Junie', he
writes in *Sur Racine*, 'est la Vierge Consolatrice par un rôle d'essence,
puisque Britannicus trouve en elle exactement ce que Néron vient y
chercher: elle est celle qui pleure et recueille les pleurs, elle est l'Eau
qui enveloppe, détend, elle est l'ombre dont Néron est le terme solaire'
['Junie is, by the very essence of her role, the consoling Virgin, since
Britannicus finds in her exactly what Néron is looking for: she is the
person who weeps and gathers up tears, she is the Water into which
one can sink and relax, she is the shade to Néron's sun'].[9] Mauron
had pointed out that Néron, like Pyrrhus in *Andromaque*, is fleeing
from a dangerous, virile, aggressive woman, able to call upon armed
support, and written that he was seeking to possess, in Junie, a 'tender-
hearted, melancholy captive, to whom he offers the sceptre and who
refuses it through faithfulness to an earlier love'. For reasons which are
manifestly clear to any Freudian who has read *Roland Barthes par Roland
Barthes*, there is a particular sensitivity in a number of Barthes's essays
to the possessive, castrating mother-figure. It is therefore not especially
surprising that his personal situation should have made him, albeit
quite unconsciously, sympathetic to certain aspects of Mauron's
approach, just as his political preferences had inclined him to accept
Goldmann's cult of intolerant absolutes. Where *L'inconscient dans
l'œuvre et la vie de Racine* strikes the English reader as a more solid and
convincing piece of work than either *Le Dieu caché* or *Sur Racine* is in
its old-fashioned, empirical approach and in its attempt to establish a
definite link between Racine the man and Racine the author of
Phèdre. Like Barthes, Mauron did adopt what one might call a 'Brighton
rock' approach. He claimed that the same patterns revealed themselves
wherever you took a 'histological section' of Racine's work, just as
Barthes was to insist that 'dans Racine, il n'y a qu'un seul rapport,
celui de Dieu et de la créature' and maintain that 'l'inceste, la rivalité
des frères, le meurtre du père, la subversion des fils' were the 'actions
fondamentales du théâtre racinien'.[10] But unlike Barthes, Mauron did

not believe sufficiently in the 'death of the author', the irrelevance of biographical details to the meaning of a work of art, to be uninterested in how this came about.

This contrast with Mauron does in fact highlight one of the major criticisms that can be levelled against Barthes's approach to literature both in *Sur Racine* and, later in his career, in *S/Z*: the narrowing down that it involves in both his own and his reader's intellectual curiosity. It is not difficult to accept his view that our aesthetic appreciation of a work of art ought to be exactly the same whether we can see a link between it and the author's life or not. What Barthes rather grandly refers to as the 'death of the author' corresponds to an idea which has been relatively commonplace in English literary criticism ever since T. S. Eliot observed in 1920 in *Tradition and the Individual Talent*, that 'Impressions and experiences which are important for the man may take no place in his poetry, and those which become important in his poetry may play quite a negligible part in the man, the personality'.[11] Strindberg's *The Father* would be no better and no worse as a play if Strindberg the man had been the happiest of husbands. It is true, as Barthes said in his review of George Painter's biography of Proust, that it is often books which enable us to understand the world and not the other way round—'Le monde ne fournit pas les clefs du livre, c'est le livre qui ouvre le monde'—and we should indeed, rather than looking to Robert de Montesquiou for the origin of the Baron de Charlus, say to ourselves that 'il y a du Charlus en Montesquiou'.[12] We shall, as Barthes argues in *Critique et Vérité*, make fewer mistakes about our social and personal experiences if we look upon fiction not as a copy of the real world but a tool by which we can better understand it. The fact nevertheless remains, to put the matter in suitably Barthesian terms, that our own culture has fashioned us in a particular way. We regard it as so natural to feel intellectual curiosity about human beings that we cannot avoid looking for a link between the author and the man. It may well be that this is only custom, and it would certainly be foolish to confuse studies of how books come to be written with the entirely different question of their literary value or their ability to function as sign systems. But neither Barthes nor anyone else has ever explained why all customs should be bad and why it is wrong to be interested in a person capable of producing a masterpiece such as *Phèdre*. Once again, it is difficult to make these very obvious points against Barthes without feeling like a cross between Polonius and Proust's Bloch. However, perhaps even pedantry is preferable to allowing a case to go by default, and the temptation to render one's own verdict in the *Querelle des Critiques* is especially strong when one feels that one of the critics mentioned though not actively involved is so much better than all the others.

The main reason for the excellence of Mauron's book can be found in the order of words in the title: *L'inconscient dans l'œuvre et la vie de Racine.* Thus, like Barthes, he begins with an analysis of the main themes in Racine's work and avoids the accusation of reductionism by not even mentioning his life until establishing beyond doubt that the patterns which he describes do exist. In establishing these patterns, Mauron also does precisely what the critic who models himself on Browning's *Fra Lippo Lippi* ought to do. He 'lends his mind out' in order that his reader may 'see . . . things he had passed a thousand times before nor cared to see'. Thus Mauron observes that in Racine's first great tragedy, *Andromaque*, the central male character, Pyrrhus, is caught between two women: the jealous, violent, aggressive Hermione, and the gentler, softer Andromaque. He then points out that the same pattern recurs in Racine's next play, *Britannicus*. There, Néron is seeking to escape from his mother, Agrippine—who like the passionate Hermione of *Andromaque* represents a fidelity to past values—into the calmer and more relaxed presence of Junie. Like Pyrrhus, Néron does not succeed, but manages none the less to transmit the violence which Agrippine aims at him on to his half-brother Britannicus.

The diagram reproduced on p. 79,[13] in which the names going from right to left in the centre line are those of Racine's male characters, while the arrow going from bottom to top on the left-hand side and from top to bottom on the right-hand side indicates the direction of aggression, makes the analysis compulsively easy to follow, and has two immense advantages over Goldmann's scheme: it is based exclusively on the plays themselves, and is completely free from any *a priori* value-judgement as to what is tragic and what is not. Admittedly, it depends in the case of Racine's third major play, *Bérénice*, on regarding the heroine as two people: the reproachful Bérénice, whom Titus had promised to marry before he became Emperor of Rome and from whom he wants to escape as Pyrrhus tried to flee from Hermione and Néron from Agrippine; and the gentler person by whose side he would like to seek refuge from a situation that has become too complicated for him. But this is not an unreasonable way of looking at *Bérénice* and the text of the next play, *Bajazet*, does not even need this slight distortion of the main character. Roxane is the most violently aggressive of Racine's possessive mother-figures, and Mauron points out that the Roxane of Segrais's *L'Amour imprudent*, one of Racine's major sources, was actually Bajazet's stepmother.[14] But before Racine gave expression to his 'theme of themes' of the incestuous mother and the fleeing son in *Phèdre*, the emphasis in the emotional patterns shifted.

Mithridate is the one secular play by Racine in which there is a dominant and capable father-figure who both acts generously in his private life and attains some kind of political victory in the outside world. His last speech contains the line 'Et mes derniers regards ont

SCHEMA DE RACINE

Andromaque-Astyanax
Junie-Britannicus

Bérénice

Atalide

Mithridate
Monime-Xipharès
Pharnace

Calchas
Agamemnon

Thésée
Aricie

Joad

Pyrrhus
Néron
Titus
Bajazet
Achille
Hippolyte

Eliacin

Agrippine
Hermione
Oreste

Bérénice

Roxane

Eriphile

Phèdre

Athalie

vu fuir les Romains', and the fact that Mithridate blessed the union
between his son Xipharès and his sometime fiancée Monime is an
intriguing example of how, for once, the patterns of what Barthes
would call the primitive horde can be made to yield to an adult
generosity of spirit. However, the psychological balance which it
represents in Racine's career does not last. Agamemnon, in *Iphigénie*,
manages to be at one and the same time both ruthless and undecided,
and this introduction of the father-figure merely brings about a shift
in the patterns of destructive aggression which so characterise Racine's
plays. The aggression now goes from the father through the son to the
violently possessive woman (see diagram), and the change is accompanied by something even more fundamental. Neither Hermione,
Agrippine, Bérénice nor Roxane feels guilty. Each is intensely unhappy,
but each utters what Barthes was later to term 'une plainte vaniteuse
et revendicative, fondée sur la bonne conscience' ['a self-centred
complaining cry, based on the knowledge that they have right on their
side'].[15] But Eriphile, Phèdre and Athalie are not only unloved. The
passion which inhabits them makes them feel guilty as well. Each
knows that she is doing wrong at the very moment when she is also
sick with jealous fury, and this ability for self-torment leads each of
them, in her own way, to self-destruction. Eriphile stabs herself on the
funeral pyre prepared for Iphigénie, Phèdre poisons herself, and
Athalie is killed, at her own urgent invitation, with the sword she had
prepared for her enemies.

The question which Mauron then sets out to answer is the intriguing
one of why these patterns in Racine's plays came to exist. For exist
they undoubtedly do, and it would really be very difficult to explain
them in terms of Picard's claim that Racine's tragedies are 'the triumph
of conscious and deliberate creation'. It is inconceivable that Racine
should have consciously chosen or remodelled each of his sources in
order to create exactly the pattern which Mauron detects. One might
as well, to take up an image which Mauron himself is fond of using,
say that the iron filings which group themselves into the lines of force
of a magnetic field are doing so in obedience to some conscious desire
on the experimenter's part to create a particular shape. The reason
why one is so often tempted to apply the word 'scientific' to Mauron—
and refuse it, in spite of all his claims, to Lucien Goldmann—is that
the former so often gives the appearance of working in the same way
as an experimental scientist. He observes phenomena, counts them
and looks for an explanatory hypothesis. He chooses the hypothesis
which seems to fit the greatest number of observed phenomena. He
then relates it, in fulfilment of the quest for general laws which characterises the scientific intellect, to a general theory governing the area
under investigation.

This appearance is, of course, to a considerable extent an illusion.

By the time he wrote *L'inconscient dans l'œuvre et la vie de Racine*, which he did between 1948 et 1954, slightly longer than it took Flaubert to write *Madame Bovary*, Mauron had been a convinced Freudian for some twenty-five years. He had consequently set out to write the book, as his Preface makes clear, in order to show how Racine's psychic structure was 'like that of any other human being, established in early childhood'.[16] But in spite of this obvious *parti pris*, Mauron still kept the scientific habit of mind which he had acquired in his first career. Originally, he had been an experimental chemist, but had lost his sight in a laboratory accident. On moving over into literary and philosophical studies, he turned his handicap to advantage by learning the texts he was studying off by heart. He then superimposed them on one another in his own mind like a comparative anatomist placing X-ray photographs of various mammals one on top of another in order to discover morphological similarities. It was this method which he had used to discover the way in which the memory of his dead sister Maria had obsessed Mallarmé, and which had made him more conscious than any previous critic had been of the emotional patterns and structure of relationships which recurred in Racine's plays. And although he must, like every French literary critic, have always known about Racine's childhood and early youth, he does manage in the second part of *L'inconscient dans l'œuvre et la vie de Racine* to give the impression of having discovered his facts by working backwards from the observable patterns in Racine's work and not of having begun with the presupposition that since Racine was himself an orphan, he would inevitably include a lot of orphans in his plays.

Racine was eleven months old when his mother died, and only three-and-a-half years old when he lost his father. This fact explains, in Mauron's view, not only the repeated presence of orphans in Racine's work—Astyanax, Bajazet, Monime, Eriphile, Eliacin—but also the more striking phenomenon of the recurrence of violent, passionate, possessive mother-figures. For after his parents' death, Racine was brought up first of all by his grandparents and subsequently by an aunt, Sœur Agnès de Sainte-Thècle, one of the most devoted and enthusiastic supporters of the Jansenist movement. From the age of nine, Racine was a boarder at the Jansenist school at Beauvais, and indeed had so close an association with the movement that it is not difficult to agree with Mauron when he claims that it was its centre at Port-Royal which served as both mother and father to him. But at no point in his childhood had Port-Royal been able to provide Racine with a father-figure on whom to model himself. Instead, by the intensely emotional and basically rather neurotic atmosphere which reigned there, it had constituted an intensely powerful mother-image which Racine sought sometimes to defy and sometimes to avoid, but whose possessive wrath he was constantly seeking to assuage. His decision to make a career in the theatre, the one activity above all others of which the Jansenists most vehemently disapproved, is presented by Mauron as an attempt at self-affirmation on Racine's part which never enabled him to develop a fully integrated adult personality. The mixture of guilt and defiance which this decision involved constitutes the psychological make-up of all the figures who represent Racine's *ego*—in his 'first cycle', Pyrrhus, Néron, Titus, Bajazet; Eriphile and Phèdre in his second—and Mauron gives a striking formulation of his basic thesis when he writes that, for Racine, happiness in love was being able to write for the theatre. 'The creation of a work of art which was at one and the same time a spectacle and a confession, linked in this way to a set of strongly sexual impulses ['une composante amoureuse très forte']¹⁷ writes Mauron, 'must have represented, for Racine's super-ego ['pour l'autorité inconsciente'], the equivalent of an act of sexual indecency', and it would be an act of intellectual self-mutilation for the sceptical reader to dismiss such language as misapplied Freudian jargon. It tells us something not only about Racine the man but also about Racine the creator of characters who, like Phèdre or the Néron of *Britannicus*, are obsessed with the experience of seeing or being seen.

Although Mauron himself played only a very small part in the *Querelle des Critiques* which followed the publication of *Nouvelle Critique ou Nouvelle Imposture* in October 1965, there is a remark in *L'inconscient dans l'œuvre et la vie de Racine* which seems almost like a direct reply to Picard's claim that Racine's tragedies were 'the triumph of deliberate and conscious creation'. 'Without knowing it', writes Mauron, 'the most lucid of our writers modelled his work on an Unconscious of which, in the course of his creation, he attained an intuitive knowledge of which he personally was not aware';¹⁸ and this is a very much more satisfying way of looking at Racine's work than Picard's insistence that it was all absolutely deliberate. Mauron did, of course, have a more celebrated theoretician in mind when he argued the case for seeing works of art as stemming from a collaboration between the artist's conscious and unconscious mind. The poet Paul Valéry had, in a number of essays, argued very vigorously in favour of seeing art as perpetually conscious fabrication, and Mauron was deliberately taking issue with him in maintaining that good art also needed the approval and contribution of that part of us which has an intuitive awareness of the unconscious.

Neither was this the only way in which Mauron put forward a more complex and satisfying account than Picard had done of the relationship between Racine the man and Racine the author of *Phèdre*. Racine, as Picard himself had brilliantly demonstrated in his monumental *La Carrière de Jean Racine*, had quite consciously pursued the ambition of carving out a place for himself in the aristocratic society of seven-teenth-century France. From relatively humble middle-class origins, he had risen to the elevated rank of historiographer to Louis XIV— who undoubtedly, as Mauron observes, preferred the account of his own military campaigns to any performance of *Phèdre*. As Picard himself insisted, and as the title of his thesis indicated quite clearly, his own aim was to study Racine's career, and he almost pointedly refrained either from suggesting why Racine was such a marvellous playwright or why so many people feel inclined to agree with Jean Pommier's remark that Racine's twelfth tragedy was his life. Indeed, Picard's approach seemed so narrow to one of Barthes's more zealous supporters that he accused him of giving more importance to Racine's laundry bills than to the writing of *Andromaque*.[19] Where Mauron's approach complemented and went beyond Picard's was in the ex-planation which it offered both for Racine's behaviour and for the contrast between the emotional richness of his imaginary universe and the intense emotional poverty of his own private life. For Racine, again as every French undergraduate knows, married a woman who never went to the theatre in her life, never read a single line of his plays, and bore him seven children. Three of the girls he succeeded in placing in convents—'Quel Agamemnon que ce père', comments Mauron, 'quelles Iphigénies que ces enfants'[20]—while his eldest son devoted himself to writing a hagiographic account of his father's life. The reason both for the emotional wealth that gave birth to Hermione, Agrippine, Roxane, Phèdre and Athalie, and for the poverty which produced the emotionally stunted self-seeker depicted in *La Carrière de Jean Racine*, lay for Mauron in Racine's childhood. The figures who belong to what he calls the order of the 'virile, castrating, all-enveloping mother-figures, Agrippine listening at keyholes, Roxane and her seraglio, Phèdre and the labyrinth' all draw their sustenance from the intense experience of Racine's early years, when Port-Royal was unconsciously building up in him 'archaic structures of an excep-tional solidity'.[21] But Racine never came consciously to terms with the emotional turmoil set up in him by his childhood, and was thus never able to develop what we would normally regard as a mature and well-balanced personality. It is this, in Mauron's view, which accounts both for the fact that Racine's most complex and emotionally charged play, *Phèdre*, was followed by a complete abandonment of the profane theatre and for the absence from his theatre of satisfactory male characters. It also explains what Mauron rightly calls 'the absence from his theatre of moral and spiritual values', and he has a similarly accurate phrase with which to modify La Bruyère's famous judgement that 'Corneille depicts men as they ought to be and Racine as they are'. Racine, he observes, 'depicts man not as he is, but a little below and beyond himself, at the moment when the other members of his family, the doctors and the lawyers, would begin to worry if it was in real life and not in the theatre'.[22]

It is in many ways a pity that while Lucien Goldmann is quite well known in England and America, and very popular with thinkers on the Left, Mauron has been discussed on this side of the Channel principally by his detractors. This is especially ironic in view of the fact that he is the one twentieth-century French critic to have known English and English literature really well—he translated, among others, Laurence Sterne, E. M. Forster, T. E. Lawrence and Virginia Woolf—and to have been associated with an important literary movement in this country. He was a close friend of Roger Fry, who translated two of his books into English—*The Nature of Beauty in Art and Literature* in 1927 and *Aesthetics and Psychology* in 1935—and is one of the few psychoanalytical critics to have asserted the primacy of literary and aesthetic considerations when studying works of art. While agreeing, in his Preface to *L'inconscient dans l'œuvre et la vie de Racine*, that art is 'essentially a restoration of "lost time", a compensa-tion·for grief and psychological ruin', he also contends that it is a compensation which is real, superabundant, and which far transcends its original cause. He is thus at the furthest possible remove from the approach of a Marxist thinker such as Tran Duc Thao, who maintained in a debate at the *Collège de Philosophie* in 1948 that Mallarmé's poetry both stemmed directly from the social conditions of his time and could be entirely explained by reference to them.[23] Indeed, the way Mauron wrote about his own work during the early part of his career has a fascinating if rather uncanny resemblance to the views on literature which Barthes himself was to develop later in his career. 'Whatever the gods of antiquity do', he wrote in *The Nature of Beauty in Art and Literature*, 'they play. And we too—actors of a miniature history which none the less surpasses us infinitely—we could not adopt a finer atti-tude'.[24] Both in *Sade, Fourier, Loyola* (1971) and in his most obscurely aphoristic work, *Le Plaisir du Texte* (1973), Barthes also insists on what he calls the ludic quality of literary activity, and emphasises the way in which the writers he admires create quite gratuitous patterns which have no necessary relationship whatsoever to real life. Mauron is less aggressive in his rejection of the mimetic illusion, but he nevertheless comes close to anticipating Barthes's later aesthetic when he compares the 'divine game' of the artist to that of a child who 'destroys a pattern of coloured cubes to build up new ones'. He also foreshadows an important part of the structuralist attitude towards art when he writes that the individuals in a situation depicted in literature 'are, as on a chess-board, pieces which count by reason of their relative situations', and the example which he chooses to illustrate his point is almost exactly the same as the one used by Saussure in the *Cours de linguistique générale*.[25] Indeed, when Mauron suggests that people are wrong to praise Proust as a great psychologist 'whereas in reality he is a great poet', he comes even closer to the ambition of Barthes and his followers to present literature as a wholly self-sufficient activity. It is indeed difficult to understand how the critics who, like R. E. Jones, consider aesthetics to be wholly absent from Mauron's work, reconcile their views with the books he actually wrote.[26]

It is nevertheless in the literary and philosophical implications of *L'inconscient dans l'œuvre et la vie de Racine* that the example of Charles Mauron is most immediately relevant to this study of Roland Barthes. For Mauron represents all that is most attractive in the new ideologies which Barthes claimed in *Critique et Vénté* in 1966 to be introducing into the allegedly out-dated world of French literary criticism. His works are all written in beautifully clear language, with sudden dramatic insights into both art and the human condition which make the experience of reading him a constant intellectual delight. He said himself in *Aesthetics and Psychology* that 'human reason has, ultimately, only one pleasure; the discovery of a new resemblance', and his method in *L'inconscient dans l'œuvre et la vie de Racine* is exactly that of the person who draws our attention to structural parallels which, as he says, 'stare us in the face' ['nous crèvent les yeux'] but which people have not noticed before. His comment, again made in 1935 in *Aesthetics and Psychology*, that 'man is perhaps only interesting as a sick and freakish animal' again has a peculiarly modern ring about it, while the observation, in his analysis of the emotional roots of Racinian tragedy, that 'la grande angoisse humaine est de tendre les bras vers un être qui se révèle meurtrier' ['the great human dread is to hold out one's arms to a being which reveals itself as murderous'][27] has the sudden depth of some of Freud's or Kierkegaard's statements about the human condition. Unlike Lucien Goldmann, who constantly presents the barbaric theology of the Jansenist movement as the one source of moral greatness in seventeenth-century France, Mauron writes of Port-Royal with a detached perceptiveness which betokens a fundamental sanity of intellectual approach. The Jansenists, he argued, were like adolescents. They wanted at one and the same time constantly to defy their parents, and yet to stay in the parental home in order to make their father and mother come round to their way of thinking. They were not even capable of genuine intellectual rebellion. Instead of going right back to St Paul, they stopped at St Augustine. Instead of honestly recognising that they were basically Protestants, they insisted on being the only true Catholics and summoned their co-religionists to instant conversion. When the Church understandably refused to jettison the theology which had taken sixteen centuries to elaborate, the Jansenists consigned ninety-nine per cent of their brethren to perdition. Underlying the whole of Mauron's attitude towards Jansenism there is a fundamental sanity and level-headedness which make him a welcome exception on the more speculative shores of modern French criticism. To say that a critical method is really worth only what its individual practitioners are worth, that it is the singer which counts and not the song, is exactly the kind of self-evident bourgeois truism of which Barthes himself would most vehemently disapprove. But like other bourgeois assumptions, it does happen to be empirically verifiable.

It is nevertheless an assumption tinged with certain presuppositions, and it is these which make Mauron attractive precisely because the comparison with Goldmann is so difficult to avoid. For Goldmann's admiration of Jansenism is strongly linked to his own political convictions. He held that Pascal's wager, the 'leap into faith' whereby Pascal accepted the humiliation of the intellect in order to be able to understand the world in Christian terms, is a kind of prototype for the Marxist wager that a socialist society will emerge from the comparable leap into faith constituted by the Revolution. To anyone with even the slightest knowledge of twentieth-century political history, it is very difficult to admire Pascal for having provided a model for this kind of thinking. The parallel is too strong between Pascal's advice to the unbeliever—'Take holy water, have masses said, that will make you stupid ['vous abêtira'] and make you believe'—and the way totalitarian governments of the Right and Left have behaved in office. They too have tried to stifle all criticism until practice and theory have attained perfect dialectical coincidence, and the initial leap into faith has been shown—retrospectively and anyone still alive—to have been fully justified.

The admiration which I myself feel for Mauron as a critic probably has deep unconscious roots whose true nature I should naturally be the last to recognise. Perhaps, however, it is merely because it is so familiar. Aldous Huxley once spoke of the 'strictly limited universe of Racine's heroines and the somewhat featureless males who serve as a pretext for their anguish',[28] and Mauron may therefore appeal because he offers an explanation for a phenomenon to which one of my favourite authors first drew my attention. Perhaps it is also because it has so unexpected a parallel with the world of P. G. Wodehouse. For the Jeeves/Bertie Wooster saga also presents us with a hero constantly fleeing from aggressively dominant and possessive females—Aunt Agatha, Honoria Glossop, Eloise Pringle, Gertrude Winkworth, Lady Florence Craye, Roberta Wickham—and it is distressingly tempting to look for the origin of this obsessively recurring structure in the experiences which the young Pelham Grenville had to undergo when spending the holidays with his Aunts while his parents were in the Far East. Indeed, in so far as Wodehouse himself transcended this traumatic experience and attained the emotional maturity which Racine so obviously lacked, one might also venture a Gallic generalisation and suggest that one of the differences between comedy and tragedy lies in the fact that the first is written by people who have obtained a fully conscious control of their childhood phobias and fantasies while the second is created by those who have only what Mauron terms an intuitive and unconscious knowledge of them.

But this generalisation, like all the others which one is tempted to make about literature, falls down on being confronted with further examples—Shakespeare and Wilde amongst them—and it is the experience of trying seriously to extend Mauron's theories to other writers which reveals how inadequate Freudianism is as an all-embracing account of human creativity. Mauron's comment that Racine's psychic structure, like that of any other human being, was fixed in his infancy certainly highlights the relationship between his childhood at Port-Royal and the plays he wrote. It is also not difficult to agree with the view that 'for Racine to think and dream with passion, it is enough (and it is essential) for maternal and religious figures to be unconsciously projected on to quite ordinary heroines'.[29] The difficulty arises when Mauron's view of literary creation is applied to almost any other writer. His own book on Giraudoux is far less satisfying than his study of Racine, and it is virtually impossible to apply his methods with any degree of success to authors such as Montaigne, Ibsen, Shakespeare, Jane Austen or Tolstoy. The whole point about a scientific explanation in such basic sciences as physics, chemistry or biology is that it should apply to random specimens as well as to those selected in advance because they happen to fit the theory. So long as the paradigm for scientific explanations remains the immensely impressive achievements of these sciences, works such as Mauron's—and, *a fortiori*, Goldmann's—will seem little more than isolated performances.

For the English empiricist, nourished in the view that the extremely complicated nature of the world makes it impossible for a sane man to adopt any attitude other than one of eclectic pluralism, this dismissal of the generalising pretensions of Mauron's approach is the most natural thing in the world. Some people, such a dogmatic disbeliever would say, have a personality which lends itself to explanations of a Freudian type. Others, to paraphrase St Augustine's remark about human beings having an *anima naturaliter Christiana*, have a naturally pagan, Marxist, Jungian, existential or even structuralist soul. However perfect and impersonal the external appearance of his plays undoubtedly was, Racine happened to belong to the Freudian category. Pascal, in contrast, happened to have the type of mind which lends itself more easily to a sympathetic interpretation in Marxist or Christian terms, just as Voltaire might be most appropriately studied in the light of the piecemeal empiricism which he did so much to popularise or Diderot from the standpoint of the Darwinian vision of nature which he anticipated in so many of his own books. This, again to use

Barthesian terms, is the self-evident corollary to the *évidence* which I have already quoted from Kipling:

> There are nine and sixty ways of constructing tribal lays,
> And–every–single–one–of–them–is–right!

No one method can be applied to every author. No critical key fits every creative door.

Barthes deliberately abstained, in *Critique et Vérité*, from answering Picard in the same aggressive style as *Nouvelle Critique ou Nouvelle Imposture*. Instead, he tried to lift the debate on to the higher plane where the real question of what literary criticism was could be meaningfully discussed. This was the issue which he had raised in the articles which originally sparked off the quarrel with Picard, *Les deux critiques* and *Qu'est-ce que la critique?*, and to which he returned with his wits sharpened even further by the need to justify his own critical method against the mockery aroused by *Nouvelle Critique ou Nouvelle Imposture*. Van Gogh once said of God that we should not judge Him on this world, which is one of His imperfectly executed sketches; and the true Barthesian would much prefer the master to be judged on *S/Z*, *L'Empire des Signes* or *Le Plaisir du Texte* than on *Sur Racine*. It is, they contend, less satisfactory an example of structuralism than *Le Dieu caché* is of Marxism or *L'inconscient dans l'œuvre et la vie de Racine* is of Freudianism, and it is obviously vulnerable to criticism in a way that Mauron's book certainly is not. Indeed, Jonathan Culler writes that it is 'marred by a misleading psychoanalytic language' and a 'needless methodological obscurity', and clearly sees the book as much less satisfying as an example of structuralism than the essays on Sade and Loyola. Not everyone, of course, agrees with this. Michael Lane, in his *Structuralism: A Reader*, argued that *Sur Racine* was 'the most significant and rewarding of all the pieces of structuralist criticism', while Thomas Merton, writing in the *Sewanee Review*, described it as a 'masterpiece of literary criticism'. He nevertheless added that its 'power and impact' might not be 'fully felt by one who has not had to study Racine in a French Lycée', and there is a sense in which Barthes's excessively assertive prose style is a kind of 'counter-violence' to the tradition whereby no pupil, on the Continent, was allowed—until 1968—to call into question the received truths dictated by the teacher.[30] If *Critique et Vérité* is in this respect a much better book than *Sur Racine*, it is precisely because it becomes a defence of the pluralist approach which *Sur Racine* so notably lacked. Indeed, one of the most unexpected features characterising the later stages of the Barthes/Picard quarrel was the fact that both sides began to claim that it was they who represented an open-minded approach and to accuse the other of intellectual intolerance.

Barthes makes this point at the very beginning of *Critique et Vérité* when he discusses the kind of language used by Picard's supporters. 'The dream', he wrote, 'has been to *wound, burst, beat, murder* the new critic, to *have him up in court on a criminal charge*, to *put him in the stocks* or *on the scaffold*',[31] and the Barthes/Picard quarrel would certainly seem to bear out the views of those popsologists[32] who contend that human beings have a psychological need to be aggressive even when circumstances in no way seem to warrant it. As far as Barthes himself was concerned, the quarrel came in what can now be seen as mid-career, and marked the point at which his ideas began to move in a more personal direction. *Le degré zéro de l'écriture* had owed a good deal to Sartre, *Mythologies* to Marx and Saussure, and *Sur Racine* to Goldmann and Mauron. Yet while his next book, *Système de la Mode* (1967), was to be in the style of thinking originally undertaken by Saussure, it already showed signs of the extreme complexity and unfamiliarity of argument which were to characterise *L'Empire des Signes*, *S/Z* and *Sade, Fourier, Loyola*. Before this unfamiliarity became too marked, however, *Critique et Vérité* set out to deal with an *évidence* that is perhaps taken even more for granted on this side of the Channel than in France.

The aim of the critic, wrote Helen Gardner in 1959, is to 'display the work in a manner which will enable it to exert its own power', and the normal assumption has been that this is best done by the critic who sees himself as a kind of 'honest broker'. In a rather similar vein, the English scholar John Cruickshank remarked in a review of Charles Mauron's work that it was really of only marginal interest to the literary critic since it in no way helped him in the task of 'evaluation and assessment' which was his central function,[33] and one of the merits of Barthes as a thinker about literature is that he does make it necessary to reassess these obvious truths. If, in the end, they emerge reinforced, Barthes still remains a man who plays an essential role in the intellectual life of modern society. He is a kind of Socratic gadfly who obliges other thinkers to carry out the process of intellectual testing which John Stuart Mill defined when he declared in his essay *On Liberty* that we can be sure of what we feel to be true only when we have tested our beliefs against all comers.

6 Politics, realism and literature

As far as Barthes himself was concerned, there was no doubt about the political nature either of Picard's attack or of the support which it received from certain sections of the French press. *Critique et Vérité* opens with a plethora of quotations from journalists who had given *Nouvelle Critique ou Nouvelle Imposture* what Barthes calls 'unreflecting, unconditional and unhesitating support', and the trouble Barthes had obviously taken to collect and quote so many of them is another indication of the almost perverse delight which he derives from the feeling that he is being persecuted. The fact that most of these articles had appeared in fairly conservative journals nevertheless did offer some evidence for his allegation that the desire to put the 'New Critics' in their place reflected a nostalgia for the Second Empire. It was then, as all French left-wing intellectuals would agree, that dissident opinions had had the most difficulty in making themselves heard, and the decision of Napoleon III's government to prosecute both Baudelaire's *Les Fleurs du Mal* and Flaubert's *Madame Bovary* when they were first published in 1857 had certainly had strong political motivation. The Second Empire is, however, regarded by left-wing intellectuals as only a runner-up in repressive conformity to the Vichy regime of 1940-4, and it was perhaps predictable that Philippe Sollers and Lucette Finas, Barthes's two closest supporters on *Tel Quel*, should equate Picard's attitude both with that of the Inquisition and with that of the supporters of Marshal Pétain.[1] The presupposition that all literary and philosophical attitudes inevitably have political implications is, of course, yet another reflection of how deeply Sartre's ideas on commitment in literature had affected the literary climate in post-war France, and there is another interesting resemblance between him and Barthes. In the 1960s and early 1970s Sartre went to immense trouble to try to force the government of the Fifth Republic to put him on trial for distributing Maoist and other far left publications. He proved, however, remarkably unsuccessful, so that his long-standing enemy François Mauriac was able to depart this life with the remark that not all Sartre's thirst for martyrdom could give the palm to someone so incurably inoffensive. Barthes allowed his publisher to put a publicity wrapper round *Critique et Vérité* bearing the words:

'Faut-il brûler Roland Barthes?' There had, as several critics observed, never been any suggestion of such a return to pre-revolutionary days, but Barthes and his supporters clearly thrived on the idea that they were being persecuted.[2]

In retrospect, however, Barthes seems to have derived nothing but profit from Picard's attack. Since he had, since 1962, been a Director of Studies at the *sixième section* of the Ecole pratique des Hautes Etudes, he could not be in any way harmed professionally. He had a tenured appointment, with all the guarantees associated with being, as all established teachers are at every level in France, a permanent civil servant. When, some nine years later, the then Secretary of State for the Universities, Jean-Pierre Soissons, decided to give the erstwhile *sixième section* the status of an independent Ecole des Hautes Etudes en Sciences Sociales, entitled to grant its own doctorates and degrees, press comment gave considerable credit to Barthes as one of those whose approach to literature and the social sciences had brought about this change. Heresy, in the words of one commentator, was receiving official status.[3] But Barthes not only used the *Querelle des Critiques* to come closer to being what Joseph Massé described in 1975 as 'cock of the walk' in the French literary scene ['celui qui tient le haut du pavé dans nos lettres'].[4] He also used the stimulus of Picard's attack to move forward from the rather derivative and not particularly convincing structuralism of *Sur Racine* to a position where he put forward a much more interesting and challenging view of what literature is and how it works.

He did this partly by expanding the ideas implicit in one of the best of the articles in *Mythologies*, 'Dominici ou le triomphe de la littérature'. In 1955, Gaston Dominici, a Provençal hill farmer, had been put on trial for murdering the English tourist Sir Jack Drummond and his family. The court proceedings struck other people apart from Barthes as decidedly odd, and the great novelist of the Manosque region, Jean Giono, wrote a devastating account of the cultural and linguistic intolerance of official French society in his *Notes sur l'Affaire Dominici*. How absurd it was, he maintained, to expect a man who had spent the whole of his long life speaking a highly local and original version of French suddenly to be judged and obliged to defend himself in an entirely different brand of French imposed by middle-class Northerners who knew nothing of his ways of thinking and expressing himself. Barthes made a very similar point, acknowledging his debt to Giono, when he wrote that the lawyers trying Dominici were thinking all the time in terms of one particular model: the vision of how people behaved instilled in them by nineteenth-century realist novelists such as Zola, Maupassant or Daudet. Because these authors had written what the bourgeoisie called 'la littérature du Document humain', the people who were putting Gaston Dominici on trial for his life were constantly imagining that they had before them a typical specimen of the peasantry as depicted in Zola's *La Terre*, or Maupassant's stories about Normandy. A picture, as Wittgenstein might have said, held them captive, and they either could not or would not cast off the *évidence*, the *Doxa*, the *ce-qui-va-de-soi* concept of what suspect Alpine peasants are like which this eminently clear and comprehensible literature had instilled into them. 'Justice', wrote Barthes, 'took on the mask of Realist literature, of the country tale, while literature itself came to the court-room to gather new "human" documents, and naïvely to seek from the face of the accused and the suspects the reflection of a psychology which, however, it had been the first to impose on them by the arm of the law.'[5] It is, in this respect, the very clarity of realist literature which makes it most dangerous. Surely, its readers think, descriptions as comprehensible as those of Maupassant must also be true.

Barthes's reply to Picard in *Critique et Vérité* contains a very similar accusation when he writes that 'ce que le vraisemblable appelle "concret" n'est, une fois de plus, que l'habituel' [Paraphrase: 'what admirers of verisimilitude call 'concrete" is merely, once again, what they are accustomed to'].[6] Picard and his supporters, argues Barthes, have a set of ready-made ideas about Racinian tragedy, much as the prosecution at the Dominici trial had of the psychology of Alpine peasants. Anything which goes against their vision of Racine the brilliant exploiter of the classical unities, Racine the creator of great female characters, Racine the incarnation of classical moderation and precursor of pure poetry, Racine the anguished Jansenist presenting *la misère de l'homme sans Dieu*, is therefore dismissed as nonsense. The 'clarity' which Picard's supporters so admire is similarly only a political language which Barthes describes as having been born at the moment when the ruling classes hoped, 'in accordance with a well-known ideological process', to 'transform the particularity of their *écriture* into a universal language', attempting to persuade people that French logic was absolute logic.[7] It is, according to Barthes, this attempt by the French bourgeoisie to secure intellectual hegemony for its speech habits which explains the intolerance shown by its spokesmen towards all other forms of language, whether the supposedly 'primitive' idioms of non-European peoples such as the Papuans or the vocabulary used by the New Critics. For Barthes, the bourgeoisie of 1965 was still guilty of trying to impose the same view of language which he had denounced at the very beginning of his career in *Le degré zéro de l'écriture*. They were still insisting on seeing it solely as a medium for the transmission of ideas which have been thought out beforehand, and refusing to recognise that it is language and language alone which constitutes the stuff of literature. It is because the *critiques universitaires* were still held captive by their own assumption that language is essentially instrumental that they were so hostile to the new critics and unable to see literature as it really is: a constant but constantly creative struggle with language itself.

As a reply to the specific criticism made of *Sur Racine* in *Nouvelle Critique ou Nouvelle Imposture*, this argument is not particularly convincing. It is one thing to accuse one's opponent, as Barthes does in *Critique et Vérité*, of blind adherence to the doctrine of manifest reason or of a consistent indulgence in the tyranny of clear ideas. The right place for common sense may well, in literary criticism as in philosophy, be where R. G. R. Mure wanted to put it: not on the Judge's bench but in the dock.[8] The fact nevertheless remains that Barthes's claim to find the same contrast between 'le soleil inquiétant et l'ombre bénéfique' ['the disturbing sun and beneficial shade'] everywhere throughout Racine's plays is not borne out by the actual events, images and relationships in the plays. To argue, as Barthes does, that the importance of an element is to be measured not by the statistical frequency of its recurrence but by the role it plays in the overall structure of a work, may well be fully justifiable. But to present such an argument as a reply to someone who has just caught you out in an exaggerated statistical claim [partout, toujours] sounds suspiciously like a desire to cancel one's bet because the horse of one's choice has fallen at the first fence.

The interest of Barthes's argument in *Critique et Vérité* does indeed lie elsewhere, and is once again best understood by going back to the first essay in *Mythologies*, 'Le Monde où l'on catche'. Indeed, the more one studies Barthes, the more does *Mythologies* become the seminal work, the book in which his major ideas are expressed not only in their most accessible form but with the greatest possibility of expansion. For it is, in 'Le Monde où l'on catche', the idea that the wrestlers are not really hurting each other, that there is no centre to the conflict which their gestures signal so ostentatiously to the audience, which is central to Barthes's argument not only in *Critique et Vérité* but also in *S/Z*, *Sade, Fourier, Loyola*, *L'Empire des Signes* and *Le Plaisir du Texte*. In his discussion of all-in wrestling, Barthes deals in fact with a problem that is, in his view, central to the whole existence of literature: how does it come about that human beings can believe in the existence of fictional characters to the point not only of being moved by their imaginary adventures but also of finding in their predicament illustrations of their own moral and intellectual dilemmas? It is not as though Emma Bovary, Becky Sharp or Ivan Karamazov ever existed as real people. Flaubert, Thackeray and Dostoyevsky are not—as a biographer would—reporting what happened; and to imagine that *Madame Bovary* is an inexhaustibly fascinating work because it depicts what Lise Delamare actually felt is as naïve as to suppose that Mick McManus inflicts genuine pain and feels genuine wrath at every moment in each appearance in the ring. Language, literature and all-in wrestling all work by codes, internally self-consistent systems of signs, in which meaning is created by the differences between the elements of which the code is made up, and not by any reference to a 'real' object lying behind the signs. The signs themselves are meaningful solely because they are familiar to us as part of a code which we already know, or are being used in a context that makes their meaning clear. Literature works, as Jonathan Culler puts it in his *Structuralist Poetics*, because human beings have a 'literary competence' analogous to the ability of native speakers to understand sentences addressed to them in their native language. It is this basic competence which new writers both exploit and expand, just as the authors of neologisms do on a linguistic level.[9]

When, for example, I first read *A Clockwork Orange*, I did not know that Anthony Burgess had placed a glossary of his neologisms at the back of the book. The meaning of terms such as 'rabbit', 'droog', 'viddy' and 'tolchock' nevertheless soon became clear to me—despite my ignorance of Russian—from the way in which they were used. It was a very Wittgensteinian experience, in that I derived the meaning from the use, and learned the language of Nadzat not by looking at its combination of English and Slavonic roots but by fitting it into another code—conventional English—which I already knew. Within another context—that of a sentimental love story, for example—the terms which Burgess had invented could well have taken on a totally different meaning. The relationship between the individual sign and the particular thing signified is, as Saussure maintained, quite arbitrary. Although the writer Anthony Burgess may have chosen to use the word 'rabbit' to mean 'work' because *rabota* means work in Russian, nothing gives the word the meaning it has in *A Clockwork Orange* except the fact of the sentences in the book being constructed in a particular way. Another writer could construct other sentences in which 'rabbit' meant 'love', 'spend money' or 'shoot'. What matters is the consistency of the structure, and the fact that the words are combined in a way that conforms to the immensely complicated pattern with which the reader's brain is familiar. In the conventions of all-in wrestling, a contestant held in a remorseless half-Nelson does not beat the canvas, as he sometimes pretends, because it is the only possible way to relieve the pain but because this is the way to indicate that he is not giving up. It is arbitrary in the sense that he could equally well kick with his right foot, blow his nose or shout 'God save Ireland'. But it is meaningful because this is the sign which the referee, his opponent and the audience recognise as indicating 'No Surrender'.

It is, for Barthes, precisely because fiction works by bringing into play the codes and structures already existing in the reader's mind that there can never be any question either of deriving information from

it or of maintaining that a novel, play or poem has one definite meaning. Novels only tell us what we already know, and appear to communicate knowledge or ideas only by making us become conscious of
something which was in our minds all the time. In this respect, Barthes's
speculations form part of the continuing process of trying to define
precisely what literature is which has been a central preoccupation
of Frer.ch writers since the second half of the nineteenth century. The
symbolists, for example, liked to distinguish between poetry and prose.
The latter, they maintained, was functional. It had no autonomous
existence and perished the moment the message it carried had been
communicated to the reader. Poetry, in contrast, did exist as an independent entity which outlived and transcended any ideas or information it might communicate, and the distinction struck Jean-Paul
Sartre as sufficiently valid to form the basis for much of his argument
in *Qu'est-ce que la littérature?* in 1947. Barthes carries the symbolist
vision of literature as a self-sufficient activity even further. For him,
books or articles with an informational content cease to be literature.
This, in contrast, is therefore paradoxically defined by what it is not.
He expresses the distinction linguistically by using the name *écrivant*
to designate anyone who uses words to communicate information or
ideas, while trying to reserve the term *écrivain* for those who pursue
what he regards as the genuine and specific activity of literature:
using words for their own sake. We shall, he writes in *Critique et Vérité*,
attain 'une certaine science de la littérature' only when we recognise
that 'l'œuvre est faite avec de l'écriture' [paraphrase: 'we shall acquire
some idea of what literature is only when we recognise that words are
made by using words in a particular manner'].[10] The object which this
'science of literature' will pursue, he continues, will not be the content
of works of art. To do so would [my parallel] be as absurd as trying to
find out who is really winning when the Iron Man meets the Red
Mask. It will be what Barthes calls 'le sens vide qui les supporte tous'
['the empty meaning which supports them all']. It is an idea which
one might illustrate in terms of English linguistic philosophy by talking
about the eggshell from which yolk and white have been blown and
on which the child draws a series of Wittgensteinian duck-rabbits:
objects whose meaning changes according to the way the spectator
looks at them.

The Barthes of *Le Monde où l'on catche* talked about 'l'évidement de
l'intériorité' as a phenomenon which characterised the wrestler's art.
They 'emptied out' what a naïve spectator would regard as the 'innerness', the essential reality of their struggle, and replaced it by what
Barthes declared in *Mythologies* to be 'the principle of triumphant
classical art': the predominance of external signs, and the exhaustion
of content by form.[11] In one of the classic *Punch* cartoons of the 1920s,
a languid young man is correcting some misconceptions which one

of his relatives has about the literary calling which he is about to adopt. 'My dear Aunt', he is saying, 'One doesn't write *about* anything. One just *writes*.' It is not a bad translation into the specific terms favoured on this side of the Channel of Barthes's attitude in *Critique et Vérité*, and the young man's Aunt would at least not have been able to accuse him of 'Just writing about yourself'. The solemn announcement of the author's death which Barthes issued in his 1968 article is already implicit in the comment in *Critique et Vérité* that 'en effaçant la signature de l'écrivain, la mort fonde la vérité de l'œuvre, qui est énigme' ['by effacing the author's signature, death founds the truth of the work: an enigma'].[12] One of the *fausses évidences* which Barthes pursues most remorselessly is the neo-Romantic notion that works of art are automatically and necessarily the expression of an author's personal feelings, and on this particular point he has the support of Proust and Camus as well as Valéry. What, for Barthes, replaces both the mimetic and the autobiographical content which earlier thinkers maintained that literature possessed is indeed what he calls 'an enigma': the ability to make people think things out for themselves.

Once again, of course, there is an obvious link between Barthes's views on literature and those that Sartre had expressed in 1947 in *Qu'est-ce que la littérature?* For Sartre, the activity of reading is possible only because the human mind is free. Free, that is to say, to pass beyond the words themselves to the meaning they evoke. When I read *Crime and Punishment*, argues Sartre, I bring the character of Raskolnikov to life by 'nihilating' the black marks on the white pages. It is because I do not have to spell each word out individually that I can go beyond them to make sense of the book as a whole, and because I am not held down by the words themselves that I bring Raskolnikov to life by lending him my own ability to feel hope, terror and despair. Such an activity, maintains Sartre, would be quite impossible if my mind were, like a snail crawling along a path, incapable of detaching itself from what is immediately there. Barthes carries this argument a stage further by also contending that our understanding of a literary text is possible only because the text itself does not have one fixed, definite, unalterable inner meaning which the mind of the reader will inevitably recognise as self-evidently true. 'If words had only one meaning', he writes in *Critique et Vérité*, 'the meaning they have in the dictionary, if a second meaning did not come along and set free what Picard calls "the certainties of language" there would be no literature.'[13] What literature does, in Barthes's view, is to set the reader a puzzle. It teases out his mind rather as Wittgenstein does by his technique in the *Philosophical Investigations*, when he constantly invites the reader to keep looking at concepts in different ways in order to free his mind from the illusion that each expression in a language must have one and only one final meaning. The meaning of a text can never be anything but the one which the reader himself chooses to give, constantly bearing in mind the infinite number of possible meanings— what Barthes will later call its 'infinite transcribability'—which it can have.

It is essentially from the standpoint of these arguments that Barthes takes issue with Raymond Picard's position in *Nouvelle Critique ou Nouvelle Imposture*. 'There is', Picard had written 'a truth about Racine on which everyone can manage to agree. By relying, in particular, on the certainties of language, the implications of psychological coherence, the structural demands of the genre, the patient and modest researcher does succeed in bringing out certain obvious facts ['le chercheur patient et modeste parvient à dégager des évidences'] which do in some way determine areas where objectivity is possible.[14] For Barthes, Picard's decision to stick to ascertainable facts betokens just as arbitrary an ideological choice as Mauron's Freudianism or Goldmann's Marxism. It presupposes that what there is to be known is empirically verifiable and that it is this knowledge which will enable us to understand Racine. But this, for Barthes, is a fundamentally misguided opinion because it presupposes that there is a Racine to know. Within the context of the ideas developed in *Critique et Vérité*, Racine is merely 'le sens vide qui les supporte tous': the empty centre around which revolve the different codes according to which his plays can be read. At the end of Ibsen's *Peer Gynt*, the central character is made to express his search for a centre to his own personality by peeling an onion. But as he removes one layer after another, the truth gradually dawns upon him that the onion does not have a centre. The essence which he is seeking lies not beneath the successive layers but only in the relationship between them. When he has laid bare what he imagined to be the centre, there is simply nothing there, and from one point of view this is a marvellous illustration of the vision of the human personality implied both by Sartrean existentialism and by the remark which David Hume made about finding within himself, when he looked, only a 'bundle of sensations'. It is also a way of looking at experience which parallels Barthes's view of what a work of literature is like. The meaning of Racine's plays does not lie hidden deep in some Platonic-type cave, solid, unchanging and accessible only to those who dive down far enough beneath the surface to find it. It consists of the patterns which the text of the plays calls into being in the minds of those who see or read them.

It also follows from the view of literature set out in *Critique et Vérité* and presented in a more complex and elaborated form in *S/Z* or *Sade, Fourier, Loyola*, that the person who goes to a work of literature expecting information about society, revelations about the author or insights into the behaviour of other human beings is making what the late Gilbert Ryle would have called a category mistake. He is looking to literature for something which it cannot give, and the man who imagines that he has really learned something about peasants from Maupassant or human sexuality from Racine is living in a fool's paradise. The only thing he has done is reinforce his previously existing notions by making Maupassant or Racine fit into the conceptual grid of ready-made notions already existing in his own mind, and this can lead him to precisely the error denounced by Flaubert in *Madame Bovary* or Barthes himself in *Dominici ou le triomphe de la littérature*: that of assuming that life is like the books he has read.[15]

As the mention of *Madame Bovary* shows, this idea of the illusions into which people can fall because they think life is like the books they read is not a new one. It is, however, rather unusual to see it put forward as a criticism of realist literature. The idea of literature as mimesis goes back a very long way in European aesthetic thought, and was central to the concept of the novel in nineteenth-century France. Balzac claimed to be merely the historian of Restoration France, Stendhal compared the novel to a mirror reflecting everything along the highway, Zola gave the Rougon-Macquart series the sub-title of *Histoire sociale et naturelle d'une famille sous le Second Empire*. The practice may well have differed from the theory, but the idea of literature as mimesis was axiomatic. One of Barthes's merits as a literary thinker lies in the way he calls this axiom into question. He suggests, to use his own terminology, that we should do much better to think of literature not in terms of mimesis but of semiosis, to see it not as the imitation of reality but as the invention of new patterns by means of signs. He is not, of course, the only person to suggest why a change in our traditional way of thinking is necessary if we are to understand such a central aspect of the human condition as the telling of stories and the understanding of stories. Malcolm Bradbury formulated the problem running through Barthes's preoccupations rather more clearly than Barthes himself when he wrote that 'Novels tell, or relate, a something; that something they invent; *this* is the central paradox of the novel'.[16] In the theatre, writers as different as Anouilh and Genet have insisted that their plays are in no way to be seen as anything but artefacts existing in their own right. Novelists such as Robbe-Grillet and Philippe Sollers have argued in theory and shown in practice that fiction can be just as non-representational as the most abstract of the visual arts. Barthes nevertheless stands out from these other writers in two ways: he is a more systematic thinker, a man whose theories have been developed in the light of ideologies such as Marxism and existentialism and who has contributed to the growth of semiology as an intellectual discipline; and he is interested in other sign systems in addition to those involved in literature. The theory of fashion developed in *Système de la Mode*, the book published immediately after *Critique et Vérité*, shows that the semiologist who had looked at non-literary culture in some of its most popular forms in *Mythologies* could still deal with a matter that impinges not only on people's daily lives but also on their own vision of themselves.

In this respect, Barthes wrote the best introduction to *Système de la Mode* retrospectively, in the preface which he published in 1972 to a collection of drawings by the fashion designer Erté. 'Fashion', he declared, 'is not erotic; it seeks clarity, not voluptuousness; the cover-girl is not a good fantasy object: she is too concerned with becoming a sign: impossible to live (in the imagination) with her, she must only be *deciphered*, or more exactly (for there is no secret in her) she must be placed in the general system of signs that makes our world intelligible, which is to say: livable.'[17] For it is with the way fashion writers try to fit women into an intelligible world of their making that *Système de la Mode* is concerned, and the subject which Barthes chose to discuss when he turned temporarily from literature is eminently Saussurian in its relevance to the central problem of how signs work in the modern world. It is also potentially Marxist in the evidence which it provides for the alienation still apparently inseparable from capitalist society.

7 Fashion, fads and language

For reasons that my own approach will already have suggested, Barthes has not so far always had a very enthusiastic reception in England. One of the self-evident truths which it is difficult to eliminate from minds brought up upon Hume, Russell or Ayer is the view that language which sets out to communicate ideas should first of all try to be clear. Similarly, the aesthetic ideas set out in *Critique et Vérité* obviously run counter to what Bernard Bergonzi described in *Encounter* in July 1975 as the English desire for poems 'to 'mean something, whatever the attractions of the symbolist claim that "a poem should not mean but be" '.[1] Yet while Bergonzi's article stands in a way as the epitome of English critical reactions to Barthes, it is far less hostile than the article which F. W. Bateson published in *The New Review* under the title *Is your Structuralism really necessary?*[2] It is certainly a question that comes irresistibly to mind when one reads *Système de la Mode*. For instead of presenting what the admirer of *Mythologies* might have expected—the hilarious spectacle of Barthes on the rag trade—the book opens with two hundred pages of head-splitting analysis of the vocabulary used in *Le Jardin des Modes*, *Elle*, *L'Echo de la Mode* and *Vogue* during the six-month period in the late 1950s. It is only in the second part of the book, 'Le système rhétorique', that *Système de la Mode* suddenly leaps to life and that the Barthes of *Mythologies* emerges from behind the austere manipulator of semiological jargon. The last seventy pages are at one and the same time so witty, accessible and obviously applicable to our daily experience, that the question inevitably arises as to precisely what purpose is served by the technical jargon and immensely complicated critical apparatus of the first three-quarters of the book which Barthes devotes to what he calls *Le code vestimentaire*.

Thus when, on page 263, Barthes analyses what he calls 'La Femme de Mode', he shows both what a splendid satirical novelist was lost to French literature when he adopted the aesthetic of *Tel Quel*, and how the ten years which had passed since the publication of *Mythologies* had in no way diminished his ability simultaneously to reproduce and dissect the dominant ethos projected by the advertising media.

Such is the Woman [he writes] normally signified by the rhetoric of fashion: imperatively feminine, young by absolute decree, endowed with a strong identity and yet with a contradictory personality. She is called Daisy or Barbara; she mixes with the Comtesse of Mun and Miss Phips; she is the manager's secretary, but her work in no way prevents her from being present at each annual or daily festive occasion; she goes away every weekend and travels constantly, to Capri, the Canary Islands, Tahiti, and yet at every trip she goes to the South of France. She never lives in any but the cleanest climate, she likes everything at one and the same time, from Pascal to cool jazz. This monster clearly exhibits the constant compromise which marks the relationship between mass culture and its consumers: the woman of fashion is at one and the same time what the woman reading the fashion pages is and what she dreams of being; her psychological profile is virtually indistinguishable from that of the celebrities daily described by mass culture. For Fashion, by what it signifies on a rhetorical plane (and, naturally, by the massive sales of its journals), stems directly from this culture.

This is a passage of more than Orwellian acuity, and also one which runs curiously parallel to Orwell's own observations about the 'unrelievedly beautiful' women who wore the clothes advertised in an American fashion magazine of the 1940s. Their clothes too were advertised in a prose style which combined 'sheer lushness with clipped and sometimes very expressive technical jargon' and which presented a world from which grey hair, fatness, middle age, birth, death and work were all equally absent.[3] Neither is it the only section in *Le système rhétorique* which shows that the social pamphleteer of *Mythologies* remained as vigorous a debunker in his mid-fifties as he had been in his late thirties and early forties. Indeed, there is even a sense in which the Barthes of *Mythologies* and *Système de la Mode* exactly fulfils the classic definition of the administrative grade civil servant: a fine mind applied to common things. The second part of *Système de la Mode* also reveals an aspect of Barthes's character and personality surprising in a man who shows himself almost over-sensitive, in *Sur Racine* and in *S/Z*, to the presence of the aggressive, domineering, castrating mother-figure. For it is a book which offers intense and intelligent support for women's lib. Fashion writers, he points out, rarely present women in anything but a subordinate role in a man's world. 'Secrétaire, j'aime être impeccable' is a typical quotation that encapsulates a whole ethos of feminine acceptance of masculine prerogatives, and which Barthes also illustrates by his remark that

when fashion allows a woman to have a job, her occupation is neither completely noble (it is not quite the thing for a woman really to compete with men) nor absolutely inferior. It is always a 'clean' job: secretary, window-dresser, librarian; and this job always remains part of those callings which can be designated as 'self-abnegatory' (as, in the past, those of nurse or companion for an elderly lady). The woman's identity is thus defined as being in the service of man (the boss), of Art, of Thought, but this submission is always sublimated by pleasant working conditions and rendered aesthetic by exhibiting an image (external appearances play an essential role here, since it is always a question of exhibiting the clothes).[4]

Germaine Greer, Kate Millett or Eva Figes could scarcely put it better, and the living individual Roland Barthes behaves in accordance with the *scripteur* of *Système de la Mode* by never dictating to a secretary.[5] His book on fashion also has strong MLF (*Mouvement pour la Libération de la Femme*) overtones in the remark that the words which it most frequently exploits (*bon, joyeux; gai, petit*) all tend to enclose women in either an infantile or a maternal role, and the whole of Barthes's analysis is shot through with the presupposition that the 50 per cent of the French female population who read fashion magazines ought really to be addressed in a more adult manner. What also characterises fashion writers, according to Barthes, is the apparently paradoxical juxtaposition between 'l'excessivement sérieux et l'excessivement futile' ['excessively serious and excessively frivolous']. Fashion is, in other words, presented at one and the same time as absolutely mandatory (you *can't* wear stiletto heels any more and you *must* have dark gloves for town) and yet based upon the most minute and unessential practical details (the cut of a coat, not its protective quality; the replacement of dots by squares). This, for Barthes, 'merely reproduces on the level of clothes the mythical status of woman in Western civilisation: simultaneously childlike and sublime',[6] and it is pleasing to see the healthy revolt against phallocracy which is so intriguing a feature of late capitalist civilisation expressed with such vigour by the man who was later to write so eulogistically of *La Déesse Homosexualité*.

All this, however, does not answer the crucial question which F. W. Bateson asked of *S/Z* but which is perhaps even more applicable to *Système de la Mode*: Is your structuralism really necessary? Surely it would have been better, if Barthes had set out with the conventional aim of communicating with his readers and influencing their way of looking at language and society, for him to have proceeded as he did in *Mythologies*: give his specific examples first and then draw them together in a concluding theoretical essay. Such a presentation would have had the immense advantage of exposing him only to the relatively minor, almost ideological objection that he exaggerates both the degree of commitment with which women read fashion magazines and the nefarious motives of the relatively small group of individuals who create and exploit the language of fashion. The not uncommon experience of an employer hearing his secretaries giggling both at the photographs illustrating new fashions and at the descriptions accompanying them is an indication that the women to whom fashion magazines are directed frequently have the same attitude to them which spectators of an all-in wrestling match have, in Barthes's own submission, towards the performers: one of detached if appreciative amusement at a well-presented confidence trick. One of the reviewers of *Mythologies* commented that Barthes over-estimated the gullibility of modern trade-unionised female workers and this is fair comment. He certainly would accept without hesitation the sociological *évidence* which Christiane Metz put forward when she wrote that 'every film for shop or factory girls pushes these girls even more deeply into their shop-girl status',[7] and here again he is a very typical middle-class left-wing intellectual. The condescension which used to characterise acts of middle-class charity has now translated itself into the efforts which middle-class men and women feel they need to make in order to liberate their oppressed proletarian sisters, and it is again a typical but unconscious left-wing characteristic of Barthes's work that his attitude to women should evoke such conservative comments.

It is nevertheless only in his exaggeration of female gullibility that the second part of *Système de la Mode* is seriously open to criticism. It is for the most part a very acute analysis of how human beings behave when they wish to use clothes both to assert what they are for themselves and to communicate this assertion to other people, and here again Barthes develops one of the ideas first suggested in *Mythologies*. He had argued there that l'Abbé Pierre's *canadienne*, close-cropped hair and flowing beard proclaimed both his ideal self-vision and the way in which he wanted other people to see him: as the absorbed incarnation of Christian charity. He was cheating, according to Barthes, in pretending that what was in fact a carefully chosen collection of signs emanated spontaneously from the inescapable inner essence of his own character, and was deliberately confusing nature and culture. He was, to take an illustration from the other end of the social and ideological scale, indulging in as blatant a form of semiological bad faith as that of the teenager who, having presented himself for a job in dirty jeans, pit-boots and a leather jacket covered with the insignia of the Afrika Korps, complains that he has been refused employment because of racial prejudice. The whole point about clothes, for Barthes, is that they express our freely elected vision of ourselves. The sin of fashion writers lies in their constant tendency to present this free choice as the inevitable consequence of what society requires us to be and of the person which we 'essentially' are.

The diagnosis of this form of intellectual cheating, of dishonesty in our attitude towards signs, of what one might describe, in English as baroque as Barthes's French, as 'semiological disingenuity', is perhaps his most important contribution to our awareness of how we behave in contemporary society. In one of the most favourable reviews to be published on *Système de la Mode*, Barthes's long-standing admirer, Pierre Lepape, claimed that semiology had become under Barthes's guidance as important as Marxism or psychoanalysis in changing man's view of himself.[8] This claim is a strong one but it might be substantiated by trying to analyse one of Barthes's own remarks towards the end of *Le système rhétorique*. He says there that in the descriptions of fashion, the rule 'always seems to be to copy the law of nature, making *homo significans* take on the mask of *homo faber*'. For just as the term *homo faber*[9] (man the maker) incarnates one of the defining characteristics of man as the animal capable of consciously changing his own environment, so the expression *homo significans* (man the meaner)—which Barthes seems to have invented—draws attention to another fundamental aspect of human experience: human beings constantly communicate with one another. They do so, moreover, in a way that is completely different from the way in which animals communicate. For human beings know, in a way that there is no evidence for saying that animals know, that there is nothing instinctive or inevitable about the way they communicate. Whereas the peacock has no choice, if it wishes to attract a mate, except to display its feathers, human beings can flaunt their sexual desires in any number of different ways: from wolf-whistles to Petrarchan sonnets or from yellow golliwogs to E-type Jaguars.

This, in biological or everyday terms, is what Ferdinand de Saussure meant when he talked about the arbitrary nature of signs: that human beings can exercise choice in the way they communicate. There is no compulsion on them always to signify anger by raising their fists. Dag Hammarskjöld used to do it by placing the points of two exquisitely sharpened pencils end to end. And just as Barthes's theory of literature extends and completes the central notion about the nature of reading put forward in Sartre's *Qu'est-ce que la littérature?*, so his prolongation of the concept of *l'arbitraire du signe* advanced by Saussure in the *Cours de linguistique générale* also has strongly Sartrean overtones. Human beings, for the early Sartre, were at one and the same time conscious of their freedom and yet constantly tempted to pretend both to themselves and to other people that they were not free. This pretence is a phenomenon which Sartre baptised as bad faith, and it is perhaps Barthes's fundamental originality as a thinker to have carried this concept over into the realm of human communication. For although human beings are, for Saussure and Barthes, always potentially conscious of the arbitrary nature of the signs they employ, they are constantly tempted to pretend that these signs are natural, inevitable, and out of their control. They are always pretending to be peacocks when they are really self-conscious chameleons. When a man makes something, Barthes suggests in the passage contrasting *homo faber* with *homo significans*, he is under two forms of constraint: the nature of the physical world, which limits his freedom in the sense that no one—in Tom Stoppard's immortal phrase—can make a Gothic arch out of junket; and the constraints stemming from the actual nature of the artefact he is constructing. In speech, writing and thought, in contrast, nobody knows what he thinks before he has said it.

The absolute distinction which Barthes insists on seeing between *homo faber* and *homo significans* may easily be shown to be excessive. Yet for all its vulnerability, it does underline the importance and independence of the notion of *homo significans* which is Barthes's principal concern. At the same time, it helps to suggest an answer to the crucial question raised by his treatment of fashion in *Système de la Mode*: why, in view of the fact that clothes not only exist as real objects but are generally presented pictorially to the prospective buyer, does he himself concentrate exclusively on language? For he does do this, and does so in full knowledge of the fact that he is thereby standing his master Saussure on his head. For Saussure stated quite clearly in the *Cours de linguistique générale* that 'language is a system of signs expressing ideas and, consequently, comparable to handwriting, deaf-and-dumb alphabets, symbolic rituals, social salutations, military signals, etc. It is merely the most important of these systems'.[10] Barthes, however, chooses to talk about a completely visual and non-verbal system of communication in a book which, as Alice would have said, has neither pictures nor conversation.

The answer is, as Barthes points out, that he is not talking about fashion itself. He is talking about the language in which fashion is presented to the readers of fashion magazines, and is doing so because, as he points out, only language enables people's thoughts to be pointed in one and only one direction. For if I am shown a picture, as Barthes himself explains both in an article entitled 'Rhétorique de l'image' and in the opening pages of *Système de la Mode*, there is always an element of uncertainty about how I am going to interpret it. This is why the label on a jar of Nescafé is made to read 'Fresh, Natural Taste', in spite of the fact that the picture of a steaming cup of beautifully brown coffee laid on a carpet of unground coffee beans should really have been capable of making this clear to the meanest intelligence. Moreover, as Barthes observes elsewhere, language is power;[11] and the history of conquest bears out the importance and validity of this idea. The famous conversation at the beginning of *Ivanhoe*, for example, is an indication that the political overtones of linguistics and semiology are neither as original nor as outlandish as Barthes's admirers or detractors are wont to maintain. For when Wamba tells the swineherd that 'old Alderman Ox continues to hold his Saxon epithet, while he is under the charge of serfs and bondsmen such as thou, but becomes Beef, a fiery French gallant, when he arrives before the worshipful jaws that are destined to consume him. Mynheer Calf, too, becomes Monsieur de Veau in the like manner; he is Saxon when he requires tendance, and takes a Norman name when he becomes matter of enjoyment', he is making a very Barthesian point. We express our mastery both over nature and over other people by the way we talk. And it is because of the language which the Norman invader used that it soon became—to use Barthes's favourite opposition —so natural to call swine 'pork' that the Saxon word took on the quaint overtones which it now has as a word designating the vulgar vices of gluttony and greed.

It is indeed because of the ability which language has to transform transient culture into apparently permanent nature that Barthes concentrates on it in his analysis of fashion. For the language of fashion, as Barthes observes, seeks not to inform but to persuade, to convince and to create dreams. This is why it so frequently employs, in French at any rate, the future tense and the imperative mood, and Barthes also points out that there is a kind of U-curve in the relationship between denotation and connotation in fashion writing.[12] The clothes intended to be bought by the rich are described in language which exactly denotes what they are made of. The rich, who can buy them, like to know. The description of clothes intended to be made or bought by working-class readers also tends to contain a number of fairly hard facts: how complicated the pattern is, what the material costs, how well it can be expected to wear. It is only in the clothes which the middle and lower middle class like to admire that denotation, according to Barthes's analysis, gives way almost completely to connotation. The aim of the writers who describe this kind of clothes is to enable the reader to dream about 'la robe que Manet aurait aimé peindre' ['the dress that Manet would have liked to paint']. For it is, as Barthes observed, a good deal easier to dream about such a dress than to buy or make it.

Barthes's point that such concepts can be communicated only by language is surely a valid one. There are nowadays in England photographs of Manet-like dresses which are actually used to advertise lavatory paper, but one would certainly not know this unless one were told so by the words accompanying the picture. It is also intriguing for an English reader to see the basic structure of Hilaire Belloc's famous poem entitled 'The Garden Party' recurring in Barthes's analysis of the language of fashion, and equally tempting for the same reader to say that Barthes is much more interesting and convincing when he is not talking about literature. This is odd in a way since everything which Barthes has ever said about himself reveals a great enthusiasm for literature, and it is fairly clear from *Système de la Mode* that he has very little sympathy for the way fashion is described. Thus when asked, in 1975, whether literature should remain on the syllabus for schools and universities, he made the Leavis-like response that it should in fact be the only subject,[13] and it is clear from the tone of *Le système rhétorique* that he regards most of what is written about fashion as an unpleasant and dishonest attempt at mystification. 'At the very moment that Fashion constructs a very strict system of signs', he writes in *Rhétorique du signe: la raison de Mode*, 'it endeavours to endow these signs with the appearance of pure reason; and it is clearly because Fashion is tyrannical and its signs arbitrary that it must convert them into natural facts or rational laws'.[14] His case against fashion writers is exactly the same as his case against the photographers of the Studio Harcourt or the make-up artists who exploited the Roman fringe benefits in *Julius Caesar*. Fashion, in the analysis presented in *Système de la Mode*, is an enormous confidence trick, a myth which is contradictory in its very essence. It not only aims to present cultural artefacts as natural products. It confers immense importance on objects which, by very definition, can only be ephemeral. Barthes is said to have devoted six years of his life to writing *Système de la Mode*, and the book was referred to by Claude Jannoud in *Le Figaro littéraire* as an 'immense travail de Bénédictin'.[15] Why, one wonders, did he labour for so long over a subject which, fundamentally, he despised?

The reason which he gives himself is that he was inspired at the time by 'un rêve euphorique de scientificité' (a euphoric dream of scientificity).[16] He wanted to write a complete explanatory grammar of a language which people used to communicate with one another in one particular area of experience. He was, in this respect, driven on by the fundamental problem which lies at the root of all enquiries in structural linguistics: what is there in a system that enables people to communicate with one another without actually understanding how this system works? And, as is so often the case when so fundamental a question is treated in any serious detail, the answer he came up with was an extremely complex and complicated one. He had, as he explained in an interview, to write the equivalent of a descriptive grammar book.[17] What corresponds in *Système de la Mode* to the nouns, adjectives and articles of an ordinary grammar book are the various terms which Barthes finds recurring in the descriptions of fashionable clothes in *Vogue*, *Elle* or *Le Jardin des Modes*: *accessoire*, *attache*, *gants*, *pantalons*, *concave*, *dégagé*, *relevé*. He lists sixty different *genres* (types) to which articles of clothing can be said to belong, and thirty different ways in which they can be related to one another. This, again, corresponds in a way to the examples of syntax contained in an ordinary grammar book, and *Système de la Mode* suffers from the immense disadvantage of all such works: it is very dull and difficult to read. It is only when one turns from Barthes's analysis to look at the actual descriptions of clothes still printed nowadays in *Elle* or *Vogue* that one realises how useful a guide he has provided, and here again his book offers a parallel with any good descriptive grammar. Once you have read it, the words which you read or hear start to fit into patterns which you had not noticed before. It is nevertheless difficult to see quite how this would occur if the book were, as Stuart Hall argued ought to happen, translated into English.[18] What Barthes so aptly calls the rhetoric of fashion is so much more a feature of the French than of the English version of *Vogue* that any translation— even assuming that a suitably dedicated Benedictine monk were available—would be as incomprehensible to the average English reader as Goldmann's analysis of Racine probably was to the students in English or American university philosophy departments who tried to read the English version of *The Hidden God. Système de la Mode* is not, in other words, any more translatable than a grammar book, complete with all its examples, would be. It is equally impossible to summarise.

Barthes's decision to embark on a structural analysis of fashion in the late 1950s was amply rewarded, in terms of his own reputation as an intellectual pace-setter, by the fact that *Système de la Mode* eventually appeared at exactly the right moment: in April 1967. The late sixties and early seventies were the great period of French structuralism, with popular guides and special numbers appearing on every side, and authors such as Jacques Lacan, Michel Foucault and Claude Lévi-Strauss taking over the position of *grands maîtres à penser* reluctantly abandoned by the Freudians, phenomenologists, Marxists and existentialists who had dominated French intellectual life during the previous thirty years. This storming of the cultural battlements of Saint-Germain-des-Prés was not accomplished without resistance or resentment, and Jean-Paul Sartre asserted in a special number which the monthly review *L'Arc* gave to the question that 'structuralism linguistics, Lacan, *Tel Quel*, are used one after the other to show the impossibility of thinking historically. Behind history, of course, the target is Marxism. The aim, with structuralism, is to build up a new ideology, the last dam which the bourgeoisie can still set up against Marx'.[19] Lucien Goldmann is also reputed to have greeted with delight the statement written up by the students occupying the Sorbonne during the rebellion of 1968: 'Le structuralisme ne descend pas dans la rue' ['Structuralism is no street fighter'][20] and for him, as for Sartre, structuralism still remained profoundly influenced by its origins. It had begun in linguistics, where it had chosen to qualify itself as synchronic. That is to say that it studied not the way language had developed historically over a period of time—the technical term is diachronically—but solely the way it actually worked at a particular moment. It consequently ignored the fundamental truth embodied in the Marxist view that all social institutions were constantly changing as a result of the class struggle and could therefore be meaningfully discussed only in a historical context. Whatever the subjective intentions of its practitioners, structuralism was therefore objectively conservative in its practice and presuppositions.

This is an interesting criticism to apply to *Système de la Mode*, since Barthes's own tastes and intentions are so obviously critical of middle-class tastes and modes of thought and his final aim is so clearly to discredit bourgeois society and all its works. His book is nevertheless vulnerable to a Marxist approach in very much the same way that *Michelet par lui-même* is open to objections based upon the more traditional method of studying an author's work in relation to his life. For although Barthes acknowledges that both fashion and the vocabulary of fashion are created by the small number of people who control the media, he makes no suggestion at all as to who they are or where they might be found. He likewise recognises that changes of fashion reflect a society whose economic well-being depends upon in-built obsolescence, but again does not follow out the implications which this idea might have when applied to the more rational organisation which will presumably prevail in a socialist state. Instead, he sticks puritanically to his linguistic last, treating the language of fashion in almost the same isolation from its technical, social or economic basis as he treated the plays of Racine in isolation from the social world in which they were created.

The consistency of Barthes's approach to phenomena as different from one another as the works of Michelet, the tragedies of Racine or the language of *Vogue* is a clear indication that he was not, in *Système de la Mode*, in any way consciously striving either to follow or inaugurate a fashion. He is what could be termed one of nature's structuralists, and the difficulty which his books present even to the initiated reader also seems to be a general feature of all structuralist writing. For neither Foucault, Lacan, Lévi-Strauss nor Roman Jakobson writes books whose meaning leaps instantly off the page, and the new obscurantism represented by this aspect of their work has moral as well as intellectual and political overtones. In the cultural life of France, their rejection of the conventional view that 'la clarté est la politesse de l'homme de lettres' is part of a political commitment. Because the traditional cult of clarity is so closely associated, as Barthes himself pointed out in *Le degré zéro de l'écriture*, with the reign of the middle class, any writer with any claim to originality feels compelled to jettison intellectual clarity along with bourgeois mystification. But in the case of Barthes, this cult of difficulty also seems associated with the neo-Protestant view that it would be morally wrong to enjoy a laugh at the rag trade without having previously demonstrated one's intellectual toughness by writing or understanding a phrase such as

> la syntaxe du vêtement écrit n'est ni une parataxe ni une rection:
> les matrices ne sont ni juxtaposées ni (linéairement) subordonnées;
> elles s'engendrent les unes les autres par extension substantielle (les
> damiers rouges et les damiers blancs forment un ensemble extensif
> à chacune de ses parties) et réduction formelle (toute une matrice
> devient simple élément de la matrice suivante).[21]

Justified though Barthes's decision to concentrate on the language of
fashion undoubtedly is, one cannot help feeling that the idea could
be more simply expressed. Barthes can write succintly when he chooses;
and the statement that 'tout signe tient son être de ses entours et non
de ses racines'[22] [paraphrase: 'every sign derives its being from the
system into which it fits and not its origins'] is as neat and useful an
expression of an act of intellectual hygiene as the Wittgensteinian
instruction 'Don't look for the meaning, look for the use' which it so
much resembles. But such phrases are, in *Système de la Mode* or *S/Z*,
few and far between.

If Barthes himself had not so fervently refused to see any connection
at all between what we might know about a writer as an individual
and what his books actually mean, an appropriate reply to these
criticisms could be found in the hedonistic attitude to literature and to
writing set out in 1973 in *Le Plaisir du Texte*. Officially, Barthes the
man is all for pleasure, and in no way insistent that enjoyment must
be bought by effort. But the practice of Barthes the writer is very
different, and his determination to send his reader over a complicated
verbal assault course is a feature of his work that it is tempting to
explain by biographical considerations. For Barthes is in another
Protestant tradition apart from that of moral endeavour. He is, for
all his formal insistence on hedonism and for all the hermetic quality
of his prose, an essentially didactic writer. *Le degré zéro de l'écriture* tries
to teach writers to be honest in acknowledging the artificial nature
of all literature, the essays on Brecht are a plea for a purified self-
awareness in our attitude to the theatre, *Mythologies* seeks to cleanse
our hearts by the purification of our signs, while *Critique et Vérité* and
S/Z require us to shake off the old Adam of the belief in the mimetic
role of literature which has bedevilled the Western approach to story
telling since Aristotle, and awaken to the new man of polyvalent
verbal structures. The third reason for which Barthes spent six years
of his life writing a book on a subject and type of writing for which he
felt little sympathy thus lay in an almost puritanical zeal to change
people's attitude towards the way they think about their clothes. He
had to deal with the language of fashion because it was for him
through language that people are encouraged to adopt a wrong
attitude towards the clothes they wear. Only through time, as T. S.

Eliot observed, is time conquered; and only through a critical analysis of language can the false visions it has created be dispelled.

The path to salvation which Barthes proposes to his followers is by now a fairly familiar one: *Larvatus Prodeo*. It is, however, one that is illustrated by examples with some unexpected political overtones, since Barthes finds the attitude he admires not in any real or even hypothetical socialist community but in the authoritarian society of the past. It is monarchical society, he claims, which

> openly presented its clothes as a set of signs and not the product of a certain number of reasons. The length of a train signalled a social condition and nothing else, no words were there to convert this lexical convention into a compelling reason [aucune parole n'était là pour convertir ce lexique en raison], to suggest that ducal dignity produced the length of the train in the same way that, in the modern text quoted above, the cold church requires a bolero of white mink at a fashionable wedding.[23]

It is not unusual for modern critics writing in French to express nostalgia for medieval or Renaissance society. Lucien Goldmann sees the Middle Ages as a state of almost perfect prelapsarian innocence before the rot of bourgeois individualism destroyed the organic nature of social relationships, while even as sane a critic as Georges Poulet cannot write about the way people think about time without somehow suggesting that they were happier in a society where everyone knew his place.[24] The Barthes of *Système de la Mode* regrets the advent of the bourgeoisie for slightly different reasons, but his nostalgia for a neo-feudal society is just as strong. And, as in the case of Goldmann or Poulet, his enthusiasm for such a social order has the same origin: a dislike of the bourgeoisie.

Like the literature admired by the middle classes, argues Barthes, the clothes they wore pretended to be natural, realistic and functional. This was a myth, since the wearing of clothes is a cultural attribute, and garments as apparently functional as a pair of overalls or a Chairman Mao jacket are just as much social signs as old school ties or college blazers. Where Barthes sees the sartorial behaviour of aristocratic or monarchical society as more honest than that of our own is in the greater recognition which he thinks then reigned of the essential artificiality of dress. When Polonius reminds Laertes that the apparel oft proclaims the man, he is speaking in very Barthesian terms. The only thing of which he fails to remind his son is that no one should imagine the clothes he wears to be the automatic embodiment of the essential inner self to which he must be true. Both the self and the clothes are, in Sartrean and Barthesian terms, equally the product of a conscious choice. To use signs honestly, whether they are verbal or visual, is thus for Barthes always a question of having the honesty to recognise them as signs. They differ from symbols precisely by their arbitrary nature and by the fact that no aspect of them ties them down to evoking one thing rather than another. A pair of scales is a symbol of a court of justice because the idea of impartiality is common to both of them. But a college tie, white shirt, dark suit and polished shoes constitute a collection of signs which could well alter its meaning if a large enough social sub-group decided to wear them to express its hatred of bourgeois society.

One of the most interesting remarks that Barthes makes in *Système de la Mode* is that fashion may often fulfil a most important psychological function: it enables a person to express what he or she either is or would like to be in terms which other people living in the same society will immediately recognise and understand.[25] Unfortunately, he observes, the terms in which fashion writers present the styles of dress available always seek to elude the need for conscious choices. The language used to describe fashion constantly tries to fool people into thinking that they have, as Barthes says, a 'personality rich enough to multiply itself, stable enough never to lose itself'.[26] It thus skates round the need which every person has to make a definite choice as to what he or she is and to express it in terms which consciously express its conscious quality. The criticism which Barthes makes of this language in *Système de la Mode* is aimed at detecting such subterfuges and obliging each person to know what he is wearing and why.

8 Balzac, fiction and Japan

I

S/Z is the only book by Barthes to concentrate exclusively on one text. It deals with 'Sarrasine', a short story by Balzac originally published in *La Revue de Paris* in November 1830 and later incorporated in the section of *La Comédie Humaine* entitled *Scènes de la vie parisienne*. The anonymous narrator is at a ball in the household of the Comte and Comtesse de Lanty. He sees a mysterious old man come and talk to the daughter of the house, Marianina, and give her a rich jewel before she spirits him away. The woman who is with the narrator, the Marquise de Rochefide, is anxious to know who he is. She implies that she will sleep with the narrator if he tells her.

The story he relates deals with a young French sculptor, Ernest-Jean Sarrasine, who goes to Italy in 1758. In Rome, at a visit to the theatre, he falls in love with a beautiful young singer known as La Zambinella. He goes back to the theatre night after night in order to watch her perform, and carves a statue of her in his workshop. After a tumultuous party, he abducts her only to discover that she is not a woman at all but a *castrato*, the favourite of Cardinal Cicognara. The Cardinal has Sarrasine assassinated, and orders a marble copy to be made of the statue of La Zambinella found in Sarrasine's workshop. This serves as a model for the painter Vien, whose portrait subsequently inspires Girodet's *Le Sommeil d'Endymion*. This, in turn, provides the starting point for yet another work of art, a portrait of Adonis which now decorates one of the salons in the Hôtel Lanty. The explanation for the mysterious old man is that he is La Zambinella, now in his/her nineties, the founder through his immensely successful career as a singer of the fortunes of the Lanty family, and the original model, at three removes, of the portrait of Adonis. Madame de Rochefide had admired this painting, wondered about the source of the Lanty family's wealth, and been curious to know about the mysterious old man. Her curiosity is satisfied, but the infectious shock of the castration theme has so affected her that she refuses to keep her side of the bargain. Although the narrator has kept his promise by telling her about the Lanty family, she refuses to sleep with him; and the story ends on a general note of disillusionment.

On a number of occasions in S/Z, Barthes declares that his fifty-eight-thousand-word analysis of the ten thousand words in Balzac's 'Sarrasine' is not an *explication de texte*, and it is easy to understand the reasons for this insistence. The technique of *explication de texte* is traditionally based on the idea that a text has one central meaning which it is the duty of the critic or commentator to bring out with absolute clarity into the full light of day. It consequently sets out from the rather curious presupposition that writers have something to say but that they somehow never quite manage to say it. It assumes—admittedly without saying so in so many words—that the critic's relationship to the creative writer resembles that of the members of the *Conseil d'Etat* to any *député* sufficiently ill-advised to bring forward a private member's bill for approval by the *Assemblée Nationale*. This body not only checks such projects to ensure that they do not contradict existing law. It also modifies the texts submitted to it 'pour les rendre plus conformes tant au droit pré-existant, qu'à la volonté réelle mais mal exprimée de leurs auteurs' ['to bring them into line either with pre-existent law and with the real but imperfectly expressed intentions of their authors'].[1]

Almost the whole of Barthes's work is devoted to refuting this view both of literature and of literary criticism. For him, nothing precedes the telling and there is no real meaning to clarify. What he seeks to put in the place of the traditional view of literature as a set of devices expressing a pre-existent content is the realisation that there is, to use the vocabulary of Saussurian linguistics, no final *signifié* behind the various *signifiants* which make up a literary text. There is, in fact, he argues in S/Z, no such thing as the 'real' meaning of a text. What gives a text its value and meaning is the extent to which it enables the reader to rewrite it for himself, and Barthes implies that the best texts are those which are infinitely rewritable. It is texts such as these which he dignifies with the evaluative adjective of 'modern', and which he contrasts with the 'classical' text. For while classical texts prevent the reader's imagination from working freely by presenting him with 'a nauseating mixture of common opinions, a smothering layer of received ideas',[2] modern texts allow and even encourage him to 'rewrite' the story for himself.

The interest of 'Sarrasine', according to S/Z, lies precisely in the way it combines these two qualities and enables the modern to triumph over the classical. For while Balzac's actual style of writing may be full of clichés and thus bog the reader down in established ideas, the underlying theme of the short story epitomises what Barthes regards as the central fallacy of supposedly realistic literature. The tragedy of the sculptor Sarrasine, argues Barthes, is that of a man who mistakes the established ideas embodied in the cultural codes of our society for reality itself. Because La Zambinella fits in with what he has been taught to think of as a woman—she is slender, beautiful, timid, sings in a high-pitched voice, is delicate and afraid of snakes—he imagines that she must be a woman. He is, of course, led into this error through ignorance. He does not know—because he is a foreigner—that real women do not appear on the Italian stage. He therefore dies, as Barthes rather ingeniously puts it, 'd'un blanc dans le discours des autres' ['of a blank in the speech of other people'].[3] His life ends tragically because he does not know how other human beings have decided to manipulate the essentially arbitrary signs of feminine sexuality. He takes, as it were, fool's gold for the real thing.

The category mistake which Sarrasine can thus be seen as making is also exemplified by his decision to try to capture the essence of La Zambinella by carving a statue of her. Since, in his view, art is essentially mimetic in nature, a perfect work of art will enable him to find his way into a deeper understanding of his beloved. But since he has misread the cultural codes which alone provide the pattern within which La Zambinella's beauty is meaningful, his statue is finally taken from him and used as a basis for other works of art which are, in turn, meaningful only within the cultural context of the society which admires them. He cannot find the secret of La Zambinella's sexuality by copying her beauty in a work of art because the whole point about 'her' sexuality is that it does not exist. The *castrato* has no sexuality. And the short story entitled 'Sarrasine' is privileged in that it denounces what one might call 'the common error of realist literature': the view that there is a 'real content' to a story which guarantees its authenticity in the same way that the gold in the vaults of the Bank of England guaranteed—in happier days—the value of the pound sterling. For Barthes, there is no such content, and Emma Bovary is a creature of paper and ink, not flesh and blood. Whatever value the pound may possess is derived from the conventions within which it circulates, not by reference to a pile of gold bars. And whatever credibility the characters of fiction may have derives from our imagination, and not from the models which the author has been copying.

It is certainly fortunate for his reputation that Barthes presents himself as a literary theoretician and not as a literary critic. Not only is he unable, in *S/Z*, to decide whether 'Sarrasine' is a 'classical' text, and therefore bad, or whether it is 'modern', and therefore good. He also leaves the reader completely in the dark about the extent to which Balzac might or might not have been aware of the implications of the story which he himself wrote. He makes great play with the five codes into which he claims that the statements in 'Sarrasine' can be classified, and gives them impressive neo-classical names in abbreviated form. HER stands for hermeneutics: the art of deciphering mysteries. SEM is short for *sème*, the unity of meaning in semantics. ACT involves both action and what the Greek rhetoricians called proairetic, the ability to think before taking action. REF, for referential, describes sentences which work by virtue of an accepted code. But he does not even seem to consider the main implication of his own remark that 'the meaning of a text can be nothing but the plurality of its systems, its infinite (circular) transcribability':[4] that to provide only five codes for an infinitely meaningful text is a shade miserly. S/Z is rather nicely dedicated to the students who attended his seminar at the Ecole pratique des Hautes Etudes in 1968 and 1969, and is described as having 'written itself according to the way they listened to it' ['qui s'est écrit selon leur écoute']. The narcissistic experience of discovering how brilliant one is by expounding one's ideas to a captive audience is one that most university teachers have enjoyed, and it is pleasant to see a foreign colleague acknowledging it so willingly. But one cannot at times help regretting that Barthes never enjoyed the slightly different opportunity of trying to explain his ideas to a British extra-mural class —or, for that matter, to an American graduate seminar.

The inquisitorial techniques practised by so many members of these groups on their course tutors would not, however, have deprived S/Z of its two most enjoyable qualities: its ingenious exploitation of sexuality and its ability to raise fundamental questions about the nature of fiction. As the analysis in 'L'Homme racinien' made fairly clear, Barthes is peculiarly aware of the presence and threat of the castrating mother-figure, and Balzac only has to mention an incident in which Madame de Lanty traps one of her lover's fingers in a door while hiding him from her husband for Barthes's Freudian preoccupation to leap into action. He immediately diagnoses yet another castration incident. One might perhaps regret Barthes's failure to extend his imagination even more fully by providing a commentary on how significant it is that La Zambinella should originally have been castrated on the orders of a Cardinal, a beskirted male who had himself forsworn sexuality in the service of the Church; but one cannot have everything in an imperfect world. Philippe Sollers did, after all, write that '*Sarrasine* is the story of a castration which takes place in the story and the story of the castration of the story as story', and Barthes himself said how sensitive the main theme of 'Sarrasine' made him to the fact that people tended to miss off the 's' from the end of his name.[5] But the main point of S/Z is not the exploitation of a theme which, as Jake Barnes ironically observed in *The Sun Also Rises*, is supposed to be very funny. It is the literary problem of trying to decide what constitutes a story and how fiction works. This is the issue which Barthes mentions in the opening pages of his book, and which he attempts to deal with by what the poet Michel Déguy would consider a typically phenomenological method: not by trying to accumulate a large number of examples, from Cervantes to Sollers, as it were, but by concentrating on one specific text which then becomes privileged and exemplary thanks to the general conclusions that can be drawn from t.[6]

The first point that strikes the English reader of *S/Z* is that Barthes s attacking, if not exactly a straw man, at least a target that has been pretty well riddled with bullets ever since the publication in 1933 of L. C. Knights's *How many children had Lady Macbeth?* 'A poem', wrote Or Knights thirty-seven years before *S/Z*, 'works by calling into play, directing and integrating certain interests', and it is fairly obvious from his examples that he takes the word 'poem' in the widest possible sense of 'imaginative literary creation'. His *bêtes noires* are Hugh Walpole, John Galsworthy and Logan Pearsall Smith, and the bourgeois *évidence* that he gives to illustrate the wrong view of how literature works is the kind of statement which Barthes would have delighted to quote if a French bourgeois novelist had offered so rash a hostage to critical fortune. 'The test of a character in any novel', writes Walpole, is that it should have existed before the book that reveals it to us began, and should continue after the book is closed',[7] and it is precisely this illusion that both Knights and Barthes are anxious to denounce. It is, of course, one shared by the listeners to *The Archers* who write to the BBC to ask whether they can spend their holidays at Ambridge, as well as by the critics who take seriously the implication of Balzac's declared ambition to 'faire concurrence à l'état civil' ['create a world with its own parish registers']. It is consequently an illusion which is remarkably difficult to destroy, and it may well be precisely because Balzac enjoys the reputation of having created a fictional world which contains real, living, autonomous characters who demonstrate their independence by recurring in different novels that Barthes chose, in *S/Z*, to attack the basic ideology of realism in its very stronghold. As Mary McCarthy observed in her famous *The Fact is Fiction* article, 'everyone knows that Balzac was a lover of fact', and can consequently be assumed to admire him as the supreme practitioner of the art form which we expect to be 'not only true to itself, like a person or a statue, but true to actual life, which is right around the corner'.[8]

There are some obvious parallels between the struggle which Barthes and his followers see themselves as waging against the literary establishment of their day and the attack delivered by Knights or Leavis against the hangover in the England of the 1930s of attitudes towards literature dating back to the Victorian period. Lanson and his disciples are the enemy for Barthes, just as Bradley had been for Knights and Leavis. Robbe-Grillet, Kafka or Philippe Sollers are the creative writers whose practice has proved the old conceptions wrong, just as T. S. Eliot was the contemporary poet who had shown that the metaphysical poets of the seventeenth century offered a more vital tradition than the Romantics. Both movements reject the biographical and intentional approach, both insist on the prime importance of language, both dwell on form rather than content, both seek to bring about a revolution in aesthetic taste in their own country, and both tend towards a totalitarian and puritanical view of literature which allows relatively few authors into the received canon. What is rather surprising is that the ideas developed in England and America in the 1920s and 1930s should have taken so long to find parallel expression in France, and should have given rise to a style of critical writing which is concerned so much with theory that it has achieved little by way of re-evaluation and reinterpretation of the established masterpieces of French literature. For fascinating though Barthes, Mauron, Goldmann or Doubrovsky may be as theoreticians about how literature works or comes to be written, their books are, as literary criticism, simply not in the same league as *The Common Pursuit*, *The Great Tradition*, *Seven Types of Ambiguity* or Wilson Knight's *The Wheel of Fire*.

It may indeed be for that reason that *S/Z* received so mixed a reception on this side of the Channel, and that few American critics have so far followed Susan Sontag's example in welcoming him as 'the most inventive, elegant and intelligent of contemporary literary critics'. There were, admittedly, some enthusiastic voices in England, and John Sturrock, writing in the *New Statesman*, produced the kind of opening paragraph which would have delighted Barthes by the accuracy with which it summed up the stereotyped notion of Balzac against which *S/Z* was rebelling.

> It is well known [declared Sturrock] that Balzac stands for sim-
> plicity; there can be nothing too deep or artificial about *La Comédie
> Humaine* because it is the very essence of Realism, an honest tran-
> scription of the state of early 19th-century France. And Balzac?
> The guileless observer who looked to life for his information not to
> books and then, allowing for one or two temperamental blockages,
> represented things as they were.[9]

This is indeed the myth which Barthes sets out to destroy in *S/Z*, showing once again that books are made with words, not out of things, and that understanding 'Sarrasine' involves seeing not what human beings or French society are like but how the words work. This is the justification for his decision to divide Balzac's text into 561 *lexies*, or units of reading, and to concentrate on showing how each one works not by referring to a fixed content in the short story but by activating certain codes in the reader's mind. It may well be that this is how fiction does work, and it is also tempting to agree with Barthes in seeing the castration theme which so vividly symbolises the emptiness lying at the centre of 'Sarrasine' as having a profound social meaning. In a feudal society, signs were meaningful because they referred to something specific: the nobleman's privileges, the artisan's labour, the king's authority. But once this stable society disappeared, social prestige depended solely on money; and money, as the story of La Zambinella illustrates, is ultimately based on a vast confidence trick which itself rests upon nothing at all. La Zambinella sings beautifully, thus evoking sexual feelings in Sarrasine, precisely because 'she' is sexless. This is a most ingenious piece of literary and sociological theorising, and Barthes illustrates it with some fascinating details— admittedly of a type which one would more normally have expected from an admirer of the positivistic methods of Gustave Lanson— about the immense earning capacity of the *castrati* in late eighteenth-century Europe.[10] But he in no way succeeds in showing how 'Sarrasine' is in any way exemplary as an illustration of how fiction works. Rastignac, after all, rises to even greater heights in post-Restoration French society largely as a result of the sexual potency which enables him to become Delphine de Nucingen's lover and thus acquire the confidence of her rich banker husband.

These criticisms do not imply that Barthes is necessarily wrong in the general theory which he puts forward in *S/Z* of how prose fiction works. The train of thought set in motion by the debate with Picard and the need to formulate his own views more clearly in *Critique et Vérité* gave rise in *S/Z* to a fascinating book. Although Frederic Raphael's claim that 'a more encouraging, or more demanding, re-habilitation of the art of fiction is hard to imagine'[11] appears a shade exaggerated, the book does effectively kill off any lingering traces which might have remained of the mimetic illusion, of the view that fiction works because it reproduces life as it 'really is'. The trouble is that it does not go for enough. *Anna Karenina, Le Grand Meaulnes, The Way of an Eagle, Dr No, Wuthering Heights* and *Right-Ho, Jeeves,* all resemble one another in being verbal artefacts which work not by reference to an underlying reality but by the exploitation of certain codes. They are nevertheless very different not only in style, tone, use of language, readership appeal and moral seriousness but in their relationship to various types of lived or imaginary experience; and while *Anna Karenina* is obviously not a better book than *The Way of an Eagle* because parts of it are based on Tolstoy's own life, this is a factor to be considered by the critic who tries to answer the question of why so many of the episodes in it ring true whereas those in *The Way of an Eagle* do not. If the ideas in *S/Z* were to be carried through to the point where they could be used as a basis for aesthetic evaluation, the book in the list which would come out top would be *Right-Ho, Jeeves.* By exploiting language and exploding established clichés ('I examined the imagination: it boggled') it does precisely what Stephen Heath claims, in his book on Barthes, that *l'écriture* can do: give a language back its liberty. It has the infinitely ludic quality praised in the book which carries on after *S/Z—Le Plaisir du Texte.* It is impeccably structured, and yet could be split into an infinite number of what one would have to call *lexias*. It clearly does not contain characters in whom one is expected to believe as real people. It holds the reader at a distance by the infinite circularity of its cultural codes ('You know your Shelley, Bertie'; 'Oh, am I?') and is constantly haunted by the invisible presence and possible return of what S/Z would call 'la Femme-Reine . . . la Figure castratrice' (Aunt Agatha). At the same time it also contains what I myself have analysed elsewhere as a double paradox: the servant is not only cleverer than his master, but saves him from matrimony instead of helping him to get the girl.[12] But although it is obviously not even intended to be judged by the same criteria as *Wuthering Heights* or *Anna Karenina*, there is nothing in Barthes's theory or practice which would even begin to explain why this is so.

But in making such points one still feels like a pedantic oaf who laboriously states the obvious when this is the last quality relevant to the debate, and it is interesting to speculate on why this is the case. The principal reason is that to judge Barthes as a critic by reference to how his theories might apply to the literature of the past is as irrelevant as to criticise Mao's China for failing to observe the etiquette of seventeenth-century Versailles. For Barthes does not set out to provide a scale whereby the merit of literary works can be assessed. As his rejection of the Aristotelian theory of catharsis in his articles on Brecht suggests, he is seeking to break with the whole Western tradition of literary thinking. And he is, in this respect, very like the Stéphane Mallarmé who once uttered the paradox that poetry went wrong with Homer. When asked what had preceded him, he replied 'Pan', and there is a comparable ambition in Barthes's later thinking about literature to go back to a similar state of artistic innocence. The wider implications of his ideas are perhaps best seen here if his theories are applied to the play which provided the first model for Western concepts of story-telling, Sophocles's *Oedipus Rex*. For the action of this play takes place linearly in time, and gradually reveals the answer to a puzzle. At the beginning, we do not know why the plague has attacked Thebes; at the end, we know everything about Oedipus and can thus explain the situation with which the play began. This is what Barthes means when he says that 'classical story-telling is constantly subjected to time and logic',[13] and it is fairly clear both from his theories and from the practice of the authors whom he most admires —Philippe Sollers, the later Joyce—what he would like to put in its place: a text in which the reader could choose to present the events to himself in any order he liked, which did not set out to explain anything, and in which, as he implies in S/Z, language is used in such a way as to demonstrate the impossibility of claiming one form of speech to be superior to all others. Texts, in the literary future that Barthes envisages, will not have a beginning, a middle and an end. In so far as they tell a story, it will be one into which the reader can enter at any time, take control of what is happening, and rewrite it for himself. It is an ideal so amusingly and effectively achieved by Gore Vidal in *Myra Breckenbridge* and *Myron* that one wonders why Barthes himself did not choose to exploit his vision in fiction which actually demonstrated the unreality of characters by creating characters and situations which were brilliantly unreal.

II

In the 1960s, Barthes had the experience of discovering a culture and civilisation in which his ideas on the nature of art, of human communication, and on the relationship between signs and the things they signified seemed to be almost miraculously exemplified. He went, in other words, to Japan, and the book which he wrote about Japanese civilisation, *L'Empire des Signes*, was published simultaneously with *S/Z*. It would be an unpardonably impertinent misunderstanding of Barthes's positions to maintain that *L'Empire des Signes* illustrates the argument of *S/Z*, for such a functional view of books and language goes against everything he stands for. But it does help the neophyte to understand what he is talking about, and it also fits into another aspect of the French tradition apart from the use of prose to express ideas: it has a remarkable if unintentional resemblance to those books which, in the eighteenth century, used the supposedly more rational standards prevailing outside Europe as a stick with which to beat the obviously imperfect society in which the writer himself actually lived. As could be expected from *Le degré zéro de l'écriture* and elsewhere, Barthes has relatively little sympathy with the prevailing intellectual atmosphere of the eighteenth century. He once wrote rather condescendingly of Voltaire as 'the last happy writer' ['Le dernier des écrivains heureux'], and his essay on *Les Planches de L'Encyclopédie* is full of a sense of effortless superiority towards people who entertained such naïve concepts as Diderot or d'Alembert held about the importance of clarity, intellectual tolerance and bourgeois democracy.[14] It is consequently a little surprising to find him writing, in *L'Empire des Signes*, a text so reminiscent in parts of Montesquieu's *Lettres persanes* or the Eldorado episode in Voltaire's *Candide*.

Barthes does, of course, differ from his eighteenth-century predecessors by having actually been to the place he describes and having greatly enjoyed himself there. Indeed, *L'Empire des Signes* is one of the most hedonistic of all his books, and the one in which he writes with the most enthusiasm about his subject-matter. He likes everything about Japan: the food, so much lighter than European food, never covered with a thick coating of sauce or shovelled into the mouth in great spoonfuls, always served almost raw and in a way that enables the diner to compose his menu in the order he prefers; the elaborate politeness of the Japanese, which seems aimed not at flattering the self-esteem of a particular person but at sketching out an abstract concept of good manners; the literary conventions of the *haïku*, in which nothing is said and where the delicacy of the form is everything, the content nothing; Japanese religion, where 'the signs are empty and the ritual without God',[15] and where no systematic theology offers a fallacious explanation in terms of intellectual concepts such as the Trinity, the Incarnation or the Real Presence; the Japanese face, in which everything is on the surface and there is no hint of a mysterious and ineffable personality lying behind the beauty of the eyes; the militant students, whom he presents with slightly disquieting enthusiasm as about to fight for the sheer delight of pure combat, unalienated and uninspired by any actual belief in the political validity of what they are doing; and, perhaps more surprisingly, the sprawling, unplanned and unmapped Japanese towns, where the absence of a centre nevertheless fits in with his permanent aesthetic preference for experiences organised around an emptiness rather than around a kernel of solid truth. Barthes was, in fact, entirely captivated by Japan, and in no other book is the world view he expresses so obviously or—if one may use a romantic cliché—so honestly based upon an immediate expression of finding himself spiritually and sensually at home.

When challenged, by an interviewer in the Communist *Les Lettres Françaises*, to explain how he reconciled his fondness for Japan with the obviously capitalist nature of its post-war economic miracle, he made the interesting reply that this particular form of capitalism was rendered livable by the survival into the twentieth century of the old, traditional feudal values. This remark not only runs curiously parallel to the nostalgia for the Middle Ages which he expressed in *Système de la Mode*, but also evinces a desire to go even further back in time. Japan, he added, derived from this survival of feudalism a partial but unquestionable superiority over our industrial societies, in which 'la libération du signifiant' [paraphrase: 'the acknowledgement of the Saussurian concept of the arbitrary nature of signs'] has been held back for two thousand years by the development of a monotheistic theology and the hypostasised entities of 'Science', 'Man' and 'Reason' accompanying it. Indeed, he made his ultimate intention in *L'Empire des Signes* even clearer by declaring that we must now replace semiology, the critical but disinterestedly passive study of signs, by semioclasm (*la sémioclastie*), the deliberately irreverent destruction of signs as we know them. 'It is Western speech as such, in its very basis and elementary forms that we have to destroy',[16] he told the respectfully attentive Raymond Bellour; and you can't, as Bingo Little observed when outlining the intentions of Charlotte Corday Rowbotham's father to massacre the bourgeoisie, sack Park Lane and disembowel the hereditary aristocracy, say fairer than that.

The revelation of this ambition to the earnest Stalinists of *Les Lettres Françaises* would not, of course, have come as a surprise to any of them who had actually read *L'Empire des Signes*. There, Barthes makes it clear from the very beginning that it is quite pointless to try to call Western society seriously into question unless one actually begins by attacking its view of language as essentially instrumental. To do otherwise, he writes, is the equivalent of trying to kill the wolf by installing oneself comfortably in its mouth, and he must for once be congratulated on making his own meaning immediately comprehensible through a vividly expressive image. Quite what Western society has done to Roland Barthes that he should raise his voice in the rich pastures of the Left Bank and call for its absolute destruction is not wholly clear, but there is certainly an impressive consistency about the lessons which he invites his readers to draw from *S/Z* and *L'Empire des Signes*. Just as Western story-telling is wrong because it has traditionally set out to help the reader see meaning in his own experience by explaining the behaviour of certain other people in rational and comprehensible terms, so Western language is wrong because it tries to express ideas. It should, instead, delight in diagrams which explain nothing because there is nothing to be explained and which consequently exist as art forms in their own right. Barthes's ideal, Robert Kanters remarked in one of those flashes of explanatory zeal which characterise the bourgeois class, was clearly to be able to write in Japanese without actually understanding the language.[17] Kanters's remark was only apparently paradoxical, and offers perhaps the best way of approaching the fundamental aesthetic and philosophical aims of Barthes as a writer. The very difficulty of his style evokes the total incomprehensibility to the Westerner of a language such as Japanese, and to read him is to indulge in the alienating but essentially enjoyable experience so well evoked by the very title of Stephen Heath's *Vertige du déplacement*. One is carried away into a splendid, vertiginous and exquisitely fascinating world, akin to that of *L'Année dernière à Marienbad* or the last sequences of *Blow-up*.

A great problem nevertheless arises when one tries to relate a comprehensible and therefore emasculated version of what Barthes is saying to one's own more conventional experience and ideas. It then becomes apparent that he is, in *S/Z* and *L'Empire des Signes*, pursuing an intriguing, fascinating, but essentially impossible ideal. For he cannot use language entirely 'for its own sake'. Precisely because he is not writing symbolist poetry or non-figurative fiction, he is caught in the corollary to the experience of the eponymous hero of T. S. Eliot's *Sweeney Agonistes* who declared that 'I gotta use words when I talk to you': every time Barthes uses words, he does talk to us. And the words that he uses express notions which then inevitably relate to other, more bourgeois and conventional ideas already in our minds. For it is very difficult not to notice that the argument in S/Z perpetually flickers from the 'is' to the 'ought', from the legitimate observation that some types of fiction work by the 'infinite circularity of signs' to the more questionable assertion that all types of fiction should be like that. It is equally hard not to be struck by the realisation that Barthes's official refusal to judge cohabits with a very clear scale of values in which Roger Martin du Gard or Somerset Maugham would come off very badly by comparison with James Joyce or Philippe Sollers, and not to wonder what Barthes could make of the argument that certain traditional novelists—Dickens or Conrad, for example—do give every illusion not only of telling us things we did not know before but of actually shaking up our normal moral conceptions. One often feels towards the Barthes of S/Z and *L'Empire des Signes* the same ambivalent emotions that Flaubert's Monsieur Homais felt towards the Racine of *Athalie*: torn between the desire to 'le couronner de ses propres mains et discuter avec lui pendant un bon quart d'heure'.

One would, in particular, like to know just what Barthes thinks about two rather different phenomena: the Marxist view of language and Danny La Rue. For if Marx was right in claiming, as he did in *The German Ideology*, that 'language *is* practical consciousness, as it exists for other men, and thus as it first really exists for myself as well. Language, like consciousness, only arises from the need, the necessity of intercourse with other men',[18] then it is extremely difficult to see how Barthes is going to invert the process and change society by starting with its language. And how could he still maintain, if he were to have the pleasure of seeing *Queen Daniella*, that it is only in Japan that the transvestite actor seeks not to be a woman but merely to 'put together the signs of Woman'?[19] For this is precisely what Danny La Rue does, and the enthusiasm with which he is invariably and justifiably greeted has strong structural affinities with the self-conscious applause that greets the performers at an all-in wrestling match. Western society, in other words, is a good deal subtler and more sophisticated in its attitude towards signs than Barthes gives it credit for, and there would seem to be—the demise of the author notwithstanding—a psychological as well as a political blockage which prevents him from recognising this.

9 Logothetes, pleasure and Sisyphus

I

In the closing pages of *The Liberal Imagination*, Lionel Trilling points out that there exists a lack of sympathy between the 'tradition of democratic liberalism as we know it' and the most significant of the modern European writers. 'Yeats and Eliot', he writes, 'Proust and Joyce, Lawrence and Gide—these men do not seem to confirm us in the social and political ideas which we hold.'[1] Trilling could have added the names of Malraux, Sartre, Kafka, Graham Greene, Aldous Huxley, Evelyn Waugh, André Breton, and the host of poets stemming from the tradition of Baudelaire, Rimbaud and Mallarmé, and brought his list to a triumphant conclusion with those of the three writers on whom Barthes chose to concentrate in his next book: Sade, Fourier and Loyola. For it would be almost impossible to find three authors more out of sympathy with the capitalist, liberal, democratic, pluralistic, secular, officially optimistic but profoundly sceptical industrial society which we have the good fortune to inhabit. Sade was a pessimistic aristocrat obsessed by the connection between sexual pleasure and physical suffering; Fourier a Utopian philosopher whose dream was of a perfectly regulated harmonious society in which differences of opinion would completely disappear; and Loyola a Catholic visionary whose whole life was devoted to establishing the authority of the Church Militant. Three of the essays making up the volume entitled *Sade, Fourier, Loyola*, published in December 1971, had originally appeared in review form in the 1960s, and the book offers no real advance on the ideas put forward in *S/Z*. What it gives us is a further application of the truism running through the whole of Barthes's thinking on literature, and which he has had the talent to present as one of the most provocative ideas of twentieth-century French literary criticism: the idea that books are made of words, not things.

The publication of *Sade, Fourier, Loyola* coincided with the appearance of a special number of *Tel Quel* on Barthes, and provided the occasion for a celebratory cocktail party at the Editions du Seuil on the evening of 8 December 1971. It is, curiously enough, not difficult to imagine how the three authors analysed in Barthes's essay would have reacted to this gathering together of the great and good of the French literary world. Donatien-Alphonse-François, Marquis de Sade (1740–1814) would have enjoyed it immensely. He was a wealthy and sexually eccentric aristocrat who had the misfortune of finding himself on the losing side in contests with four forms of authority: his mother-in-law, the police force of the *ancien régime*, the government of revolutionary France, and Napoleon I. Each succeeded in putting him in prison, his mother-in-law by the use of the *lettre de cachet*, the others by the more conventional authority vested in them. He consequently spent a total of twenty-seven years locked away from his fellow men, composing a series of books glorifying the sacrifice of the weak to the strong, systematically cataloguing all possible forms of sexual perversion, and urging men to compete with Nature in the one area where she was supreme but where rivalry was nevertheless possible: cruelty and destruction. He was, in point of fact, rather a mild man who carried his moral and intellectual disapproval of the death penalty to the point where, sitting in judgement on his mother-in-law during his brief spell as head of a revolutionary *Section* during the Terror, he saved her from the guillotine. He had, ever since Apollinaire had greeted him in 1909 as the thinker who would dominate the twentieth century, been something of a cult figure in the French literary world, and there was in fact something rather conventional—in left-wing circles, at any rate—in Barthes's decision to discuss him in such detail.

Charles Fourier (1772–1837) would have been an equally popular figure at the gathering. His own failure in business had helped to make him acutely aware of the disadvantages of capitalism. He had suggested, as an alternative, the creation of a number of collective units of production known as *phalanges*, each of which was to occupy an area of territory known as a *phalanstère*. Each *phalanstère* would become entirely self-sufficient, and each *phalange* cater for all possible varieties and combinations of human passions. Indeed, the driving force behind the *phalange* was to be made up of the passions of the people inhabiting it, and Fourier had calculated that these could be divided into eight hundred and ten different groupings. Each person living in the *phalange* would therefore be able to find and perform a job which satisfied his or her ruling passion; and everyone would find a partner whose sexual tastes corresponded to his or her own. Work would thus cease to be an imposition and become a pleasure, and the harmony attained in human society would at last equal the universal Newtonian harmony observable in the movement of the planets and the other heavenly bodies. No one would go hungry, each man would willingly help his neighbour, co-operation would reign supreme, and nobody could ever again possibly be unhappy.

Fourier had also become, though less noticeably than the Marquis de Sade, one of the heroes of the French intellectual left. As far back as 1947, André Breton had written an ode to him; the student revolutionaries of 1968 had declared, as Fourier had, that the quest for pleasure and happiness should dominate all other considerations and seen him as one of their patron saints; those responsible for putting up the barricades in the rue Gay-Lussac in March 1969 had re-erected his statue; and a twelve-volume edition of his works had been published by the Editions Anthropos between 1966 and 1968.[2] Any enemy of capitalism is a friend of the French intellectual Left, and it cannot have been wholly an accident that Barthes should originally have written about the precursor of the *communes* in *Tel Quel*, a review even more enthusiastic about the Cultural Revolution than the Chinese masses themselves. Fourier might even have proved a useful man to have had around if the drink began to run out. While there is no record of his actually changing water into wine, he apparently believed that the harmony inseparable from the eventual triumph of his system would make the sea turn into lemonade.

The only odd man out would really have been the third of Barthes logothetes, or creators of worlds through language, Ignatius of Loyola. An ex-military man, he would have been ill at ease in a crowd of voluble literary intellectuals; while as the Founder of an Order based upon the principles of poverty, chastity and obedience, he would scarcely have found any other aspect of the gathering particularly congenial. The memory of his canonisation in 1622, like that of the importance which his Order had placed upon a disciplined approach to classical texts, would have made him look equally askance at Barthes's ludic attitude towards literature, at his rejection of the technique of *explication de texte*, and at the remark in *Sade, Fourier, Loyola* that the ability to spell correctly has no intrinsic educational merit but is merely the sign that one belongs to the middle class.[3] The Hispanic austerity of his personal life would have clashed with the cult of pleasure characteristic not only of Sade and Fourier but also of Barthes himself, and it is doubtful whether his deep sense of sin and constant awareness of the need to train his disciples to obey *perinde ac cadaver* (just like a corpse) would have let him linger over the Cinzano and canapés for very long.

But there are only commas to separate the names *Sade, Fourier, Loyola* on the cover of his book, and the presence of Ignatius of Loyola as the third person in this trinity of the bad, the mad and the sad is eminently justifiable in terms of the structuralist and non-representational approach to literature which informs the whole of Barthes's work. For the Catholic Saint, like the wicked aristocrat and the lunatic philosopher, is obsessed with counting. He enumerates sins, types of prayer, modes of spiritual preparation and the times of day most suitable for entering into contact with God. He is therefore, from the standpoint of Barthesian structuralism, like the Fourier who counts pleasures, types of fruit, concepts of true happiness in Rome at the time of the Emperor Varro (278) or individuals in France capable of equalling Homer (45,000). Content, for the structuralist, is infinitely less important than form, so that the Saint and the Utopian are brothers in words to the imprisoned and frustrated sexual fanatic who classified and analysed crimes, sexual perversions and different types of death, established for his libertines a strict timetable for digestion, copulation and evacuation, and created—as do Fourier and Ignatius—a world which exists in total isolation from the normal business of conventional society. All three authors, by creating a world exclusively through language (*écriture*), transcend the narrowly utilitarian function attributed to words by bourgeois society. And even the Jesuit Saint, by inventing a language in which the believer may speak to God, is carrying out a revolutionary act. He is enabling people to escape from the *Doxa*, the received opinions, the ready-made ideas which habitually glue them down to conventional modes of discourse.

If one were to count the number of pages in *Sade, Fourier, Loyola* devoted to each writer, Sade would undoubtedly come out top. There are two essays on him as against one on each of the other two logo-thetes, and it is in the second essay on Sade that Barthes makes the alliterative epigram which most neatly summarises his approach to literature. Commenting on the physical impossibility of the orgies described in Sade's work, and noting how incredible it is that the four libertines of *Les Cent-Vingt Journées de Sodome* should rule alone and without opposition over a whole castle-full of victims, he asks: 'Pourquoi le livre ne serait-il pas programme, plutôt que peinture?' ['Why should a book not present a programme rather than a painting?']⁴ and the reader is once again comfortably back on the lines of argument suggested by *Le Monde où l'on catche, Critique et Vérité* or *S/Z*. It is also when talking about Sade that Barthes again involuntarily makes the English reader feel at home by reminding him of the later philosophy of Wittgenstein. For when he writes 'there is no meta-language; or rather: there are nothing but meta-languages: language on language, like an apple turnover with no fruit, or better still, for no language has a permanent hold over the other, like scissors–paper–stone',⁵ he is putting forward a view that has strong analogies with the interpretation which can be placed on Wittgenstein's theory of language games. There is, for Barthes as for Wittgenstein, no language which enjoys pride of place over other languages, and consequently no such thing as a supreme, metaphysical form of knowledge. All ways of finding out about human behaviour or the constitution of the physical world are equally valid, since each illuminates a different aspect of the pheno-menon being studied. Indeed a strict Barthesian would go so far as to say that there is not even a real phenomenon to be studied. There are only the empty constructs which the language we elect to use brings into being, and there is no way of deciding whether the construct created by the Marxist is better or worse than those conjured up by the Freudian, the phenomenologist, the Hegelian idealist or the Popperian positivist. Aldous Huxley had had a similar intuition in *Those Barren Leaves*, in 1925, when he made Calamy discuss the impossibility of finding any common ground between the descriptions which the physicist, the chemist, the biologist or the moralist might give of his hand. Each would be quite right in his own terms, but there would be no common ground between the biologist's analysis of it in terms of blood, skin, muscles and nerves, and the physicist's presentation of a mass of electrons whirling round a collection of invisible neutrons. This is, however, a fairly traditional problem, and the familiarity to any literate Englishman or American of the actual ideas expressed in *Sade, Fourier, Loyola* might perhaps justify as well as explain the peculiarities of Barthes's own *écriture*. Both when everything has been said, and when there is nothing actually lying behind language waiting to be said, only an unusual way of saying can justify a writer's activity.

Barthes does not, however, stick entirely to the austere principles of pure semiosis when discussing the works of Sade. Just as the fascinating details about the earning power of eighteenth-century *castrati* provided an unexpected bonus of bourgeois positivism for the unregenerate reader of S/Z, so the essays on Sade occasionally allow a mimetic detail to slip through as well. The presence in one of the scenes evoked in the *Les Cent-Vingt Journées de Sodome* of an enormous looking-glass capable of reflecting all the details of all the orgies is, Barthes observes, an indication of the tremendous wealth enjoyed by Sade's aristocratic libertines. In the eighteenth century, he claims, owning a looking-glass was akin to owning a private yacht today, and the bourgeois reader may regret that Barthes does not allow his structuralist mask to slip more often. At one point, Barthes even goes so far as to claim that 'the Sadian novel is more real than the social novel (which is realist)' and justifies this by a comment rich with mimetic overtones: that while the activities of Sade's libertines may seem highly improbable in twentieth-century Western Europe, they could very well take place even nowadays in an underdeveloped country. For one would find there, as one could have found in eighteenth-century France, the same strict social divisions, the same availability of victims, the same isolation from the rest of society, and the same immunity from the laws. Geoffrey Gorer, in what is still the best and most perceptive of all the books on Sade, observed how fully his analysis of human behaviour anticipated the concentration camps of Nazi Germany, and there is no doubt about the relevance of the content as well as the form of Sade's works to our own preoccupations.[6] As in his books on Michelet and Racine, Barthes is more hindered than helped in *Sade, Fourier, Loyola* by his attempt to apply structuralist methodology to authors who did in fact have something to say.

The unremittingly gallocentric nature of Barthes's frame of historical reference comes out very clearly in his assertion that Fourier lived through 'the two great events of modern History: the Revolution and the Empire', and he seems to feel no hesitation in suggesting that novelists could be classified 'according to the frankness with which they talk about food' without mentioning Dickens. Fourier's totalitarian Harmony is naturally presented as inferior to 'the modern State in which the pious organisation of leisure is matched by a pitiless censure exercised over pleasure', while the other left-wing cliché of the 1960s about 'repressive tolerance' recurs in the claim that 'repressive liberal discourse' seeks constantly to smother the 'déploiement victorieux du texte signifiant' ['victorious unfolding of the physically meaningful text'].[7] There is also a typically left-wing zeal to explain the events of the past in socio-economic terms while commenting on what is happening nowadays largely as an illustration of the way the bourgeois media use language. Thus while Ignatius of Loyola's attempt to calculate the relative gravity of sins is seen in very Marxist terms as reflecting 'the new capitalist ideology, based at one and the same time on the individualistic concept of the person and the enumeration of the goods which, by belonging to him, make him what he is',[8] Barthes has a very different attitude elsewhere towards the quadrupling in the price of oil. Thus he declared, in his preface to Gérard Miller's *Les pousse-au-jouir du meréchal Pétain*, that the oil crisis 'thanks to the co-operative insistence of the State radio, has gradually become a pure, natural occurrence, analogous to the great physical calamities or epidemics of the past',[9] and his remark is again interesting as a reflection of the impact which the French radio has on its more critical listeners. Barthes does, however, carefully refrain from mentioning that the price of oil was originally increased in order to try to blackmail the West into handing the Israelis over to the tender mercies of Yassir Arafat.

It is indeed very difficult, when reading Barthes, to refrain from the bourgeois habit of remembering what actually happened, and from judging so obviously political a text as Barthes's preface to Miller's book by one's own political criteria. One does, of course, thus provide a portrait of oneself and of one's standards but bourgeois customs do have some advantages: one can condescend to give credit where credit is due and comment that Barthes's *écriture* is at times so splendidly rich that it does, as his own literary ideology requires, quite outweigh the oddity of what he is actually saying. Thus the threat constantly hanging over the imprisoned Marquis de Sade of being refused exercise-time or pen and paper calls forth the comment that: 'Ce qui est censuré, c'est la main, le muscle, le sang, le doigt qui pointe le mot au-dessus de la plume. La castration est circonscrite, le sperme scriptural ne peut plus couler: la détention devient rétention: sans promenade et sans plume Sade s'engorge, devient eunuque.' ['This censorship strikes the hand, the muscle, the blood, the finger pointing the pen towards the word. Castration is circumscribed, the scriptural sperm can no longer flow; detention becomes retention; unable to walk or to write, Sade swells up, gross as a eunuch.']10 Elsewhere in *Sade, Fourier, Loyola* Barthes comments that the creation of neologisms is an erotic act and claims that this is why it 'never escapes the censure of pedants'.11 Nowhere in his work does the remark that his ideal would be to write in Japanese without understanding the language become more applicable than in *Sade, Fourier, Loyola* or the book which he published in 1973, *Le Plaisir du Texte*.

II

He had by then, as he remarks on a number of occasions, fallen greatly under the influence of Nietzsche, both ideologically and in the form of his work. The quotation from Nietzsche which Jonathan Culler makes in his *Structuralist Poetics*12—'I fear we are not getting rid of God because we still believe in grammar'—exactly fits the attitude towards language in *L'Empire des Signes*, and *Le Plaisir du Texte* shows the formal influence by being written as a series of aphorisms rather than a continuous argument. It must be admitted, however, that some now familiar theses again do not take long to make themselves felt. A descriptive sentence, argues Barthes, does not tell us anything about the world. It is a kind of 'lexicographical artefact' which must be seen as existing in its own right. Adjectives are merely 'the doors through which ideology comes pouring in'; and since all ideologies are stulti-fying and abominable, one assumes that all adjectives are automatic-ally bad. The ideal use of words takes place in what Barthes calls a 'texte de jouissance'. There, the effect is to shake all established habits of thought, and thus contribute to the destruction of all ideologies. Literary value-judgements based upon reasoned argument are in the context of *Le Plaisir du Texte* both impossible and undesirable: all the critic can say is: 'c'est cela pour moi'. In Flaubert, 'il n'y a plus que la langue' ['nothing is left except language'], and it is a complete error to think that texts can in any way imitate reality. All that classical texts do is confirm our existing views and hypnotise us into believing that certain ways of talking are truer than others. The supreme value lies in what Barthes calls, in another of his neologisms, 'la signifiance', and which he defines as 'the meaning which it is possible to produce sensually'.13 There is a good deal of insistence both in *Sade, Fourier, Loyola* and *Le Plaisir du Texte* on the idea of reacting physically to the books we read, deciphering them with our very bodies, even going back to the custom of reading them aloud. This very welcome idea that we read for enjoyment nevertheless goes hand in hand with the almost obsessive but typically left-wing feeling which Barthes still has that he is being persecuted by the society in which he lives. For pleasure, he argues, is under attack both from the platitudinous conservative majority and from the progressive minority. The former regard it with suspicion as an instrument for dissolving established verbal habits and social values, while the second take the puritanical view that enjoyment is a distraction from the needs of the revolution. Nobody, according to Barthes, bases his regret that only 50 per cent of the French population ever reads a book on the idea of the pleasure they are missing.[14]

For Barthes to accuse other people of puritanism is a little surprising when one considers how many kinds of literature he would like to discourage, but a consciously hedonistic approach to experience is clearly part of the ideal self-image which he is seeking to project in the later part of his career. It became quite fashionable, in reviews of *Le Plaisir du Texte*, to refer to it as an intellectual *Karma Sutra*,[15] and the description is really quite a good one. For just as erotic manuals presuppose a detached and intellectualised attitude towards sex which is as far removed from the Grand Passion as it is from the more relaxed felicities of married bliss, so Barthes's approach to literature is one that eschews both the enraptured forgetfulness of self in a powerful story and the interested amusement procured by good satire or clever comedy. What it puts in their place, according to the comparison at the beginning of *Le Plaisir du Texte*, is the very different delight of the libertine choosing the very moment of orgasm to cut the rope by which he is hanging himself. Elsewhere in the book, Barthes presents writing as an essentially Oedipal activity: one that involves making love to one's *langue maternelle*, taking it to pieces in the kind of joyous rape which James Joyce accomplished in *Finnegan's Wake*, and there can be few books on literature which present its pleasures in so consistently erotic a series of comparisons.

This cult of cruel and unusual ecstasies is nevertheless accompanied by an austere and suspicious attitude towards ordinary language which has strong analogies with the preoccupations of Antoine Roquentin, the hero of the novel which Sartre published in 1938 under the title of *La Nausée*. For just as Roquentin felt disgusted at the way all the words he has to use are shopsoiled through hanging about in other people's minds, so Barthes longs to strip language free of the thick layers of dead skin that centuries of usage have deposited upon it. His desire here seems akin to that of Mallarmé and T. S. Eliot to 'donner un sens plus pur aux mots de la tribu' ['purify the dialect of the tribe'], and there is clearly the same puritanical drive at work in *Le Plaisir du Texte* as there was in *Mythologies* or *Système de la Mode*.

There is also the same proselytising zeal to replace the old-fashioned view of language as an instrument of communication by the new, purified vision of language as the creator of its own reality, and even a New Testament implication that the new wine of semiosis, the creation of meaning, cannot be put into the empties left over from the outdated concept of mimesis, or imitation of reality.

III

The closing sentence of Camus's *Le Mythe de Sisyphe* invited the reader to imagine Sisyphus as happy. The consciousness which he had of the futility of his task heightened the pleasure he derived from his physical contact with the stone, while the sights and scents of his mountain each offered an infinitely rewarding world of enjoyment and contemplation. It is a vision which almost inevitably springs to mind when one considers both Barthes's ultimate, long-term aim and the way in which he has chosen to spend his life. For to attempt to destroy intellectual and cultural habits so deeply rooted as the belief in language as communication or the vision of literature as mimesis is a Sisyphean task which Barthes seems blissfully happy to have undertaken. No trace of romantic anguish or existentialist despair hangs about his elegant frame, and if he looks, as Roy McMullen remarked, like a deposed Bourbon monarch, there is no nostalgia for a lost or inaccessible kingdom. When, in 1974, he chaired a session at the First International Congress of Semiotics, he did so with 'suavity, wit and good sense', wearing a 'Mao-Nehru-Cardin jacket' as a consciously adopted sign of his political sympathies and concept of sartorial pleasure.[16] *Roland Barthes par Roland Barthes*, his last work to date, is shot through with visions of different types of happiness, from his list of favourite fruits to his discussion of friendship and from remarks about music to the notation of the pleasures of provincial life. Even the evocation of his rather sad childhood has an air of amused, interested acceptance about it. The book also contains some excellent passages about both orthodox and unorthodox sex, including a brilliant defence of prostitution. This is based, as Barthes observes, on a very honest contract which frees you from trying to imagine what the other person is thinking. You are thus not distracted from your own pleasure by any vain attempt to coincide with an entirely mythical vision.[17] Barthes also suggests that people always tend to underestimate the pleasure which perversions such as homosexuality or the smoking of hashish procure, and it is a mistake for his conservative critics to take his rejection of petty bourgeois concepts too much for granted. It does, after all, enable him to be very frank about himself in print.

The explanatory image which recurs throughout *Roland Barthes par Roland Barthes* is that of the vessel *Argos*, which retained its identity in spite of the fact that not a single one of the pieces composing it was the one originally put there when the ship was built. Its structure, however, had remained the same, and the example is a useful mnemonic device for starting a discussion on the structuralist approach which Barthes has done so much to take an integral part of the modern cultural scene. The results of trying to apply this way of thinking either to our personal experiences or to the books we read could also be salutary as well as strange. It is obviously good for us to realise that we tend to make new experiences and ideas fit into pre-existing patterns, structuring each new event to bring it into line with everything we have caused to happen to us before. But it is very difficult to dismiss as completely misguided the more orthodox view that the things happening to us do have a form and content of their own, and this example of how Barthes's ideas might work out in practice is almost an epitome of the intellectual problem which he presents. What he says is fascinating and challenging. It teaches us a new way of looking at our own experience. After a reading of Barthes, even the worst film or most nauseating advertisement becomes fascinating. We watch how the signs are manipulated, and rejoice in our ability to stand analytically aloof. But what he presents as the whole truth about the relationship between society and the communication codes it uses is rarely capable of completely replacing our existing concepts. This is equally true of his views on literature, where his perception that works of fiction are essentially verbal artefacts is an excellent antidote to the simplistic concept of 'a good book because true to life'. But this is not the only way in which we can usefully look at literature, or even the way which would—to use Barthes's own most recent criterion—give most people the greatest pleasure.

Barthes's ability to provoke his critics into such constant restatement of truisms is perhaps his most enviable talent as a writer. He makes us acutely conscious of what John Weightman, reviewing the English translation of *The Pleasure of the Text*, rather ironically called our 'benighted provincial rationalism',[18] and of our consequent inability ever really to know whether or not we have understood him well enough either to sympathise with what he is saying or to dismiss it as nonsense. But one of the most frequent reactions of both French and English critics to *Le Plaisir du Texte* was to make jokes about it, referring to Barthes as an 'obsédé textuel', or saying, as Paul Theroux did in the *New Statesman*, that he would sooner let Barthes get near his sister than his library,[19] and this tendency highlights a different aspect of Barthes's relationship with contemporary society. Because of the in-built pluralism which characterises Western democracy, we are capable of treating the revolutionary thinker in the one way really certain both to neutralise and to annoy him. We absorb what he has to say, use it to enrich our perception of the immensely complex nature of human experience, but never change our way of thinking in anything like the dramatic way that he demands. We take what he presents as a whole truth, destined in his view to change the world by the compelling logic of its argument, and turn it into a half-truth or quarter-truth which merely shifts the emphasis of our thinking without destroying the basic make-up of our mind. Avant-garde absurdist writers find themselves being offered the Nobel Prize, Marxist radicals are appointed to rich professorships or even richer pickings in the Polytechnics, the Surrealist movement reaches its logical apotheosis in *Monty Python's Flying Circus*, and somebody is probably even now looking at the commercial possibilities of rewriting the Japanese translation of a Balzac short story as a deliciously erotic ballet danced around an empty effigy of Michelet by seven self-consciously clad all-in wrestlers pursued by Racine's Agrippine with a carving knife. The smug ability of modern democratic society to absorb all the attacks delivered by left-wing intellectuals must surely constitute in their eyes its most infuriating characteristic, the final proof that it is, from a cultural standpoint, as structurally sound as the good ship *Argos*. What a pity the oil sheiks and trade unionists are not held off quite so easily.

10 Conclusion

In the article which he devoted in 1955 to Alain Robbe-Grillet's *Le Voyeur*, Barthes recalled how an anthropologist had once shown the same film on underwater fishing to a group of Congolese negroes and to a number of Belgian undergraduates. The Congolese, Barthes observed, gave a 'purely descriptive, precise and concrete account' of what they had seen without making anything up ['sans aucune fabulation']. The Belgians, in contrast, had no clear recollection of what they had seen, could remember few details accurately, made up stories to explain what they imagined they had seen, filled their account with literary effects and tried to bring back the feelings and emotions which the film had inspired in them.[1] The novels of Robbe-Grillet, Barthes proceeded to argue, were aimed precisely at curing us of this habit of distorting what we see by constantly interpreting it through our memories of what we have read, and the example which Barthes used in this essay to explain Robbe-Grillet's work might well provide a microcosm to illustrate the central ambition of his own. For in his most recent book of literary theory, *Le Plaisir du Texte*, he explains what he means by the new term *l'inter-texte* by coming back to what is basically the same idea. It is 'the impossibility of living outside the infinite text—whether this text be Proust or the daily newspaper or the television screen: the book creates the meaning, the meaning creates life'.[2] In Barthes's view, we are perpetually caught up, at every moment of our experience, by a mesh of words that prevents us from seeing what is really happening. Like the Belgian students—or like Don Quixote or Emma Bovary—we perpetually see life in terms of the books we have read, and have quite lost the ability to see physical objects as they actually are. In so far as it ties us down to a predigested version of the way somebody else first saw the world and expressed it for us, this habit prevents us from realising our full potential as free human beings. It is consequently—though here I am extrapolating from Barthes's work, not referring to any formal statement which he has made—the task of the person who writes either about literature or about language to make people conscious of the distortions created by the way verbal communication works. The missionary role thus entrusted to the linguist or literary critic constitutes the most important conclusion which Barthes has drawn from Saussure's insistence on the arbitrary nature of signs, and provides both the central theme linking the whole of his work together and his most significant contribution to the intellectual life of the mid to late twentieth-century. When in May 1970 he told an interviewer in *L'Express* that his ambition was to 'battre en brèche la naturalité du signe' ['attack and destroy the idea that signs are natural'],[3] he was justifying this way of looking at his work as the most fruitful approach that a beginner could adopt.

Such an account of Barthes's attitude towards language cannot, however, fail to remind his disciples and admirers of the anecdote about the Scotsman who sent his wife to church and asked her, on her return, to tell him about the sermon. 'It was about sin', she replied. 'Yes, but what did the Minister say?', he asked. 'He were agin it' was the response; and had the Minister been present he would have rightly raised his hands to Heaven at this reduction of his complex analysis of original sin, salvation by Grace, the impiety of modern thought, Where We Differ From Rome and the Nature of our Redemption to this one laconic utterance. For where in this vision of Barthes's work, the insider in semiology might ask, is the analysis of *écriture*, *signifiance* or *inter-textualité*? What becomes of the essential distinction between *plaisir* and *jouissance*, *dénotation* and *connotation* or *référent* and *signifié*? Where is the recognition that the technical concepts he has taken over from linguistics give Barthes's thinking on literature an entirely new dimension? For he is not, such an admirer might argue, just the latest in the long line of philosophers who, like Kant, have warned human beings against the danger of seeing the categories of their mind as the ultimate reality, or who, like the later Wittgenstein, have denounced the error of imagining that one form of language can reign supreme over all the others. He is an original thinker whose work can only be flattened to banality by these constant comparisons with established figures from the past.

There are several replies to these objections. If the husband had really been disappointed by his wife's account, the solution would still be in his own hands: he could go to church himself next time. Barthes himself is justifiably derisive, in *Sade, Fourier, Loyola*, at the expense of those critics who merely reproduce in an edulcorated form what the writer has already said perfectly adequately in his own words. The answer to what Barthes means by *ludisme*, *archi-vestème* or *uchronie* can be found in the text of *Système de la Mode*, just as the usefulness of the terms *syntagme*, *adéquation* or *pertinence* can be assessed only by reading the *Eléments de Sémiologie*. There is also a remark by André Gide which could justify the brevity and simplicity of the wife's reply. 'Je suis loin', he once said, 'd'abonder dans mon sens' ['I am far from enthusiastically espousing my own point of view'], and a refusal to plunge into the doctrine of the Atonement may well have reflected an uncertainty

on the Scottish housewife's part as to whether she really had understood everything the Minister had just said. This is very much my
position with regard to the more technical aspects of Barthes's work. I
think I have understood him in the terms set out in the book, but am
so little attached to my own account that anyone who writes to tell
me where I have gone wrong can count on the most enthusiastically
inquisitive reply. Stephen Heath describes S/Z as an attempt to
'pluraliser la critique, recueillir le pluriel du texte' ['pluralise criticism,
welcome the plural meanings of a text'],[4] and I am certainly enough
of a Barthesian to recognise that mine is only one of many different
accounts that can be given of his work. A critic who considered the
Eléments de Sémiologie rather than *Le monde où l'on catche* to be the best
expression of Barthes's attitude would probably come up with a very
different account of his principal preoccupations.

There is, of course, something rather odd about needing to hedge
one's account of a man frequently regarded as a literary critic by so
many caveats about the possibility that one may not have understood
him. It is hard to shake off the traditional view of the critic as someone who writes in order to enable other people to understand and
appreciate a literary text, and consequently difficult to find an ade-
quate reply to the Plain Man's objection that the critic should not add
to the existing difficulties of the text by writing in an opaque and
elusive style. But Barthes is more a philosopher of language than a
literary critic, and there is therefore some justification for his work
being so difficult to understand. I would nevertheless maintain that to
see him as a man determined to free people from preconceived ideas
by pointing carefully at the individual strands in the mesh of language
holding them captive is to look at his work from the most fruitful
point of view. He described himself, in *Roland Barthes par Roland Barthes*,
as a man who *sees* language,[5] and each one of his books can be read
as an attempt to make people conscious of how completely the way
we express ourselves conditions our vision of the world. *Le degré zéro
de l'écriture* denounces the illusion that any form of literary language
can be natural, and warns against the trap of assuming that because
an account of experience is immediately comprehensible, it is therefore
innocent of pre-conceived ideas. *Mythologies* is shot through with an
insistence on the need to avoid 'la naturalité du signe' by constantly
emphasising the artificial nature of all communication systems, while
Système de la Mode is dominated by the realisation that we can be
honest with our fellow human beings and ourselves only by seeing the
clothes we wear as consciously expressing the deliberate choice which
we make of how we would like other people to see us. *Sade, Fourier,
Loyola* carries Barthes's position in *Le degré zéro*, *Mythologies* and S/Z
to its logical conclusion by recognising that the role of language is to
enable the writer to create his own autonomous world, while *Le*

Plaisir du Texte uses the neologism *signifiance* to embody the notion that it is only when we have freed ourselves of the illusion that words reflect reality—or even, perhaps, that there is a reality to be reflected—that we shall begin to see language as creating our awareness of meaning by the physical impact which it makes upon our senses.

In this reading of his work, Barthes's ideas evolve only by becoming a more self-confident and positive expression of the same basic attitude, and there is an interesting illustration of this in his ideas on music. In November 1956, in an article subsequently republished in *Mythologies*, he criticised Gérard Souzay for constantly singing in a way that emphasised the meaning of the words, and in 1967 he implied that the same defects of explanatory dramatisation and exaggeration recurred in Fischer-Dieskau. In 1972, on the other hand, he showed what kind of singing he preferred by praising the much older singer Panzera for enabling his audiences to hear 'le grain de la voix' ['the texture of his voice'], and there is an immediate parallel with one of the most eloquent pages in *Le Plaisir du Texte*. Thus he writes there that:

Il suffit en effet que le cinéma prenne *de très près* le son de la parole (c'est en somme la définition généralisée du 'grain' de l'écriture) et fasse entendre dans leur matérialité, dans leur sensualité, le souffle, la rocaille, la pulpe des lèvres, toute une présence du museau humain (que la voix, que l'écriture soient fraîches, souples, lubrifiées, finement granuleuses et vibrantes comme le museau d'un animal, pour qu'il réussisse à déporter le signifié très loin et à jeter, pour ainsi dire, le corps anonyme de l'acteur dans mon oreille: ça granule, ça grésille, ça caresse, ça rape, ça coupe: ça jouit.
[In fact, it suffices that the cinema capture the sound of speech *close up* (this is, in fact, the generalised definition of the 'grain' of writing) and make us hear in their materiality, their sensuality, the breath, the gutturals, the fleshiness of the lips, a whole presence of the human muzzle (that the voice, that writing, be as fresh, supple, lubricated, delicately granular and vibrant as an animal's muzzle), to succeed in shifting the signified a great distance and in throwing, so to speak, the anonymous body of the actor into my ear: it granulates, it crackles, it caresses, it grates, it cuts, it comes: that is bliss.]

and it is fascinating to see how the text on Panzera develops the same ideas in a different context. For whereas Fischer-Dieskau never allows us, according to Barthes, to hear 'the tongue, the glottis, the teeth, the inner lining of the mouth, or the nose', Panzera deliberately avoided an 'expressive' way of singing in order to bring out, in contrast, the physical working of language, the 'very friction of the music'. It is for this reason, Barthes argues, that Panzera would not have enjoyed the same kind of success which, in our own day, uses a 'positive censorship' to make it impossible for anyone who does not happen to like Fischer-Dieskau to enjoy recordings of Schubert. Panzera lived before what Barthes called 'le micro-sillon de masse' (mass-produced LPs for everyone) which has enabled Fischer-Dieskau to monopolise the market. But he would not, in any case, have lent himself to the essentially petty-bourgeois art which smothers the physical 'significance' beneath the intellectualised 'signification'.[6] He delighted in words and music for their physical texture, not for the expression which they could give to the ideas or feelings supposedly lying behind them, and the text entitled *Le grain de la voix* again emphasises what is perhaps Barthes's most fundamental recommendation. Since, in his view, language is going to stand in our way in any contact which we try to make with the real world, we might just as well enjoy every detail of the obstacle. Far from worrying because we cannot break through the mesh surrounding us, we should rejoice in the pleasure which an intense contemplation of its texture can procure us.

The idea of pleasure is never wholly absent from Barthes's work and can also be seen as one of its unifying themes. In the seminal essay on all-in wrestling, he appreciates the way in which 'un catcheur du caractère arrogant et ridicule, . . . Armand Mazaud, met toujours la salle en joie par la rigueur mathématique de ses transcriptions' ['a wrestler of an arrogant and ridiculous character, . . . Armand Mazaud, always delights the audience by the mathematical rigour of his transcriptions'].[7] What matters, for Barthes, is the detail of the gestures, not the final outcome of the contest. Since the result has in any case been fixed in advance, the real pleasure for the spectator lies in consciously witnessing how it all appears to be happening, and here again there is more of an intensification of Barthes's ideas than any fundamental change as he moves from *Le monde où l'on catche* to *Sade, Fourier, Loyola* or *Le Plaisir du Texte*. What he appreciates in Fourier is 'le détail adorable',[8] and one of the passages which he quotes to illustrate the kind of pleasure that the text can give us is the suggestion by Leibnitz that pocket watches 'marquaient les heures par une certaine faculté *horodéictique*, sans avoir besoin de roues, ou comme si les moulins brisaient les grains par une certaine qualité *fractive*, sans avoir besoin de rien qui ressemblât aux meules' ['told time by means of a certain *horodeictic* faculty, without requiring springs, or as though mills ground grain by means of a *fractive* quality, without requiring anything of the order of millstones'].[9] There is thus a very positive counterpart to the intense mistrust of language which informs *Mythologies*, *S/Z* or *Système de la Mode* and which gives Barthes's work the essential unity which I spoke of earlier: a delight in language for its own sake. Once the illusion that words might mean something has been cast away, Barthes revels in their sound and shape. In *Michelet par lui-même* and *Sur Racine*, the two major books in which he is not primarily concerned with how language itself and the literary use of language in particular distort our vision of reality, it is the texture of Michelet's prose and the sensual power of Racine's language which attract Barthes's attention and inspire some of the best prose that he himself has written. Indeed, the opening passage of *Sur Racine*:

> ... les grands tableaux raciniens présentent toujours ce grand combat mythique (et théâtral) de l'ombre et de la lumière: d'un côté, la nuit, les ombres, les cendres, les larmes, le sommeil, le silence, la douceur timide, la présence continue; de l'autre, tous les objets de la stridence: les armes, les aigles, les faisceaux, les flambeaux, les étendards, les cris, les vêtements éclatants, le lin, la pourpre, l'or, l'acier, le bûcher, les flammes, le sang.
> [... the great Racinian pictures always present this vast mythical (and theatrical) conflict between light and shade: on the one hand, night, shadows, ashes, tears, sleep, silence, gentle shyness, continual presence; on the other all is stridency: weapons, eagles, fasces, torches, shouts, fine raiment, linen, purple, gold, steel, funeral pyres, flames, blood.][10]

is itself an excellent illustration of what language used for its own sake can be. If, as Barthes himself claims, the experience of *seeing* language is an illness from which he suffers, one hopes there is no cure. Its side-effects give too much pleasure to his readers as well as to himself.

It is in this hedonistic approach both to language itself and to everyday experience that Barthes is most attractive, both as a writer and as a man. The endearing honesty about sexual activities which led him, in *Roland Barthes par Roland Barthes*, to enumerate the advantages of prostitution, also inspires the remark in *Sade, Fourier, Loyola*, that the visitor to a foreign country who goes in search of his sexual prey (*le dragueur*) has a more open attitude to experience than the tourist. Because the latter is 'tout engoncé dans des stéréotypes de monuments' ['stiffly encased in the obligatory tourist round'], he never escapes from the ready-made set of ideas which petit-bourgeois culture has imposed upon him,[11] and it is excellent that Barthes should seek, through sex and writing, to make people more intensely aware of the extensive and peculiar experiences available to them. Barthes is also, in *Sade, Fourier, Loyola*, very good on money. He underlines the hypocrisy with which most philosophers have denounced money in the past—again unconsciously emphasising his similarity to the Orwell of *Keep the Aspidistra Flying*—and points out how right Fourier is to insist that money is an indispensable element in any combination of factors leading to happiness. Both Barthes and Fourier here show an admirable ability to go against the *Doxa* of the left—Marxists, observes Barthes, agree with Freudians and Christians in seeing money as a 'damned, fetishistic, excremental commodity'[12]—and there is no doubt that

Barthes is much more satisfying a writer when taken at his own valuation as a guide to the erotic zones of inter-textuality than when seen as a literary critic. Susan Sontag is indeed right to insist that it is 'an obvious injustice' to cast him in such a role, and Barthes himself argues both in *Critique et Vérité* and in *Le Plaisir du Texte* that because literary criticism in the past has been so concerned with passing judgements and not with formulating delights, it is not possible for any modern writer who respects the intellectual freedom of his readers to admit to being a critic.[13]

In a way, of course, Barthes is being over-modest in also refusing to be associated with the other traditional function of the critic: that of opening people's eyes to books and writers they might not otherwise appreciate. Indeed, the American critic Robert Alter went so far as to claim that Barthes was even more interesting as a critic than the creative writers whom he chose to discuss, and wrote in *Tri-Quarterly* that 'None of Robbe-Grillet's novels really equals in fascination Roland Barthes's brilliant descriptions of them.'[14] It is nevertheless not only his virtues which make it difficult to describe Barthes as a critic. For although Susan Sontag may be right in maintaining that 'only if the ideal of criticism is enlarged to take in a wide variety of discourse, both theoretical and descriptive, about culture, language and contemporary consciousness, can Barthes be plausibly called a critic',[15] there are sometimes less flattering reasons why one would hesitate to discuss him in the terms applicable to an Arnold, a Leavis, a Trilling, an I. A. Richards or an Empson.

Barthes does, of course, make a genuinely original contribution to literary discourse by the implications which he sees in the fact that there is no necessary connection between the word 'rose' and the flower it signifies. His ambition to 'battre en brèche la naturalité du signe' ['attack and destroy the idea that signs are natural'] is both laudable and intelligible, and his application of it to the novel is a valuable step in clear thinking about how language functions in a literary context. Frederic Raphael expressed the same notion from the other side when he said that he realised, as a working novelist, that what you say cannot finally be distinguished from the way you say it,[16] and his remark underlines how foolish it would be to think, for example, that Pickwick or Emma Bovary would not change as characters if their adventures were described in different language. The whole difference between fiction and reality lies in the fact that since characters in fiction exist only by virtue of the black marks on white paper which bring them to life in the reader's imagination, there is no possibility of going behind the pages of the book to check whether the author has described them correctly or not. Once the sign has changed, the thing it represents changes as well. Since there never was a real Emma Bovary, the character in Flaubert's novel can perfectly well have brown eyes, blue eyes or black eyes according to the whim of her creator. We may, of course, when the colour of Emma's eyes changes in this way from one chapter to the next, fault the novelist for an inconsistency in the presentation of his imaginary universe.[17] But what we cannot do is say that since the 'real' Emma had blue eyes, the linguistic sign 'blue' is the only appropriate one to describe them.

It is nevertheless more difficult, both on logical and on empirical grounds, to follow Barthes in the next step which he takes in applying the idea of the arbitrary nature of signs to literature. For while there is no difficulty in using it to reinforce one's rejection of the naïve notion that *Madame Bovary* is a good novel because it tells the literal truth about a particular person, it is quite another thing to argue, as Barthes does in *S/Z*, that there is never any 'content' whatsoever in works of art. Flaubert may not be the master of representational art that some of his theories suggest and that many of his nineteenth-century admirers considered him to be. But neither is *Madame Bovary* the work he evoked when he gave free reign to the non-representational side of his literary personality and talked about his desire to write:

> un livre sur rien, un livre sans attache extérieure, qui se tiendrait lui-même par la force interne de son style, comme la terre sans être soutenue se tient en l'air, un livre qui n'aurait presque pas de sujet, ou du moins où le sujet serait presque invisible, si cela se peut.
> [a book about nothing, a book with no external links, which would stand up by itself through the inner force of its style, as the earth hangs with no support in the air, a book almost without a subject, or in which the subject would be almost invisible, if such a thing be possible.][18]

It is clearly 'about' a large number of things—the status of women in nineteenth-century France, the relationship between fiction and reality, the dullness of provincial life, the dissemination of Voltairean scepticism among the half-educated, the physical appearance of the Normandy countryside—and one of its many virtues lies in the way it enables the reader to participate, through an imaginative reading of the text, in experiences which can by definition never be his own. There is certainly a place for non-representational art of the type that Barthes admires in Robbe-Grillet's *Le Voyeur* or Philippe Soller's *Le Parc*, and nobody would nowadays contend that *Madame Bovary* was a real story told in the only possible way dictated by a pre-existent subject-matter. But to deny the interest and validity of all attempts at representational art, as Barthes does when he writes that realism 'consists not of copying reality but of copying a painted copy of reality',[19] is to throw out the baby of Flaubert's complex literary achievement with the bathwater of late nineteenth-century theories about the inevitability of realism.

There are naturally passages in Barthes's work that show a more subtle awareness of how complex a phenomenon literature is and how difficult it is to define. Thus when he stated, in *Essais Critiques* in 1964, that literature inevitably had an 'unrealistic status' ['un statut fatalement irréaliste'][20] because it could evoke reality only through the intermediate stage of language, he did chose a form of words which is less open to the criticism that he makes sweeping statements supported by inadequate evidence. Since, he argued, language has only an institutional and not a natural relationship with things as they are, it can never have the more direct access to reality enjoyed by the visual arts. Whereas the blue on the canvas can make us immediately think of the blue of the sky, literature can work only because of the more complex and entirely arbitrary link between the word 'blue' and the blue sky. Barthes made a similar point in another of the *Essais Critiques* when he said that literature is 'condemned to mediation, that is to say to telling lies'.[21] Balzac, he explained, was able to describe the society of his time with the realism that Marx so much admired only because he was looking at it through the distorting glass of his Monarchist, Catholic philosophy. It is precisely, argues Barthes, because modern realists try to describe the social world exactly as it is and in the most 'natural' way possible that social realism produces so many bad novels.

This indirect recognition that W. H. Auden was right when he wrote that the 'truest poetry is the most feigning'[22] is one of the most interesting themes running through the *Essais Critiques*. It is in this book that Barthes most obviously struggles with language to bring out the extreme oddness of the phènomenon whereby the twenty-six letters of the alphabet can be combined in an infinite number of ways to make us believe in worlds as different as those of Barchester, Baker Street, or the Bordeaux of François Mauriac. He does not then always give his sentences the absolutist quality which makes an English empiricist's hackles rise so abruptly as the statement in *S/Z* that 'speech has no responsibility towards reality' ['le discours n'a aucune responsabilité envers le réel'],[23] and he consequently comes closer to making us more conscious of one of the central paradoxes of the novel: that although there never was a 'real' Bernard Desqueyroux that Mauriac copied, it is Mauriac's knowledge of the Bordeaux area that enabled him to create, in Bernard, a far truer incarnation of a *bourgeois bordelais* than one could ever hope to find in real life. For it is all very well for Barthes to argue, as he does both in *S/Z* and in *Sade, Fourier, Loyola*, that nobody could actually re-enact every detail in all the scenes in a supposedly realistic novel. The fact remains that some writers have written great books by basing themselves at least in part on the world around them. André Malraux may have been quite right to say that one becomes an artist in the first instance by looking not at the outside world but at the work of other artists. But no artist, and especially no novelist, could keep his readers very long if he did not take an occasional look at what was happening around him and try to write down something of what he saw.

It is one of the more embarrassing peculiarities of Barthes's work that he should inspire such laboured restatements of the obvious, and it is partly for this reason that the refusal to call him a critic is not always entirely a compliment. For it is surely—to invoke a central *Doxa* of English literary thinking—an openness to as many different kinds of literary experience as possible that characterises the good literary critic and is essential to the great one. One might, of course, explain this aspect of his work by biographical considerations. Barthes constantly evokes, in the remarks which he makes about contemporary French society and the intellectual atmosphere in which he is obliged to live, the vision of a vast conspiracy aimed at perpetuating a whole series of oppressive myths against which he is fighting. The French bourgeoisie, if one is to believe in what he says about it, still uses language to perpetuate its domination over other classes, still maintains a strict hierarchy of linguistic usage to match the social hierarchy which it imposes upon other people, severely censures both the frivolous use of language and any cult of physical pleasure, is intensely suspicious of any intellectual activity—'on sait qu'en France l'art est suspect, s'il pense'[24]—and refuses to entertain the possibility that the link between the thing said and the word which says it is anything but wholly natural. It is perhaps this feeling which he has of being persecuted that explains why Barthes should himself adopt so intolerant a stance as a means of defending himself against his attackers, and there is again, for the English reader, a curious biographical similarity to F. R. Leavis. Yet while both men have the same sense of being cold-shouldered by the academic establishment of their day, there is much less justification for Barthes to see himself as a martyr in the cause of intellectual progress. He has not done all that badly and has in fact, as John Weightman predicted, ended up as a member of the *Collège de France*—'than which there is no higher consecration here below'.[25] The intolerant strain that is often apparent in Barthes's attitude towards literature cannot therefore be explained away as a justified riposte to genuine oppression, and is, to the conservative foreign observer, a serious flaw in his work. This is even more the case when it is accompanied by the second reason for which one would hesitate to flatter Barthes by calling him a critic: an apparent inability to distinguish between the prescriptive and the descriptive use of language.

Thus he frequently presents, as statements about writers or about literature in general, ideas which are fascinating when read as suggestions as to how a new type of literature might develop or as descriptions of certain books which exemplify this development, but which are patently absurd when read in the highly general form that he gives them. For example, he writes in the essay *Ecrivains et Ecrivants*, first published in 1960 and reprinted in *Essais Critiques* in 1964, that since 'écrire est un verbe intransitif' ['writing is an intransitive verb'], 'la littérature est toujours irréaliste' ['literature is always unrealistic'],[26] and there is obviously a way in which this statement is a valuable antidote to the naïve concept of realism which presents books as photocopies of reality. Even if it were possible for a writer to be a camera, the angle from which he took his shots would still mean that he was composing a picture rather than reproducing the world absolutely as it is. But since there is no indication that Barthes is writing metaphorically rather than literally, the other implications of his statement are decidedly odd. The 'toujours' can only mean that Thomas Hardy tells us nothing about rural England before the impact of the industrial revolution, that Jane Austen's novels have no interest as a portrait of the English gentry at the time of the Napoleonic wars, or that the characters in *War and Peace* bear no resemblance to early nineteenth-century Russian aristocrats. And when Barthes also declares, in *Le Plaisir du Texte*, 'Tout écrivain dira donc: *fou ne puis, sain ne daigne, névrosé je suis*' ['Any writer will thus say: I cannot be mad, I deign not to be sane, I am neurotic'],[27] he reacts even more like a man who is putting Humpty-Dumpty's advice about language quite seriously into practice. Words do mean, for him, exactly what he wants them to mean, neither more nor less, and this is again the case when he proclaims, in *Sade, Fourier, Loyola*, that ' "poetry", which is the very language of transgression against language, thus always calls into question the very nature of things' ['est toujours contestataire']. All that this purely private use of language tells us is that words such as 'writer' or 'poetry' are used in a very odd way by certain modern French literary intellectuals and have no possible application outside the Left Bank.

Barthes is nevertheless writing in a well-established French rhetorical tradition whereby ideas are stated in what is sometimes rather an exaggerated form in order to produce more of an effect. Thus at this end of his long analysis, in *Les Mots et les Choses*, of how the relationship between language and the world has evolved since the Middle Ages, Michel Foucault makes the statement I have already quoted in my discussion of *Sur Racine*: 'L'homme est une invention dont l'archéologie de notre pensée montre aisément la date récente; et peut-être la fin prochaine' ['Man is an invention which the archaeology of our thought can easily show as having come to birth fairly recently: and which may well soon disappear']. It is a remark which led R. D. Laing to state that: 'When Foucault in one of his books said that man as a historical subject is dead, his sentence reverberated round the European intellectual scene with something of the same resonance as Nietzsche's statement that God is dead';[28] and the phrase certainly has a fairly dramatic ring to it. It does not, however, have quite the literal meaning which someone who thought that words meant what they said might give it: that the recognition of *Homo Sapiens* as a distinct biological species is a relatively recent intellectual event, and that human beings will soon cease to be distinguishable from other animals. All Foucault is saying, if one places the sentence in the context of his general argument, is that while in the last three hundred years most literate Europeans have had a fairly clear idea of what human beings were like, how their minds worked and what they ought to try to become, we can now see that this consensus no longer exists in quite the same form. What the sentence loses in dramatic effect it gains in verifiability, and there is also a sense in which it is equally useful to translate Barthes's highly autocratic statement, at the beginning of *S/Z*, that 'il y a d'un côte ce qu'il est possible d'écrire et de l'autre ce qu'il n'est plus possible d'écrire' ['on the one hand, there is what it is possible to write and, on the other, what it is no longer possible to write'][29] in a similar way. This gives something like:

> There are some books from the past which I like to talk about because they have points in common with those I find satisfying nowadays; but, in contrast, there are other books which, for aesthetic reasons which I shall now explain, seem so old-fashioned that they no longer inspire me with the desire to write about them, and do not, in my view, offer useful examples for modern writers to follow.

Strange though such 'translations' of Barthes's remarks into the longer sentences and flatter prose favoured by British twentieth-century linguistic philosophers may appear, they in fact present his work in a much less hostile way than the alternative: asking how statements about poetry being 'toujours contestataire' could possibly apply to English poets such as John Betjeman or Philip Larkin.*

* (*a*) Statements about literature are verifiable only by reference to existing literary works.

(*b*) Betjeman and Larkin are both poets whose work is recognised and admired by the majority of people who read and enjoy poetry.

(*c*) Although both of them criticise certain important aspects of modern society, neither writes poetry which is *contestataire* in the sense of calling the world in general or society as a whole into question.

(*d*) It is therefore inaccurate and misleading to say that poetry is always *contestataire*. Some of it is, and Barthes has every right to admire poets who, like Rimbaud, express feelings of revolt. But to state his own tastes in this absolute form is to reveal either extreme ignorance, or intense narrow-mindedness, or both.

Indeed, in so far as Barthes's own ambition in the rest of his work can so often be seen as that of trying to 'purify the dialect of the tribe' by inviting his readers to become aware of the prison in which certain forms of language have enclosed them, it might even be a rather Barthesian exercise to see how his views on literature do appear when expressed in a language different from his own. On the other hand, however, since it implies both that language is a tool for expressing ideas and that ideas remain basically the same whatever the language chosen to express them may be, such an exercise could be seen as a complete denial of everything Barthes stands for. One of the clearest statements of his position in this respect is in a reply which he made in March 1957 to a survey organised by the literary newspaper *Arts* on the question of why Joseph Conrad had chosen to write in English rather than in Polish. It was not, said Barthes, because English was a better medium than Polish for writing about the sea. Indeed, the very act of asking such a question showed a fundamental misunderstanding of the very nature of language. This is not an 'instrument that one chooses as one might choose a weapon in an armoury or a monkey wrench from a tool kit'.[30] Language, and particularly the language used by an imaginative writer, is 'a structure and a mode of awareness' ['une structure et une conscience']. The decision to write in one language rather than another cannot be separated from the choice which one has made of one's whole identity as a person, and from one's fundamental attitude towards experience. When Conrad decided to write in English rather than in Polish, he was acting in accordance with a deeper, existential preference which he had already expressed for what Barthes calls *la britannité* over what one would, in a comparable neologism, have to call *la polonnité*. It follows from this that any attempt to 'say what Barthes really means in your own words' is by very definition a betrayal of his whole philosophy of language. It is, to revert to the story about the churchgoing Scottish housewife and her heathen if inquisitive husband, the equivalent of trying to talk about St Paul while eschewing all use of terms such as 'God', 'grace', 'sin', 'salvation' or 'spirit'. The temptation nevertheless exists, and Barthes's own *francité* is too intriguing a challenge to the intellectual imperialism of English empiricism to be seriously resisted. It may well be, to revert for one last time to *Le monde où l'on catche*, as misguided an exercise as trying to explain what really happens when the Black Mask meets the Mad Monk. But at least it is not so disappointing an experience as seeing the Mad Monk eventually defeated and forced to remove his cowl. For what we see then is merely an ape-like countenance indistinguishable from the one that the audience has already beheld glowering above the massive shoulders of his opponent. Barthes, in contrast, is still sufficiently interesting as what he himself would call an *écrivant*—someone who does use language instrumentally—for the way he thinks to be discussed in isolation from the way he writes. Although he may be most successful when writing as an *écrivain*, giving full rein to his zest for language by evoking rather than communicating the world view of the designer Erté or the pleasures of the table enumerated in Brillat-Savarin, he cannot prevent his basic attitude from being sufficiently coherent to be meaningfully discussed with reference to another cultural tradition.

Indeed, the very way in which he chooses to write is a means of ensuring that this will happen. Like Michel Foucault, Jacques Derrida, Julia Kristeva or Jacques Lacan, he deliberately adopts a style of writing which is not immediately comprehensible, and does so precisely in order to make his reader think things out for himself. This is not merely a condescendingly charitable explanation of his often very opaque prose. Instant accessibility is, in his view, a dangerous trick, and Stephen Heath[31] quotes a very characteristic passage from the 1973 text *Aujourd'hui, Michelet* to illustrate this idea. The concept of clarity [clarté], writes Barthes, can exist only within 'a classical conception of the sign, with the *signifiant* on one side, and the *référent* on the other, the first in the service of the second'. The whole of Barthes's career so far has been devoted to overthrowing this idea and replacing it with a vision of language in which man, recognising that he lives, moves and has his being in and through words, can at last begin to enjoy the experience for its own sake.

Postscript

In April 1977, Barthes published his fourteenth book: *Fragments d'un discours amoureux*. Like his twelfth one, *Le Plaisir du Texte*, it consists of a series of extracts arranged in alphabetical order,[1] and like all the others it deals with the problem of language and communication. Unlike his previous books, however, *Fragments d'un discours amoureux* has its starting point not in literature, mass culture, fashion or foreign travel, but in personal relationships. In talking about love—a subject which, Barthes argues, is neglected in our current obsession with sex—it explores what at first might appear to be a paradox: that the person who loves—*l'amoureux* —is essentially passive. Although he may take the initiative in pursuing his beloved, he does so in order that he himself may be recognised and loved. 'Un homme n'est pas féminisé parce qu'il est inverti', writes

Barthes at the very beginning of the book,[2] 'mais parce qu'il est amoureux' ['A man is not feminised because he is a homosexual, but because he is in love']. This passivity is most marked when we suffer from the loved one's absence, and Barthes is attractively open about the personal experience which led him to the recognition of the ideas exposed and analysed in *Fragments d'un discours amoureux*. As a child, he explains, he had not learned the adult art of temporarily forgetting the loved one when he or she is not there. When his mother went out to work, a long way from home, he lived through 'interminable, abandoned days'. In the evening, when she was due to return, he would go and wait for her at the *U bis* bus stop at Sèvres-Babylone. 'The buses went past,' he writes, 'one after another. She was in none of them.'[3]

The idea that our aim in loving is to be loved ourselves is not, of course, a new one either in other people's experience or in French or English literature. Sartre's analysis of our relationship with other people in *L'Etre et le Néant* centres around the view that I am always trying to make the other person think of me in a particular way. For, argues Sartre, if The Other can be made to 'consecrate me with his glance', I can escape temporarily from the uncertainty about my own identity which is normally inseparable from my self-awareness. If I can make the other person love me, then I can bask in the sunlight of his gaze, reassured both about what I am and about my right to be it. In *September 1st, 1939*, W. H. Auden declared that

> What mad Nijinsky wrote
> About Diaghilev
> Is true of the human heart;
> For the error bred in the bone
> Of each woman and each man
> Craves what it cannot have,
> Not universal love
> But to be loved alone

and several of Barthes's analyses evoke a similarly impossible but nevertheless universal desire. What we want, he argues, is to have the loved one concerned exclusively with us, to be looked at, listened to and understood as if we and only we existed.[4] Since Rimbaud, claims Barthes, literary madness has been held to lie in the phrase 'Je est un autre', and madness in an experience of depersonalisation. But what Barthes in love realises is that, on the contrary, madness is something quite different: it is the impossibility of escaping from oneself. I realise, when I love, that I have been sentenced to be what I am. I can come to terms with this only if the person I love will accept and love me as I am for myself.[5]

At an earlier period of French literature, Barthes's intuition about the fundamental but conventionally unavowable ambition which makes us 'fall in love' would have been expressed in poetry or fiction. *Fragments d'un discours amoureux* is full of the unashamedly romantic longings which have, in the past, been the traditional subject matter for lyric poetry, and also contains a considerable amount of what one is initially tempted to call 'psychological analysis'. This led Hector Bianciotti, reviewing the book in *Le Nouvel Observateur*,[6] to go so far as to describe it as the 'photographic negative' of a novel which Barthes's concept of literature forbad him to write, and a number of passages do in fact evoke the maxims, portraits and attempts to distinguish between different states of mind which eventually gave rise, in the seventeenth century, to the tradition of psychological analysis that once characterised French literature. The general tone of *Fragments d'un discours amoureux* also seems to indicate that Barthes's work is now moving away from the approach to experience represented by *Sur Racine*, *S/Z*, or *Sade, Fourier, Loyola*, and back to a more human and humane tradition. It is becoming much less strident and intellectual, much less concerned to prove a thesis, much less obviously the product of the French Left Wing. But Barthes is still too closely wedded to the aesthetic of *Tel Quel*—the collection in which the book is published—to agree to tell a story or create characters. The fragments are arranged in alphabetical order, he explains, precisely in order to discourage what he calls 'la tentation du sens' ['the temptation to find a meaning'], and the book is very much a 'Do it yourself' kit for the understanding and appreciation of human emotions. Far from imprisoning the reader in what Barthes would regard as the established notions inseparable from conventional fiction, it both obliges and enables him to make up his own picture of how he personally feels and thinks. It is, as Barthes's and Sartre's theory of literature requires, a homage to the reader's emotional and intellectual freedom.

In this respect, of course, it also fits very neatly into the aesthetic put forward in *Le Plaisir du Texte*. Barthes suggested there that we never read any work of fiction with equal attention to every page, and he describes elsewhere how he himself reads *A la recherche du temps perdu* not as a continuous narrative but sometimes on the Albertine code and sometimes on the code for Charlus.[7] This is very much the way to read *Fragments d'un discours amoureux*. One can choose to follow out the references to *Werther* or to Plato's *Symposium*. One can decide to note how frequently Barthes goes back to the child's relationship with its mother as providing the starting point and paradigm case for all forms of emotional attachment. Alternatively, one can trace how Barthes's obsession with language recurs in his analysis of the way in which the desire for love embodies the longing to be understood in what I say as well as in what I am. Or again, one can recognise some familiar friends in his gallocentricity and apparently permanent vision of contemporary French society as stifling and intolerant. For he claims at one point that none of the 'langages reçus' [received languages] allows love anything but a 'devalued place', and he presents these languages as only three in number: the Christian, the psycho-analytic and the Marxist. The first, he maintains, if it still exists, exhorts the lover to repress or sublimate his language and feelings. The second 'l'engage à faire le deuil de son Imaginaire' ['urges him to give up his imaginary world'], while Marxist speech says nothing.[8]

It would nevertheless be unfair and unrewarding to dwell on the evidence which *Fragments d'un discours amoureux* thus offers for the continued existence of Barthes's persecution complex. To do so would lead one to neglect the way in which he succeeds in putting into practice a much more generous theory of writing than is suggested in any of his earlier work and which he expressed, after the book had been published, in a review of Jean Daniel's collection of childhood reminiscences, *Le Refuge et la Source*.[9] What characterises a human being, he wrote—'ce qui fait l'homme'—is the fact of having had a childhood. Not, he adds, a childhood as it is occasionally lived in practice—as Barthes confesses his own to have been—with long stretches of boredom, but childhood as a period of time in which 'Je suis encore proche de la mère et que j'ai la vie éternelle devant moi—autrement dit, je suis immortel' ['I am still close to the mother and have eternal life before me—in other words, I am immortal']. Such a stage in our life, he writes, can be rediscovered only through the verbal notation of direct physical memories, and he continues

il n'y a pas d'écriture sans une décision de générosité à l'égard du monde. Il existe une éthique de l'écriture (j'appelle ainsi l'ensemble des valeurs fines qui donnent envie et raison de vivre); ou mieux: l'écriture est d'emblée un acte éthique: l'écriture, c'est un peu, à chaque fois, une 'crise de bonté'. Cette bonté, bien entendu, l'écriture ne l'énonce jamais; c'est lorsque nous avons fini le texte, c'est alors seulement que nous faisons une sorte de total indéfini de ce que nous avons lu, et que nous nous sentons 'bien'.

[there can be no writing without a decision to be generous towards the world. There is an ethic to writing (this is what I call the set of delicate values which make us want to live and give us reason for living); or better still: writing is from the very outset an ethical act: every time you write, it is as though you were going through a 'crisis of goodness' towards the world. This goodness, of course, is not something which writing openly states; it is when we finish a text, and only then, that we make up a kind of indefinite total of what we have read, and that we 'feel good'.][10]

This remarkably frank and almost sentimental attitude towards

writing also has the advantage of evoking a solution to the problem
which Barthes discussed in his inaugural lecture at the *Collège de France*
in January 1977: how can the person who does not wish to dominate
his fellows escape from the fact that language is power and the very
act of speaking an involuntary move to imprison other people in the
network of the words we utter? For there is normally, Barthes argues
in *Fragments d'un discours amoureux*, 'no benevolence in the act of writing'.
What it contains is a 'terror' which 'suffocates the other person'. Far
from seeing a book dedicated to him as a gift, the recipient reads it as
'an assertion of mastery, of power, of delight, of solitude'. The only way
to escape the 'cruel paradox of a dedication'—'At all costs, I want to
give you what stifles you'—is to weave the name and personality of the
loved one into the very texture of the work. The other person then takes
on a new power of her or his own—rather as Elizabeth Barrett Browning
does in *One Word More**—and escapes from the tyranny that normally
characterises the relationship between the speaker and the person
spoken to.[11] Running through the whole of *Fragments d'un discours
amoureux* is a concern to free other people from being the object of our
discourse. It is a concern that was not always so visible in Barthes's
earlier work, and which more than makes up for the accusations of
sentimentality which *la critique parlée* addressed to Barthes when the book
was first published.

If such criticisms were mentioned in print, it was to be immediately
rebutted; and one of the great virtues of *Fragments d'un discours amoureux*
—for the middle-class Puritan, at any rate—lies in the fact that Barthes
scrupulously avoids any evocation of the sexual aspects of love. He
concentrates instead, as he puts it in one of his better puns, on those
physical contacts which, like holding hands, are 'une fête, non des sens,
mais du sens' ['a feast, not of the senses, but of meaning']. It is because
a loving relationship with another person is above all else the means
whereby we feel ourselves to be at home and understood in the universe
that language is such a central part of it. 'Depuis que l'homme existe,
ça ne cesse de parler'[12] writes Barthes towards the end of the book, and it
is only through language that I can, according to *Fragments d'un discours
amoureux*, satisfy the innermost desire which is common to all people:
that of being told, by someone I love, what I am truly worth. For most
of the time, of course, the reassurance that I do have value in the eyes
of the person I love escapes me. Indeed, I must often suffer what Barthes
brilliantly analyses as the ultimate relegation to meaninglessness which
occurs when the loved one refuses even to reply to my question. It can
also happen that I have to undergo the comparable torment of being

* Here they are, my fifty men and women
  Naming me the fifty poems finished!
  Take them, Love, the book and me together:
  Where the heart lies, let the brain lie also.

'aligné au rang des fâcheux: ceux qui pèsent, gênent, empiètent, compliquent, demandent, intimident (ou, tout simplement; ceux qui parlent)' ['classed as a bore: someone who is in the way, embarrassing, intrusive, asking for something, intimidating (or, more simply, someone who talks)'],[13] and it is in passages like this, which are numerous in *Fragments d'un discours amoureux*, that there is, perhaps for the first time in Barthes's career as a writer, a perfect and deliberate alliance, both for himself and his readers, between heart and head. He uses the language which has always obsessed him and which, as he says, he has always *seen*, to understand his own emotions and to offer his readers the same opportunity to understand theirs. And it does indeed happen, as one reads *Fragments d'un discours amoureux*, that the words which often come most spontaneously to mind are those which Montaigne used to justify his somewhat different and rather more urbane essays in introspection: 'Chaque homme porte la forme entière de l'humaine condition' ['Each man carries within himself the entire form of the human condition'].

For the genuinely conservative and bourgeois reader of Barthes's works, this reaction is nevertheless a surprising one. *Roland Barthes par Roland Barthes* makes no secret of the fact that Barthes is not interested in women, and *Fragments d'un discours amoureux* leaves very much the same impression. The love of parents for their children, or of a man for his wife, is consequently absent from his book, and it is tempting to explain the frequency with which the themes of jealousy, loneliness and desertion recur in *Fragments d'un discours amoureux* by invoking the essential impermanency which writers such as Proust and Genet have depicted as characterising homosexual relationships. It could also be argued that Barthes is so very much more sensitive than the common run of humanity that even the analyses in *Fragments d'un discours amoureux* do not offer the basis for a reply to the question which my golf-playing neighbour never fails to ask me when I tell him that I am writing a book about yet another French writer: 'Yes, but what is there going to be in it for *me*?'. For has this neighbour, I wonder, ever had an experience which would make him be grateful to Barthes for confessing in public that the act of loving makes me cruelly vulnerable to the realisation that 'nobody really needs me'?[14] Or, to take a less sentimental example, would any of the solid, sun-burnt men whom I see driving their Jaguars along the Harrogate road see Barthes's description of the emotions he has on contemplating his loved one's body as expressing feelings which they have had?

> Je voyais tout de son visage, de son corps, froidement: ses cils, l'ongle de son orteil, la minceur de ses sourcils, de ses lèvres, l'émail de ses yeux, tel grain de beauté, une façon d'étendre les doigts en fumant; j'étais fasciné—la fascination n'étant en somme que

l'extrémité du détachement—par cette sorte de figurine coloriée, faïencée, vitrifiée, où je pouvais lire, sans rien y comprendre, *la cause de mon désir.*

[I looked at the whole of his [or her] face, of his body, dispassionately: the eyelashes, the toenails, the slenderness of the eyebrows and lips, the enamel of the eyes, a beauty spot, a way of stretching out the fingers when smoking; I was fascinated—fascination being in point of fact merely an extreme form of detachment—by this kind of coloured, glazed, vitrified figurine in which I could read, in total incomprehension, *the cause of my desire.*][15]

There are two answers to this question, the conventional and the Barthesian. The conventional response is to make mock of the illusion whereby the literary intellectual assumes that the granitic face of the man on the Clapham omnibus hides a heart of steel, and point out that although everyone undoubtedly has the emotions analysed by Barthes, most have the decency to keep quiet about them. From this standpoint, *Fragments d'un discours amoureux* expresses what everyone 'really' feels but is too sensible or too embarrassed to admit, and the book could certainly be defended—as the equally intense and despairing vision of the human emotions in Proust could be defended—on these grounds. The more original, Barthesian answer is to develop the vision running through his whole work that man is first and foremost *homo communicans*—a communicating animal. He is, moreover, an animal that communicates in everything that he does, in actions as well as words, in what he feels as in what he thinks. The physical response of the person I love is important not because it adds to my sensual pleasure—as Barthes observes in *Roland Barthes par Roland Barthes*, the great value of prostitution lies in the fact that it enables me to concentrate on enjoying my sensations without worrying about my partner's—but because it reassures me that I am not mad, not alone and not talking to myself. And while the physical response of the loved one to my desire is important, it matters less, in a way, than the verbal reply to my desire to be loved. It is less important than the words 'I love you' which in certain rare, unpredictable, almost miraculous moments of absolute bliss are uttered by my partner at the very moment that I pronounce them myself.[16]

It is easy to see why Barthes did not develop what Hector Bianciotti referred to as the 'photographic negatives' of *Fragments d'un discours amoureux* into a traditional novel of psychological analysis. To do so would not only, by requiring the invention of imaginary characters in whom the reader was expected to believe as real people, have gone against the whole rejection of the mimetic illusion in *S/Z*. It would also have distracted Barthes from giving all his attention to analysing the way in which language and other forces of meaningful behaviour structure our experience and make communication with other people both possible and unavoidable. One of the most important aspects of structuralism, at least in the form which Barthes has given it, lies in what he would call the 'rejection of the myth of innerness'. Language, for him, does not serve to elucidate what we feel deep down within us, but to make our experience meaningful by casting it into forms which we ourselves recognise as sharing with other individuals. At the same time, of course, language always threatens to stifle the individuality of my experience under the weight of the accepted, ready-made formulae which constitute the *Doxa*, and at least two passages in *Fragments d'un discours amoureux* reveal how preoccupied Barthes still remains with the involuntary persecution to which the public use of language inevitably subjects us. He is, he confesses, always reluctant to accept other people's evaluation of his relationships, even when this is favourable, since it 'flattens their special nature under a conventional formula', and he also objects to the way in which mass culture is a 'machine for showing desire'. ' "This is what ought to interest you", it says, as though men were incapable of finding out for themselves what they desire.'[17] What matters to Barthes is the precise meaning and implications of the words which we use to formulate ideals, to designate states of mind or describe types of behaviour, and in this respect *Fragments d'un discours amoureux* makes a particular appeal to those who admire him within the English as well as from the old and new aspects of the French tradition.

Thus at one point, he looks at what would be involved in trying to apply to our own experience Clotilde de Vaux's remark that it is 'unworthy of noble minds to spread around them the emotions which they feel'. He begins by observing that it is impossible wholly to hide one's passions. This is not only because human beings lack the moral strength to do so. It is also because passions are 'made to be seen', are above all else a means whereby we communicate with other people. The person I love has to see the fact that I am hiding my love, for otherwise this love does not really exist. If it is to exist, my secret passion has to fulfil the paradoxical condition of being seen to be hidden. We can never escape from the signs which relate us to other people, and to put on dark glasses to disguise the fact that I have been crying is, however great my desire to hide my red and swollen eyelids may be, involuntarily to fall into the condition of the Roman actor who comes forward, *Larvatus Prodeo*, pointing at his mask.[18] The other may, of course, fail to recognise this half-intentional, half-deliberate sign, but there is nevertheless nothing that I can do to prevent my language, my emotions or my physical appearance from meaning something. If I feel jealous, Barthes argues in another passage, I suffer not only by being left out or abandoned, but from the awareness that the loved one will notice my jealousy—will see it as a sign—and either be wounded by it or join me in my own self-condemnation for giving way to so vulgar and negative an emotion.[19] The experiences which Barthes is analysing in these and other passages are what a phenomenologist would call our 'modes of relationship with other people'. The emotions which give rise to them do not need to be examined in some mysterious 'inner self' to which only the 'skilled psychologist' or the 'novelist of the human heart' has access. They are, as Sartre put it in 1938 in his famous essay on Husserl, 'out there, in the world of men', accessible in the words we use, the gestures we make, the understanding which the existence of other people enables us to have of our own ambitions and desires.[20] This understanding is mediated in its most complex, interesting and accessible form through language, and it is with this that Barthes is concerned in *Fragments d'un discours amoureux*. This role of language is also the proper concern both of the French tradition of psychological analysis which Barthes has so frequently sought to reject and of the central tradition in English linguistic philosophy.

The last thing one discovers when writing a book, said Pascal, is what ought to have come first. This is especially the case when one ventures to write about a living author who can always confound judgements and prognostications by producing an unexpected book, and had *Fragments d'un discours amoureux* been available before *Roland Barthes: a Conservative Estimate* had been set up in proof, the opening chapters of this study might have been rather different. For *Fragments d'un discours amoureux* does project a far more interesting and attractive attitude towards language and communication than the sweeping generalisations of *Le degré zéro de l'écriture*, and reveals Barthes as belonging to that enviable category of writers who, as the classical tradition would put it, improve with age. The estimate of him put forward in this book would have undoubtedly been a far less conservative one had I been able to begin with the intuitions of *Fragments d'un discours amoureux* rather than with the hackneyed Marxist notion that the crucial date in literary history is 1848.[21]

Bibliography

The works of Roland Barthes published in book form are:

1. *Le degré zéro de l'écriture*, Editions du Seuil, 'Pierres vives', 1953. Reprinted as a paperback in 1965 with Barthes's *Eléments de Sémiologie* (Gonthier, 'Médiations'). Reprinted with the *Nouveaux Essais Critiques*, Editions du Seuil, 'Points', 1972. Translated into English by Annette Lavers and Colin Smith and published in England by Jonathan Cape (1967), in America by Hill & Wang (1968). The American edition has a long preface by Susan Sontag.
2. *Michelet par lui-même*, Editions du Seuil, 'Ecrivains de toujours', 1954.
3. *Mythologies*, Editions du Seuil, 'Pierres vives', 1957. Reprinted in 1965 and published as a paperback in the series 'Points' in 1970. Twenty-eight of the original *mythologies*, together with the long essay 'Myth To-day', were translated into English by Annette Lavers and published in England by Jonathan Cape and in America by Hill & Wang in 1972. Republished as a Paladin paperback in 1973.
4. *Sur Racine*, Editions du Seuil, 'Pierres vives', 1963. Translated into English by Richard Howard and published in America by Hill & Wang, 1964.
5. *Essais Critiques*, Editions du Seuil, 'Tel Quel', 1964. Translated by Richard Howard, Northwestern University Press, 1972.
6. *Eléments de Sémiologie*. Originally published in the review *Communications*, 4 (November 1964). Published in book form in 1965 as a double volume with *Le degré zéro de l'écriture*. Translated into English by Annette Lavers and Colin Smith and published by Jonathan Cape in England (1967) and Hill & Wang in America (1968); and as a Beacon paperback (1970).
7. *Critique et Vérité*, Editions du Seuil, 'Tel Quel', 1966.
8. *Système de la Mode*, Editions du Seuil, 1967.
9. *S/Z*, Editions du Seuil, 'Tel Quel', 1970. Reprinted in the series 'Points' in 1976. Translated into English by Richard Miller and published by Jonathan Cape and Hill & Wang, 1975.
10. *L'Empire des Signes*, Geneva, Skira, 'Les Sentiers de la création', 1970.

11. *Sade, Fourier, Loyola*, Editions du Seuil, 'Tel Quel', 1971.
12. *Le Plaisir du Texte*, Editions du Seuil, 'Tel Quel', 1973. Translated into English by Richard Miller and published by Jonathan Cape (1976) and by Hill & Wang (1975).
13. *Roland Barthes par Roland Barthes*, Editions du Seuil, 'Ecrivains de toujours', 1975.
14. *Fragments d'un discours amoureux*, Editions du Seuil, 'Tel Quel', 1977.

There have been a number of critical studies on Barthes in French. The best of these, Stephen Heath's *Vertige du déplacement: lecture de Barthes*, Fayard, 'Digraphe', 1974, contains an excellent bibliography. The special number of *Tel Quel* (47, autumn 1971) on Barthes also has a very full bibliography. So too does the special number of *Le Magazine littéraire*, 97 (February 1975). Other critical studies include L.-J. Calvet: *Roland Barthes. Un regard politique sur le signe*, Petite Bibliothèque Payot, 1973; and Guy de Mallac and Margaret Eberbach: *Barthes*, 'Psychothèque', Editions Universitaires, 1971.

Of particular interest are the two articles which Barthes devoted to Biblical texts and which have not yet been reprinted in book form: *L'Analyse structurale du récit: A propos de Actes X-XI* in *Exégèse et Herméneutique*, Seuil, 1971; and *La lutte avec l'Ange: Analyse textuelle de Genèse*, 32, 23-33 in *Analyse structurale et exégèse biblique*, Seuil, 1973. In a rather different vein, Barthes's preface to the latest edition of Brillat-Savarin's *Physiologie du goût* (Hermann, 1975) brings together his love of pleasure, his liking for wood, and his continued interest in the existential thematics of substances.

Notes and references

ABBREVIATIONS

CV: *Critique et Vérité*
DZ: *Le degré zéro de l'écriture*
Michelet: *Michelet par lui-même*
NCNI: *Nouvelle Critique ou Nouvelle Imposture*
PT: *Le Plaisir du Texte*
RB: *Roland Barthes par Roland Barthes*
SFL: *Sade, Fourier, Loyola*
SM: *Système de la Mode*

CHAPTER 1

1. See *L'Echo du Sud-Ouest*, 2 Mar 1973; see also Barthes's reply to *Tel Quel*, 47 (autumn 1971) p. 90.
2. See *RB*, pp. 49 and 130 (Oedipus); interview in *Gulliver*, Mar 1973 (Oedipus); holidays in the provinces: *RB*, *passim*.
3. Interview in *Gulliver*, Mar 1973. See also *RB*, p. 130, for Barthes's own recognition that 'le seul Père que j'ai connu (que je me suis donné) a été le Père politique'.
4. 'Politics versus Literature: an examination of *Gulliver's Travels*', in *Collected Essays, Journalism and Letters*, Secker & Warburg, 1968, vol. IV, p. 209.
5. *Contre Sainte-Beuve*, Pléiade, 1971, pp. 221–2.
6. *Mantéia*, No. 5, Marseilles, 1968, pp. 12–17. See also an interview in *Les Lettres Françaises*, 9 Feb 1972, in which Barthes told Jean Riotat that 'Genet est dans ses livres en tant que personnage de papier. C'est là, la réussite de son œuvre: en tant que personnage entièrement exhérédé [disinherited], débarrassé de toute hérédité par rapport à lui-même en tant que référent'.
7. *S/Z*, p. 126. Translated by Richard Miller, Cape, 1975, p. 120.
8. See Chapter 8 for a fuller discussion of this point. For Barthes's own review of *RB*, see *La Quinzaine Littéraire*, 1 Mar 1975. For *La Déesse Homosexualité*, see *RB*, p. 79.
9. *RB*, p. 50. Orwell on genteel poverty: *Coming Up for Air* (1939), Penguin, 1962, p. 137. Barthes on same: *RB*, pp. 49–50.
10. *RB*, p. 134.
11. See the excellent bibliography in Stephen Heath's book *Vertige du déplacement: lecture de Barthes*, Fayard, 1974. See *Combat*, 27 Jan 1972, for details of how Maurice Nadeau helped him in the early stages of his career. See

also the long interview which Barthes gave to *Tel Quel*, 47 (autumn 1971)
p. 92.

12. Cf. Guy Dumur, *France-Observateur*, 6 June 1963.

13. *Le degré zéro de l'écriture, suivi de Nouveaux essais critiques*, Editions du Seuil,
'Points', 1972, p. 44. All references are to this edition.

14. Ibid., p. 38.

15. *Qu'est-ce que la littérature?*, Gallimard, 1947, p. 314.

16. *DZ*, p. 49.

17. Ibid., p. 39.

18. Ibid., p. 56.

19. See '*L'Etranger*', *roman solaire*, Bulletin du Club français du livre, April
1954. An article reprinted in *Les Critiques de notre temps et Camus*, Garnier,
1970.

20. See entry no. 21620, June 1953. For a change of view on Barthes in the
Bulletin critique, see entry 59826 praising *Sur Racine* in November 1963, and
entry 70433 in June 1967 praising *Système de la Mode* and observing that
'un assez vaste public admire le brillant essayiste des *Mythologies*'.

    DZ was also enthusiastically welcomed in the April–June 1954 number
of the *Journal des Ingénieurs*, albeit with the remark that their scientific
training led engineers to take as their literary ideal 'cette forme artisanale
de l'écriture qualifiée par l'auteur de littérature bourgeoise'.

21. See *Le Monde*, 3 Oct 1953, and *Critique*, no. 80, pp. 1–13.

22. Cf. John Fletcher, *Claude Simon and Fiction Now*, Calder & Boyars, 1975,
p. 201.

23. *DZ*, p. 19.

24. Thus, according to Mathieu Galey, writing in *Arts*, 9 Apr 1964, Barthes's
famous article on *Les Gommes* ('Littérature objective', in *Critique*, July–Aug
1954; reprinted in *Essais Critiques*) showed Robbe-Grillet what he was
really doing. Dominique Rolin, in *Le Point*, 6 Mar 1973, asked 'Que
seraient Robbe-Grillet, Butor, sans lui?', and commented on the fact that
Barthes was the only author to have had a special number of 'un mouvement littéraire aussi terroriste que *Tel Quel*' devoted to his work.

25. See Heath's article *Changer de langue* in the special number (97, Feb 1975)
which *Le Magazine littéraire* published on Barthes.

CHAPTER 2

1. See his interview with Claude Jannaud in *Le Figaro*, 27 Sep 1974, for the
first remark, and with Gilles Laponge in *La Quinzaine littéraire*, 1 Dec 1971,
for the second. Barthes also told Laponge that he did not consider himself
an intellectual. But see *Le Nouvel Observateur*, 10 Jan 1977.

2. *CV*, p. 14. In her preface to the translation, *Writing Degree Zero*, which
Hill & Wang published in New York in 1967, Susan Sontag wrote that
'to describe Roland Barthes as a literary critic does him an obvious
injustice. As a man of prodigious learning, unflagging mental energy, and
acutely original sensibility, he has established his credentials as an aestheti-
cian, literary and theatre critic, sociologist, metapsychologist, social critic,
historian of ideas and cultural journalist. Only if the ideal of criticism is
enlarged to take in a wide variety of discourse, both theoretical and

descriptive, about culture, language and contemporary consciousness, can Barthes be plausibly called a critic.' When Jonathan Cape published the same translation in London, Miss Sontag's preface was not used.

3. *RB*, p. 164.
4. *Michelet*, p. 12.
5. Ibid., p. 187.
6. Ibid., p. 86.
7. Ibid., p. 168, quoting the passage from Volume II of *L'Histoire de la Révolution* (1847) in which Michelet describes how the revolutionaries of 1793 justified each act of violence on the grounds that only one more crime was needed to bring about the millennium.
8. Quoted by Maurice Chapelan in his review of *PT*, *Le Figaro*, 17 Feb 1973.
9. Cf. *Tel Quel*, 47, p. 94.
10. *Michelet*, p. 105.
11. *Tel Quel*, 47, p. 94.
12. *Mythologies*, Editions du Seuil, 'Points', 1970, p. 128. All references are to this edition. Annette Lavers's translation, Paladin, 1973, p. 78. For the quotations from *Michelet*, see pp. 158, 134, 160; on *nappé*, *RB*, pp. 156–7.
    For other references to smooth, unctuous surfaces, see *Michelet*, pp. 33, 35, 74, 75; *Essais Critiques*, p. 33—'la nappe homogène d'une matière idéale'; see also the quotations on p. 114.
13. *Le Monde*, 10 May 1954. For an equally hostile reaction, see *Le Bulletin de Lettres de Lyon*, 15 May 1954: 'le volume le plus aberrant et le plus insupportable de la série'.
14. *Michelet*, p. 78.
15. Migraine: *RB*, pp. 128–9, *Michelet*, p. 17. For 'mouvements essentiels', see *Michelet*, p. 82.
16. *Michelet*, p. 154. See also pp. 131, 142 and 144.
17. *Le Monde*, 22 June 1957. In No. 884 of *Lectures Culturelles*, August 1954, a certain J. G. also said that *Michelet par lui-même* was not a book which young girls ought to be allowed to read.
18. *Michelet*, p. 129.
19. See Emile Henriot, *Le Monde*, 1 Apr 1959. For details concerning the *Combat* article, published on 24 Apr 1954, see Bernard Dort, *Critique*, no. 88, pp. 725–32: 'Vers une critique totalitaire'.
20. See *Bulletin des Lettres*, 15 Oct 1962, pp. 333–7.
21. See E. F. K. Koerner, *Ferdinand de Saussure. Origin and Development of his Linguistic Thought in Western Studies of Language*, Braunschweig, Vieweg, 1973, pp. 23–5, for the quotation from Leroy. Koerner also quotes G. C. Lepschy, *A Survey of Structural Linguistics*, Faber, 1970, p. 42: 'Saussure's discoveries depend on an analysis which to-day we would not hesitate to call structural. Taking into account the whole system, he postulates elements of an abstract character which are defined on the basis of their structural function rather than their phonetic shape.' I am indebted to my friend and colleague G. O. Rees for this particular reference.
22. *Mallarmé l'Obscur*, Denoël, 1940, p. 48.
23. Henri Mondor, *Vie de Mallarmé*, Gallimard 1941, p. 55. Mallarmé's letter was written on 1 Aug 1862.
24. *Le Figaro*, 27 Sep 1963.

25. *Aesthetics and Psychology*, Hogarth Press, 1935, p. 62. The work does not seem to have been published in French.
26. Michelet's *Journal* eventually appeared in four volumes, Gallimard, 1959–62 (1828–60, ed. by Paul Viallaneix); 1976 (1861–74, ed. Claude Digeon).
27. *Le Monde*, 14 Sep 1960.
28. *Michelet*, pp. 145–6.
29. Ibid., p. 148.
30. *Mercure de France*, July 1955, pp. 494–9.
31. See *La Force de l'Age*, Gallimard, 1960, p. 135.
32. E.g. Henri Bonnier, *Le Provençal*, 12 June 1966, discussing the reissue of the *Histoire de la Révolution Française* in the 'Pléiade' series, and Claude Mettra in his preface to his shortened edition of *Histoire de France* in the 'J'ai lu' series in 1966. Guy Dumur, reviewing *Michelet par lui-même* in *Médecine de France*, vol. LIV (1954) had commented earlier how Michelet's works could only be found on second-hand bookstalls, where nobody wanted to buy them.
33. *Tel Quel*, 47 (1971) p. 95.
34. See *Essais Critiques*, p. 57. The first number of *Théâtre Populaire* appeared in June 1953, and Barthes remained an active member of the Editorial Board for several years. His more important articles were reprinted in *Essais Critiques*. For Camus, see *Copeau, seul maître, Théâtre, Récits, Nouvelles*, Pléiade, 1962, pp. 1697–8.
35. *Essais Critiques*, p. 75.
36. See *Theatre Arts*, July 1946: 'Forgers of Myths. The new playwrights of France', pp. 324–5.
37. See his article 'Théâtre moderne et public populaire', in the special number which *Esprit* published on the theatre in May 1965, pp. 834–6.
38. *Essais Critiques*, p. 87. An article reprinted from *Arguments*.
39. *Essais Critiques*, pp. 48–50.
40. *RB*, p. 59.
41. *Mythologies*, p. 69.
42. *Essais Critiques*, p. 77.
43. *Sur Racine*, p. 85.
44. *Situations III*, Gallimard 1949, p. 191.
45. *Essais Critiques*, p. 88.
46. *Esprit*, May 1965, pp. 834–6. See also Chapter 10, n. 24 for further references to Barthes's feeling of being persecuted.
47. Garnier, 1973, pp. 91–3.
48. Loc.cit., p. 92.
49. *Théâtre Populaire*, July-August, 1955, p. 70.
50. Ibid., July 1953, pp. 12–22, 'Pouvoirs de la tragédie antique', an article not reprinted in *Essais Critiques*.
51. *TLS*, 8 Oct 1971, p. 1203.

CHAPTER 3

1. *Education Physique et Sport*, no. 39 (Mar 1958). 'Le Monde où l'on catche' is not the only one of Barthes's essays to have gained admiration from a

wholly non-literary body. In March 1973, the *Centre de Perfectionnement des Journalistes et des cadres de la presse* devoted one of its study sessions to the *fait divers* [odd news item] and presented Barthes's 'Structure du fait divers', first published in *Communications* in 1962, reprinted in *Essais Critiques* in 1964, as the best analysis of the section to which, it appears, 80 per cent of the readers of *Ouest-France* turn on opening the paper. Barthes saw the structure of the *fait divers* as epitomised by the Latin *cum* . . . *tum:* at the very moment when the husband was preparing to forgive his wife, her lover killed him. See *Essais Critiques*, p. 195.

2. *Cours de linguistique générale*, Payot, 1969, p. 33. Saussure himself published very little during his lifetime, and the *Cours* was put together after his death by two of his disciples: Charles Bally and Albert Sechehaye. It was based upon lectures given by Saussure in Geneva between 1906 and 1911.

3. *Tel Quel*, 47, p. 96.

4. See *Introduction à la Sémiologie*, Seuil, 1971, pp. 189–97: 'La sémiologie de Roland Barthes'.

5. *Mythologies*, p. 23.

6. *SFL*, p. 41.

7. *Mythologies*, p. 22.

8. Ibid., p. 16.

9. Ibid., p. 14.

10. Ibid., pp. 28–9, 67–9, 41–2.

11. Ibid., p. 175.

12. Ibid., p. 173.

13. *Collected Essays, Journalism and Letters*, Secker & Warburg, 1968, Vol. I, p. 481.

14. *Le Magazine littéraire*, no. 97 (Feb 1975) p. 11. A selection of essays was translated into French by Philip Thody and published in Gallimard's 'Du Monde Entier' series in 1960.

15. *New Society*, 6 Feb 1972.

16. *Times Higher Education Supplement*, 21 Apr 1972; *Sunday Times*, 5 Mar 1972. The comparison between Barthes and Katharine Whitehorn is an intriguing one. A *mythologie* such as 'Jouets', with its plea for toys made out of wood, a substance which is unbreakable, has no cutting edges, is long-lasting, able to live with the child and modify its relationship with him as he grows older, rather than 'the mechanical toys which collapse with the hernia of a broken spring', is very much in the *Which?* or *Observer* tradition of improving the quality of middle-class consumer products.

17. *New Yorker*, 9 Sep 1972. In France, the fellow-travelling *Libération* and *France Observateur*, like the socialist *Europe*, each welcomed the book. In the first (3 Apr 1957) Claude Roy compared it to Bayle's *Dictionnaire historique et critique* or Voltaire's *Dictionnaire philosophique* and Flaubert's *Dictionnaire des idées reçues*, while in the second (21 Mar 1957) Maurice Nadeau fully endorsed Barthes's analysis of the mass media as the new opium of the people. In the third (Aug 1957), Jean Baumier found it lacking only in a detailed analysis of how the myths were deliberately created by Citroën, Astra and the textile millionaire Prouvost. In *Rivarol* (28 May 1957), in contrast, P.-A. Cousteau described Barthes's style as 'l'inimitable jargon que les cuistres pelliculeux de l'Underground sartrien substituèrent,

dans l'immédiat après-guerre, à la langue française', and his comments anticipated the good, albeit predictable, joke which Léon Treich made in the almost equally right-wing *L'Aurore* on 29 Mar 1964: that Barthes's books were written 'au seuil de la langue française, de toute évidence' ['clearly on the threshold of the French language']. In *Le Rappel* (31 Mar 1957) Jean Anouilh's admirer Pol Vandromme also advised the translation of *Mythologies* into French, while Michel Vivier in the equally right-wing *La Nation Française* (31 Sep 1957) wryly observed that Barthes's political ideals could be realised only with a proletariat which gave up reading *France-Soir* and being interested in professional cyclists. *L'Express* (22 Mar 1957) was not enthusiastic about *Mythologies;* perhaps because of that review's association with François Mauriac.

18. *Mythologies*, p. 141.
19. Ibid., p. 79: 'Bifteak et frites'.
20. Op.cit., vol. IV, p. 136.
21. *Mythologies*, p. 140.
22. *L'Express*, 18 May 1954.
23. Barthes did in fact reply to an enquiry on the then new Gaullist regime in 1959 with the suggestion that a file should be kept on the myths which it propagated (Heath, op.cit., p. 32). It is interesting to compare his attitude with that of Robbe-Grillet, who was one of the first to sign the *Manifeste des 121* but who deliberately excluded all conscious political themes from his work. (See *Nouveau Roman, Hier, Aujourd'hui*, Collection 10/18, 1972, p. 173.)
24. *La Littérature en France depuis 1945*, Bordas, 1970, p. 831.
25. *Sunday Times*, 5 Mar 1972. Cf. also Christopher Prendergast, *The Cambridge Review*, 2 June 1972; Don Locke, *The London Magazine*, Jan–July 1972, pp. 163–6. Cf. p. 88 of Annette Lavers's translation (*Mythologies*, p. 150) for the actual quotation about the Citroën. Casey: *Spectator*, 18 Mar 1972; *New York Review of Books*, 18 May 1972.
26. Loc.cit., 12 Apr 1957. Morillon also commented that 'La midinette a peut-être le cœur tendre, mais elle est syndiquée.'
27. See Michel Vivier, in *La Nation Française*, 31 Sep 1957; Marcel Thiébaut in *La Revue de Paris*, Oct 1957, p. 158; and the Rev. Father Michel Ulrich in *Radio Vatican*, 24 Feb 1958.
28. *Mythologies*, p. 196. For 'battre en brèche', see interview in *L'Express*, 31 May 1970.
29. Ibid., p. 234.
30. Ibid., p. 56. In 1945 Sartre commented in his *Présentation* of *Les Temps Modernes* that 'Bourgeois charity maintains the myth of fraternity'.
31. *Esprit*, 1971, pp. 613–15.
32. Loc.cit., 20 May 1970.
33. *Mythologies*, p. 84. Since the *mythologie* entitled 'Publicité et Profondeur' was not included in Annette Lavers's translation, I have had to use my own.

CHAPTER 4

1. See especially the *mythologies* entitled 'Martiens', 'Bichon chez les Nègres' and 'Continent perdu'.

2. See the articles in *L'Express*, 21 Oct 1974, and in *Le Nouvel Observateur*, 7 Nov 1974, for details of this new title and the view that Barthes's determination to mingle different disciplines was partially responsible for this welcome change in status.

3. Charles Mauron also comments in the 'Note Annexe' to *Le dernier Baudelaire* on the refusal of the Sorbonne to provide systematic teaching on any aspect of Freudian psychoanalysis.

4. *Tel Quel*, 47, p. 90.

5. *Esprit*, May 1965, pp. 834–6.

6. *Sur Racine*, p. 136.

7. *Sur Racine*, p. 143.

8. *Revue des Sciences Humaines*, July–Sep 1957, pp. 335–9.

9. *La Dépêche du Midi*, 3 May 1966.

10. *TLS*, 27 Sep 1963.

11. *Esprit*, Nov 1955, pp. 1778–81.

12. *Le Monde*, 28 Mar 1964.

13. Cf. *Arts*, 22 May 1963; *Combat*, 30 May 1963; *Tribune de Genève*, 3 Aug 1963. For this definition of structuralism see *Essais Critiques*, p. 214.

14. *France Nouvelle*, 5 May 1975. Although Barthes does not figure in Alain Schnapp's and Pierre Vidal-Naquet's *Journal de la Commune étudiante* (Seuil, 1969), critics writing before 1968 commented on the hostility to traditional academic methods implied by *Sur Racine* and *Critique et Vérité*. Thus Guy Dumur, in the left-wing *France Observateur*, wrote on 6 June 1963 that Barthes had succeeded in discovering the complexity of Racine's universe precisely by giving up traditional explanations, while Renaud Matignon expressed a very frequent point of view when he commented (8 May 1966): 'Au fond de l'ancienne critique, il y a un postulat autoritaire: la raison, la clarté française, les certitudes psychologiques'; and added that it was 'grand temps de rénover quelque peu la philosophie des *Classiques Larousse* . . . et de s'interroger sur l'art autrement que comme un médecin qui étudierait le système nerveux sur l'homme de Neanderthal'. In *La Gauche* for 17 May 1966, André Franklin accused what he called the 'Journal de tendance fasciste, *Europe-Action*' of unfairly and systematically praising Picard at the expense of 'le progressiste R. Barthes'.

15. Jean-Jacques Brochier, *Les Temps Modernes*, Dec 1965, pp. 1140–2. Brochier also argued that Picard's attack stemmed from the fact that *Sur Racine* was widely read whereas *La Carrière de Jean Racine* was not.

16. See *Revue des Sciences Humaines*, Jan–Mar 1965, pp. 28–49.

17. *En France*, Julliard, 1965, p. 42.

18. *NCNI*, p. 128. In *Climats*, 15 Apr 1954, Morvan Lebesque had earlier used the X-ray comparison to praise Barthes's method in *Michelet par lui-même*.

19. Allemand, op.cit. (A la Baconnière, 1967), p. 25.

20. *NCNI*, pp. 123–6.

21. *Le dernier Baudelaire*, Corti, 1966, pp. 171–86. What Mauron calls 'la querelle héroï-comique' sparked off by Picard was summarised in appropriate language by Dominique Noguez in *Arts*, 6 July 1966:

En l'an 12 de l'ère barthienne, frappé d'un obscur centurion Picardius d'un coup de pique en pleine poitrine et voué, tout aussitot, aux ricanements et crachats d'une certaine tourbe à stylos ou bicornes, Roland Barthes est mort et a été enseveli. La foudre est tombée aux Hautes Etudes; la terre s'est entr'ouverte à Saint-Germain-des-Prés; les Saintes Femmes de 'Tel Quel' ont gémi; le bronze d'imprimerie de *Critique* a sué, cependant que des rustres jouaient *Sur Racine* aux dés. Mais le troisième jour, le maître est ressuscité, d'entre les morts, et est monté au *Seuil*, d'où il devait redescendre quelques mois plus tard, pour faire passer à ses disciples recueillis le Saint Esprit de *Critique et Vérité*, 79 pages, 4F 50. Or déjà Jean Genette appareillait pour Patmos et Saül-Doubrovsky trottinait vers Damas.

22. *La Nouvelle Critique et Racine*, Nizet, 1970.

23. The papers read at *Les chemins actuels de la critique* were published by Plon in 1966; those on *L'enseignement de la littérature* in 1971. Roger Laufer expressed a widely held viewpoint when he wrote (p. 361 of *L'enseignement de la littérature*) that the teaching of French literature enclosed both teachers and pupils in a tradition which they rejected.

24. *NCNI*, p. 91.

25. *Sur Racine*, p. 20.

26. Ibid., p. 26.

27. Ibid., p. 34. Barthes is nevertheless far from being the only critic to see a dichotomy between Racine's official Christianity and the moral universe of his plays. Thus Antoine Adam writes, in his authoritative and highly respectable *Histoire de la Littérature française au XVIIe siècle* that the theology implicit in *Phèdre* is analogous to that of the Marquis de Sade, being one in which 'the world is given over to wicked gods, who derive pleasure from human suffering, who compel men to commit crimes so as to have the right to damn them' (Vol. IV, p. 405, Domat, 1954).

28. Ibid., p. 61.

29. Loc.cit., pp. 410–11.

30. *Au sujet du 'Cimetière marin'*, *Œuvres* (Pléiade), Vol. II, p. 1507.

31. *Pour une sociologie du roman*, Gallimard, 'Bibliothèque des Idées', 1964, pp. 11 and 28–9.

32. *Les Mots et les Choses*, Gallimard, 1966, p. 398.

33. Op.cit., p. 20.

CHAPTER 5

1. Goldmann, *Sciences humaines et création culturelle*, Anthropos, 1970, p. 472. Revel, *La Quinzaine littéraire*, 15 Apr 1966.

2. *Le dernier Baudelaire*, p. 185.

3. *Situation de la critique racinienne*, L'Arche, 1971, p. 113.

4. Alistair MacIntyre, *Encounter*, Oct 1964, p. 70. Raymond Williams: Lecture at Lady Mitchell Hall, Cambridge; reprinted in the *New Left Review*, Mar–June 1971, and as an Introduction to Alastair Hamilton's translation of Goldmann's book on Racine (Cambridge: Rivers Press, 1972).

5. Goldmann's most detailed exposition of his thesis is in *Le Dieu caché*, Gallimard, 'Bibliothèque des Idées', 1956 (English translation: *The Hidden God*, Routledge & Kegan Paul, 1964). However, he also repeated the

same basic arguments in *Racine* (L'Arche, 1970); in *Sciences humaines et philosophie* (Gonthier, 1971); and in *Situation de la critique racinienne* (L'Arche, 1971).

6. *Le Dieu caché*, p. 383.
7. Cf. Miller's Preface to his *Collected Plays*, Cresset Press, 1956.
8. *Sur Racine*, p. 109.
9. Ibid., p. 93. Cf. Mauron, *L'inconscient dans l'œuvre et la vie de Racine*, Annales de la Faculté des Lettres d'Aix-en-Provence, 1957, p. 71.
10. *Sur Racine*, pp. 55 and 21.
11. In *The Sacred Wood*, 1920, University Paperback, 1960, p. 56.
12. *La Quinzaine littéraire*, 15 Mar 1966.
13. Cf. Mauron, op.cit., p. 27.
14. Ibid., pp. 96–7.
15. *Sur Racine*, p. 40.
16. Op.cit., p. 19.
17. Ibid., p. 260.
18. Ibid., p. 181; Picard, op.cit., p. 91.
19. J.-J. Brochier, *Les Temps Modernes*, Dec 1965, pp. 1140–2.
20. Op.cit., p. 219.
21. Op.cit., pp. 307, 286.
22. Op.cit., pp. 262, 150.
23. Mauron, op.cit., p. 9. For Tran Duc Thao on Mallarmé, see Maurice Lefebvre, *La Pensée et les Hommes*, 10 July 1966.
24. Mauron, *The Nature of Beauty in Art and Literature*, translated by Roger Fry, Hogarth Press, 1927, pp. 53–4.
25. Mauron, op.cit., p. 81; Saussure, op.cit., p. 43.
26. Mauron on Proust—op.cit., p. 70; R. E. Jones, *La Nouvelle Critique en France*, Société d'Edition d'Enseignement Supérieur, 1968, pp. 151–81; p. 164. Mr Jones does, on the other hand, have a very high opinion of Jean-Paul Weber.
27. See *Aesthetics and Psychology*, pp. 102, 107; *L'inconscient dans l'œuvre et la vie de Racine*, p. 36.
28. *The Devils of Loudun*, Chatto & Windus, 1961, p. 96.
29. Op.cit., p. 260.
30. Jonathan Culler, *Structuralist Poetics*, Routledge & Kegan Paul, 1975, p. 100; Michael Lane, *Structuralism: a Reader*, Jonathan Cape, 1970, p. 37; Thomas Merton, *The Sewanee Review*, July 1969, pp. 536–42. Mr Merton also mentioned William Styron's then recent book on Nat Turner as an example of the 'good writing' denounced in *Le degré zéro de l'écriture*, said that it was misleading to call Barthes a structuralist, and described him as 'one of the most articulate and important literary critics writing to-day'.
31. *CV*, pp. 10–11.
32. Barthes is not alone in enjoying neologisms. I claim to be the originator of 'Popsology' (the popularised science of sociology) and 'popsologist' (a popularising sociologist). See 'Grammar and stereotypes. Some problems in popsology' in *International Social Science Journal*, XXVIII (2) (1976) 375–84.
33. Helen Gardner, *The Business of Criticism*, Oxford, Clarendon Press, 1959, p. 17; John Cruickshank, *British Journal of Aesthetics*, Apr 1964, pp. 155–60, esp. p. 159.

CHAPTER 6

1. Thus Philippe Sollers wrote in *Tel Quel* (24, winter 1966, p. 92) that 'Ce serait peu de dire de ce discours qu'il est réactionnaire. Il semble incarner l'ordre moral lui-même'. Lucette Finas, in *La Quinzaine Littéraire*, 15 Oct 1966, compared Barthes to Galileo, victim of a new kind of Inquisition.

2. Cf. Lucien Guissard in *La Croix* (9 Nov 1966), who pointed out that Barthes had chosen to quote only the unfavourable remarks which he had made about *Sur Racine*. Cf. also *L'Hôpital*, Nov 1966, p. 848, and *Le Figaro littéraire*, 24 Mar 1966. But see *La Gauche*, 17 May 1966, and *L'Express*, 8 May 1966, for the view that there is a strongly authoritarian element in traditional French criticism, against which Barthes is legitimately rebelling. The *TLS*, however (23 June 1966), observed that Picard was concerned not with politics but with accuracy. For Mauriac's remark on Sartre see the *Observer*, 'Sayings of the Week', 26 July 1970.

3. See *L'Express*, 21 Oct 1974 and *Le Nouvel Observateur*, 9 Nov 1974.

4. *Gazette Médicale de France*, 25 Apr 1975.

5. *Mythologies*, p. 53. Annette Lavers's translation, Paladin, p. 46.

6. *CV*, p. 24.

7. Ibid., p. 28.

8. *Retreat from Truth*, Oxford, Blackwell, 1958, p. 153. 'In a philosophical court, the place for common sense is in the dock, or on occasion the witness box, never on the bench.'

9. Op.cit., ch. VI, pp. 120–5.

10. *CV*, p. 57.

11. Op.cit., p. 17.

12. *CV*, p. 60.

13. *CV*, p. 52.

14. *NCNI*, p. 69.

15. For a fuller statement of this attitude, couched in the language in which Barthes and his followers so frequently and so successfully hide their meaning, see Barthes's own article 'Drame, Poème, Roman' in *Tel Quel: Théorie d'ensemble*, Editions du Seuil, 1968, p. 29:

    L'évacuation de la 'psychologie', depuis si longtemps investie dans le roman traditionnel, de type bourgeois, n'est pas seulement une affaire de littérature. La psychologie est aussi dans l'écriture de la mondanité, dans ce livre que nous croyons intérieur, que nous appelons, en l'opposant bien naïvement au monde des livres, 'la vie': tout notre imaginaire quotidien, parlé en dehors de toute situation d'écrivain ou d'artiste, est essentiellement psychologique. L'œuvre fondée en psychologie est toujours claire, parce que notre vie nous vient de nos livres, d'une immense géologie d'écritures psychologiques; ou plutôt: nous appelons clarté cette circulation égale des codes dont s'écrivent à la fois nos livres et notre vie: l'une n'est jamais que la translitération des autres. Changer le livre, c'est donc bien, selon le premier mot de la modernité, changer la vie.

16. *Possibilities. Essays on the State of the Novel*, Oxford Paperbacks, 1973, the essay entitled 'The Novel and its Poetics', p. 285.

17. The volume entitled *Erté* was published in a limited edition by Maria Ricci, in Parma, in July 1972. Barthes's preface was translated by William Weaver.

CHAPTER 7

1. Loc.cit., pp. 52–8. For a similarly dismissive view, see also George Watson, *Encounter*, Feb 1975, pp. 48–54, *Old Furniture and "Nouvelle Critique"*, especially the remark: 'The ultimate puzzle of "advanced" French criticism is its continuing success in isolating itself from the intellectual life of the Western world.'

2. Vol. 2 (1975) no. 14.

3. *Collected Essays, Journalism and Letters*, vol. iv, p. 234.

4. *SM*, p. 256.

5. Cf. *Le Monde*. 27 Sep 1973, where Barthes also told his interviewer, Jean-Louis de Rambures, that he always used a fountain-pen and not a biro. 'J'irai même', he added, 'jusqu'à dire qu'il existe un "style bic" qui est vraiment de la "pisse-copie", une écriture purement transitive de la pensée.'

6. *SM*, p. 246.

7. Quoted in Paul Angenot, *Le roman populaire*, Presses de l'Université de Québec, 1975, p. 12. Cf. also Chapter 3 n. 26.

8. Cf. *Paris–Normandie*, 19 May 1967.

9. *SM*, p. 270. The term *homo significans* struck John Sturrock as sufficiently meaningful to serve as a title for his long review of Jonathan Culler's *Structuralist Poetics* in *The New Review*, vol. 1, no. 12, 1975.

10. Op.cit., p. 33.

11. 'Le langage, c'est toujours de la puissance, parler, c'est exercer une volonté de pouvoir', *Tel Quel*, 47, p. 4.

12. *SM*, p. 247. For a similar observation about cookery, see *Cuisine Ornementale* in *Mythologies*, where Barthes contrasts the impossibly elaborate dishes described in magazines read by a mainly working-class public, such as *Elle*, with the more practical recipes published in the predominantly middle-class *L'Express*.

13. Interview in *France Nouvelle*, 5 May 1975.

14. *SM*, p. 265.

15. *Le Figaro Littéraire*, 24 July 1967.

16. *Le Magazine littéraire*, no. 97, p. 20.

17. Interview in *Sept Jours*, 8 July 1967.

18. *Guardian*, 2 Mar 1972.

19. For Sartre, see *L'Arc*, no. 30 (1967) pp. 87–96.

20. For the Goldmann remark, see *La Nouvelle Critique*, July 1972, pp. 610–22.

21. *SM*, p. 93.

22. Ibid., p. 37.

23. Ibid., p. 269.

24. Cf. *Etudes sur le temps humain*, Edinburgh, 1949, p. 13 and p. 19.

25. *SM*, p. 258.

26. Ibid., p. 260.

CHAPTER 8

1. A traditional formula confirmed by practice.

2. *S/Z*, p. 211. See Chapter 2, n. 12, for other examples of Barthes's obsession

with smooth coatings. See also his remark on *L'Etranger* to the effect that Camus does not offer his readers 'un acte tout englué dans la nappe des causes' ('L'Etranger, roman solaire', in *Les Critiques de notre temps et Camus*, Garnier, 1970, pp. 60–4).

3. *S/Z*, p. 190.

4. Ibid., p. 126.

5. *La Quinzaine littéraire*, 1 May 1970. For Barthes on Barthe, see *L'Express*, 31 May 1970. Barthes himself also claimed in this interview that he was in fact completely carried away by the story on his first reading of a Balzac novel ('Mais moi-meme, je marche à fond quand je lis Balzac, croyez-le bien'), but that he then had a more critical look.

In spite of the fact that it put forward almost as eccentric a view of Balzac as Barthes's earlier essays had done of Michelet and Racine, *S/Z* provoked relatively little public argument in France. There was an exchange of views in *Le Monde* (9 May 1970) between Raymond Jean, who maintained that *S/Z* explained why the Ancients were right to consider the commentator as the most active form of critic, and Pierre Citron, editor of the *Comédie humaine* in the 'L'Intégrale' series, who pointed out how arbitrary Barthes's analytical codes really were, regretted his neglect of Jean Seznec's discovery that there actually had been a French eighteenth-century sculptor called Sarrazin, and observed how odd it was that Barthes should describe Sarrasine as being 'vierge' on his arrival in Rome when the story mentions his having a mistress in Paris. *L'Année balzacienne* (1971, pp. 109–23) also published an intelligently critical review by Pierre Barbéris pointing out how much Barthes's critical method led him to ignore: the historical significance of 1830, the fact that Balzac's family name had originally been Balssa, etc., etc.

6. Thus, commenting on the Barthes-Picard quarrel in *L'enseignement de la littérature* (Plon, 1971), Déguy had claimed that Picard's approach was entirely wrong because he relied on an inductive approach based on empirical evidence. He was consequently deaf to 'l'intuition eidétique, c'est-à-dire à un mode de constitution de l'objet intelligible telle que la phénoménologie nous l'a appris—ou réappris' (pp. 410–11). In such a mode of argument, according to Déguy, the interpretation of works of art should be based upon one example, provided that it is the best one available, and he makes no mention of the fact that Barthes had in fact gone completely against this principle precisely by generalising not about one play but about the whole of Racine's theatre. Like most of the contributors to *L'enseignement de la littérature*, Déguy maintained that the teaching of French at both secondary school and university level was consciously aimed at maintaining the bourgeoisie as the political and intellectual governing class. By inculcating in their charges a respect for empirical evidence, Cartesian logic, the technique of *explication de texte* and the need to present essays with a carefully planned beginning, middle and end, the teachers of the Fifth Republic were ensuring that the revolutionary ideologies of Marxism, Freudianism and phenomenology were kept, like the working class, firmly in their place.

7. I am naturally not the only person to have been struck by the similarity between Barthes's approach and that of his Anglo-Saxon predecessors. Lowry

Nelson Jr., describing the First International Congress of Semiotics (held in Milan, in June 1974), wrote that 'In all this, as in Barthes's *S/Z* (a minute analysis of Balzac's *Sarrasine* which is very much in the E. T. A. Hoffmann mode) there is not much new for Anglo-American rhetoricians of prose fiction. That is not to say that the aesthetic problems of fictionality and 'narrative' (speaker, omniscience, inner monologue, frame, point of view) should not receive widening attention, but that much of the old New Criticism is still new to the *Nouvelle Critique*.' 'European critics', he continued, 'breaking away from the old university orthodoxy, are bringing about a revolution of sorts about thirty years after the Americans have done what they did' (*Yale Review*, 1975, pp. 297–320).

8. L. C. Knights's pamphlet was based on a lecture given in King's college, London, and published by the Minority Press, Cambridge, in 1933. See page 37 and page 2 for the quotations. Miss McCarthy's essay appeared in *Partisan Review* in summer 1960 (pp. 438–58) and is perhaps the most unambiguous statement ever made of what Barthes and his followers would call the mimetic illusion. Her claim that all novelists are characterised by 'a deep love of fact, of the empiric nature of experience' is fascinating to compare with the claim of Philippe Sollers in *La Quinzaine littéraire*, 15 Apr 1968, that 'on écrit un texte avec des textes'.

9. Miss Sontag's view is quoted from Robert Nye's review in the *Scotsman*, 15 Mar 1975. On 24 Nov 1975, John Updike described her as 'our glamorous camp follower of the French avant-garde' (*New Yorker*). For John Sturrock, see the *New Statesman*, 8 Aug 1975. David Lodge, writing in *The Tablet* for 19 Apr 1975, was equally enthusiastic. In the *Scotsman* for 15 Mar 1975, however, Robert Nye compared Barthes to an academic ant crawling up the Scott Monument, and observed that there was little in Barthes which had not already been better expressed by Empson. Martin Dodsworth also observed in the *Guardian* (6 Mar 1975) that 'at the Arnoldian feast, Barthes is but a jester', and it would seem that the closer one comes to the steady centre of English cultural life, the more mitigated does enthusiasm for Barthes tend to become. Derwent May entitled his review in *The Listener* (20 Mar 1975) 'Code in the Head' and commented that there was something 'fundamentally misguided and bizarre about what these structuralists are doing', compared to the best examples of alert reading provided by Empson.

10. Thus Richard Miller's translation reads as follows: 'We must here recall that in the eighteenth century a castrato could occupy the position and amass the fortune of a great international star. Caffarelli bought a duchy (San Donato), became a duke, and built himself a magnificent palace. Farinelli ('il ragazzo') left England (where he had triumphed over Handel) covered with gold; proceeding to Spain, he cured the mystic lethargy of Philip V by singing to him daily (moreover, always the same song); and for ten years received from the king an annual pension of 14 million old francs; discharged by Charles III, he built himself a superb palace in Bologna' (*SZ*, pp. 192–3; English translation, pp. 186–7).

11. *Sunday Times*, 13 Apr 1975.

12. In 'Jeeves, Dostoyevsky and the Double Paradox', *University of Leeds Review*, Oct 1971. For an even stricter application of Lucien Goldmann's

genetic structuralism, see also my article, 'The Cosmic Pessimism of Hilaire Belloc', ibid., May 1970.

13. 'Le récit classique est fondamentalement soumis à l'ordre logico-temporel' (p. 58).
14. See 'Le dernier des écrivains heureux', in *Essais Critiques*, pp. 94–101; 'Les planches de l'Encyclopédie', in *Nouveaux Essais Critiques*, pp. 89–106.
15. *L'Empire des Signes*, p. 148.
16. *Les Lettres Françaises*, 20 May 1970.
17. *Le Figaro littéraire*, 20 May 1970.
18. *The German Ideology*. Quoted on pp. 85–6 of Karl Marx, *Selected Writings in Sociology and Social Philosophy*, ed. Boltomore and Rubel, Pelican, 1963.
19. *L'Empire des Signes*, p. 123.

CHAPTER 9

1. *The Liberal Imagination*, Secker & Warburg, 1951, p. 301.
2. See *Arts*, 19 Apr 1972, 'Il y a deux cents ans naissait Charles Fourier'.
3. *SFL*, p. 168.
4. Ibid., p. 140.
5. Ibid., p. 169.
6. For social divisions, see *SFL*, p. 135. Geoffrey Gorer's book was first published by Peter Owen in 1934 and reprinted in an enlarged and revised edition in 1953.
7. *SFL*, pp. 187, 129, 16.
8. Ibid., p. 75.
9. Cf. Preface to Gérard Miller, *Les pousse-au-jouir du Maréchal Pétain*, Editions du Seuil, 1975.
10. *SFL*, p. 186.
11. Ibid., p. 87.
12. Op.cit., p. 96.
13. *PT*, p. 25, 24, 97.
14. *PT*, p. 91; a claim repeated in *Le Monde*, 15 Feb 1973.
15. Cf. *La Revue Générale*, May 1973; *Le Nouvel Observateur*, 6 Dec 1973.
16. See *Horizon*, vol. XVII no. 2 (spring 1975) pp. 33–37; and *Yale Review*, 1975, p. 298. Mr McMullen added that the *New York Times* had hailed Barthes as the creator of 'a world of pure light and coherence', and observed that 'Madison Avenue has been working on the two semiotic levels long enough to do it sometimes just for laughs'.
17. *RB*, p. 64.
18. *Observer*, 22 Feb 1976.
19. *New Statesman*, 20 Feb 1976.

CHAPTER 10

1. *Essais Critiques*, p. 64.
2. *PT*, p. 59. Miller's translation, p. 36.
3. *L'Express*, 31 May 1970.
4. Heath, op.cit., p. 131.
5. *RB*, p. 164.

6. Cf. *PT*, p. 105 (Miller's translation, p. 67); *Mythologies*, pp. 168–9; *Tel Quel*, 47, p. 90; *Musique en jeu*, 9 Nov 1972, pp. 57–63.
7. *Mythologies*, p. 17.
8. *SFL*, p. 108.
9. *PT*, p. 68. Miller's translation, p. 42.
10. *Sur Racine*, pp. 32–3.
11. *SFL*, p. 154.
12. Ibid., p. 92.
13. *CV*, p. 14; *PT*, p. 24, p. 37.
14. Robert Alter, 'The self-conscious moment: reflections on the aftermath of modernism', *Tri-Quarterly*, spring 1975, pp. 209–54; p. 211.
15. Cf. her preface to the American translation of *Le degré zéro de l'écriture*, published by Hill & Wang in 1968. Barthes was first brought to the attention of Hill & Wang by Richard Howard.
16. *The Novelist's Art*, BBC3, 22 Sep 1976.
17. *Madame Bovary*, Conard edition, 1930, pp. 19, 45, 69, 114, 180 and 324. See also B. F. Bart, 'Flaubert's documentation goes awry or What color were Emma Bovary's eyes?' *Romance Notes*, v, 2 (spring 1964) p. 138.
18. Letter to Louise Colet, 16 Jan 1852.
19. *S/Z*, p. 61.
20. *Essais Critiques*, p. 264.
21. Ibid., p. 133.
22. *Collected Poems*, Faber & Faber, 1976, p. 470. Used by Laurence Lerner as the title of his excellent book on theories of literature (Hamish Hamilton, 1959).
23. *S/Z*, p. 87.
24. *Essais Critiques*, p. 60. For other evidence of Barthes's vision of a hostile, simple-minded and oppressive modern French society, cf. ibid., pp. 60, 85, 86; *SFL*, pp. 4, 89, 99, 102; *PT*, pp. 62, 74, 101.
25. Review of *Mythologies* (in translation), *Observer*, 12 Mar 1972. See *Le Monde*, 10 Jan 1977 for extracts from Barthes's inaugural lecture at the *Collège de France*.
26. *Essais Critiques*, p. 149.
27. *PT*, p. 13.
28. See Max Charlesworth, *The Existentialists*, University of Queensland Press, 1976, p. 48.
29. *S/Z*, p. 10.
30. *Arts*, 20 Mar 1957.
31. Op.cit., p. 162.

POSTSCRIPT

1. See the Index to *PT*, which indicates this to be the case.
2. Editions du Seuil, 1977, p. 20. Cf. also pp. 72, 148, 161 and 231.
3. Ibid., p. 21.
4. Ibid., p. 127. Many of the examples and illustrations in *Fragments d'un discours amoureux* are taken from *Werther*, a text which Barthes studied at length in his seminar at the *Ecole pratique des Hautes Etudes* in 1974–75.
5. Ibid., p. 142.

6. 25 April 1977.
7. *PT*, p. 23.
8. *Fragments*, p. 250.
9. Grasset, 1977.
10. *Le Nouvel Observateur*, 9 May 1977.
11. *Fragments*, pp. 93–4.
12. Ibid., p. 246.
13. Ibid., pp. 178, 198.
14. Ibid., p. 231.
15. Ibid., p. 86.
16. Ibid., p. 179.
17. Ibid., pp. 34, 163.
18. Ibid., pp. 52–3.
19. Ibid., p. 173.
20. Cf. *Situations I*, Gallimard, 1947, pp. 31–5.
21. Cf. *Marxists on Literature. An Anthology*, edited by David Craig, Penguin Books, 1975, *passim*. For other examples of Barthes's ability, in *Fragments d'un discours amoureux*, to elucidate what we mean by the terms applied to certain states of mind, see p. 69—the suffering of the loved one annihilates me by excluding me from what he feels most intensely; p. 79—rivalry— useful because it reassures me that I am not idiosyncratic in my desires; p. 148—the power the loved one has over me by inexplicably varying his moods; p. 161—to tell somebody that I shall never understand them means that I shall never really know what they think of me; p. 233—the word 'ravish' (*ravir*) has quite changed its meaning. Far from describing how I, as in the case of the Sabine women, carry off the one I desire, it now evokes the loss of control over myself in relation to the one I love. I thus do not quite agree with the implications of Christine Brooke-Rose's remark in *The Times* of 31 May 1977 that *Fragments d'un discours amoureux* is 'extremely personal'.

Selective Index

This is the first study to be published in English on Roland Barthes, probably the most influential of modern French literary critics, and which is also written from an essentially Anglo-Saxon, empirical standpoint.

Professor Thody, who is already well-known for his studies on Anouilh, Camus, Genet, Huxley, Laclos and Sartre, gives a succinct account of Barthes' career and principal ideas. He relates these ideas to comparable movements in English and American literary thinking and illustrates them by reference to specific works taken from both the English and the French tradition.

At the same time as he provides a clear account of Barthes' principal themes, Professor Thody also offers a reasoned and systematic criticism of them, underlining both their originality and their often controversial nature. In particular, he analyses the famous dispute sparked off by the publication of Barthes' book on Racine in 1963, and relates Barthes' works to other critical tendencies such as Freudianism and Marxism.

The book contains a bibliography of Barthes' works, together with a description of the critical reception enjoyed by each of his books. Since Barthes is interested not only in literature but also in the general problem of communication, Professor Thody's study is likely to be of interest to sociologists, social scientists and students of politics. It introduces the reader to concepts such as semiology and structuralism which have been frequently discussed but rarely defined.